INSATIABLE

A PASSION-FOR-LIFE MEMOIR

BACKPACKING AROUND THE WORLD

INSATIABLE

A PASSION-FOR-LIFE MEMOIR

BACKPACKING AROUND THE WORLD

Scott Stone

ISBN: 1500665878
ISBN 13: 9781500665876
Library Of Congress Control Number: 2014914141
CreateSpace Independent Publishing Platform
North Charleston South Carolina
*Please note when necessary names of people and places may be changed for protective
purpose.

To order a copy of this book please visit www.amazon.com

To my mother . . . your zest for living, curiosity, and ongoing mantra of "expand your horizons" was my greatest inspiration to travel.

AUTHOR'S NOTE

A brief introductory, explanatory note about the book's organizational structure . . .

   Please check the TABLE OF CONTENTS.

Notice my world journey is not routinely mapped out in a typical linear, chronological itinerary format.

Instead it flows freely in a flexible, fluid format. The thirty-six true stories (CHAPTERS), all documented in my original travel journals are organized into eleven broad THEMATIC SECTIONS. Their headings, in large bold print, provide instant visual organization and clarity.

This FORMAT creates a rich, varied tapestry of stories woven together from different times, different places, different people, situations and settings; creating a compelling, comparative diversity. This unique organizational structure better captures the spirit of this passion-for-life journey.

CONTENTS

EVERY JOURNEY HAS A BEGINNING . . .

1 The Best of Times: QE2 Crossing
   Welcome Aboard! Welcome to the World!   1

2 The Journal:
   Shipboard Scribblings   5

3 Bon Voyage!
   First Port of Call: London   9

4 Last Night in Paris   12

5 Moving On . . . No Return Date   18

**CHALLENGE: HOW TO PAY FOR A PRICELESS
GLOBAL ODYSSEY? (Work/Hitchiking)**

6 Au Revoir Paris! Hello Hitchhiking!   25

7 Portugal The "Magic Message:"
   Lost in Translation   30

8 Very Much Alive in a Swedish Cemetery   34

9 Auvergne: Toiling the Fields of France   44

10 Austria: Snow Shoveling Czar   51

11 Hunger's Drive to Desperate Deeds:
    I was Shameless   66

BREAKING BREAD AROUND THE WORLD

12   Cassoulet Nirvana in Castelnaudary   71

13   Philippine Pig Roast! Praise The Lord!   79

14   Thai Family Dinner with All the Trimmings
     (Daughter for Dessert)   86

15   Brittany Belly Buster   92

WHAT'S A GUY LIKE YOU . . .
DOING IN A PLACE LIKE THIS?

16   Switzerland:
     Swinging, Jet Setting, St. Moritz   101

17   Morocco: Bat Cave at Knife Point   110

18   Singapore Sling: Brothel Gets Nasty   129

THE KINDNESS OF STRANGERS

19   Scotland Pastry Shop:
     Two Angels and a Wee Bit O' Heaven   141

20   Munich Trolley Stalker   146

21   Burma: My Buddhist Savior - Hero   155

22   Kindness and Kimchi in Korea   173

TRAVELS WITH "PETE" (MOM)

23   Travels With "Pete" (Mom)
     (Greece, Turkey, Italy)   187

MELANCHOLY MOMENTS

24 Norway: Coming in From the Cold   199

25 India: When the Going Gets Tough   201

26 Austrian Ski Resort:
    The Worst of the *Wurst*   208

ROMANCE OF THE ROAD

27 Florence: Uffizi Gallery
    Titian Art Treasure Leads to Botticelli Beauty   217

28 Afghanistan: Romance and Rapture
    In the Hindu Kush   224

29 Yugoslavia: Raucous Family and Rakia
    Do Not a Romantic Rendezvous Make   240

ONWARD! EVER ONWARD! EASTWARD HO!

30 Istanbul: "Crossroads of The Backpacker's Universe"   247

31 Overland Asia to India
    (Turkey, Iran, Afghanistan, Pakistan)   251

32 Sri Lanka: "Paradise Found"   277

33 Palembang – Bukittinggi Agony Express
    (Sumatra, Indonesia)   289

INDIA: "THE AGONY AND THE ECSTACY"

34 India Weaves Its Spell   305

35 The Hindu Pilgrimage: On Being Deified   307

HOMEWARD BOUND

36   Homeward Bound   343

About the Author   351

EVERY JOURNEY HAS A BEGINNING . . .

THE BEST OF TIMES: QE2 CROSSING WELCOME ABOARD! WELCOME TO THE WORLD!

Mark Twain grabbed my attention and captured my imagination when he wrote:

> "Twenty years from now you will be more disappointed by the things you didn't do than by the ones you did do. So throw off the bow lines. Sail away from the safe harbor. Catch the trade winds in your sails."

Who amongst us does not yearn at times, to "throw off the bow lines and sail away?" So sail away I did that summer long ago, following college graduation.

And not returning until many seasons and many journals later, after backpacking around-the-world. The year was 1976.

I remember well the first day at sea, reclining comfortably in a deck chair and recalling again Twain's compelling words. My parents were the "trade winds" that helped launch that first "sailing away" on my first trans-Atlantic crossing on the luxury liner the Queen Elizabeth 2.

It was their proud, college graduation gift to me, accompanied by a handsome leather journal. The first page inscribed:

> "A symbolic gift . . . CONGRATULATIONS, SON!
> WELCOME ABOARD!
> WELCOME TO THE WORLD!"

It was to be a brief ten day trip, focusing only on Paris and London. But all that was to change.

I adjusted the deck chair back another notch and stretched out. The sun was warm and gentle, the breeze soothing, the sound of the sea hypnotic.

Gazing out to sea, my mind started drifting as freely as the cirrus clouds floating above me . . . I was thinking . . . now out of college my life priorities were not motivated by greed. Power, prestige and possessions were not my goal.

My most treasured possession was a passport. My short term goal was to travel.

My long term goal was expressed by poet Frederick Franck:

> "I know artists whose medium is life itself.
> Whatever their hand touches has increased life.
> They see and don't have to draw.
> They are the artists of being alive."

My thoughts started rushing in, rolling over, like the rhythmic waves surrounding me. "Artist of being alive" . . . a lofty goal indeed.

My thoughts now turned homeward . . . The night before I left home, at dusk, mom and I walked to the lake, to our special, secluded place at the very end of the longest dock for a last "mother-son talk." We had done this through the years, and I have always valued this time shared. I called them our "Pearls of Wisdom Bull Sessions."

Mom had prepared a well thought-out master list for me to take on the trip. It began: with practical hints such as how to avoid mildew with damp clothes in my backpack. It progressed: to how a great opportunity had been given to me and how to best maximize it. And concluded: with a promise to keep up my journal. I did not do so well with the mildew. But I excelled with keeping up my journal.

In a small "P.S." at the bottom of the page, I was glad to see a parting "Pearls of Wisdom" quote from mom. This one was from Emerson.

"Though we travel the world over
To find the beautiful,
We must carry it with us
Or we will find it not."

I would put it in the pocket flap of my journal, where I would not lose it. Thoughts now drifted back to shipboard.

I grinned as I remembered my last night on board: the image of me in my first Black Tie, dreamily dancing in too tight shoes to the shipboard orchestra's rendition of the old Sinatra classic "I've Got The World On A String."

As I was dozing off, I was now humming the lyrics:

"Got the world on a string
Sitting on a rainbow
Got the string around my finger
What a world! What a life!
I'm in love!"

And I was in love. Passionately. Hopelessly. Wholeheartedly with life. Fully and completely at age twenty-two.

My last waking thought was this is a love of life and travel that must be documented. I felt wonderfully "alive," as I surrendered to sleep, knowing there would be many more "being alive" moments to record in my Journal.

Boarding the QE2: Welcome to the World

Chapter 2

THE JOURNAL: SHIPBOARD SCRIBBLINGS

The long lazy days at sea, on the QE2 crossing, was the ideal time to break in my new journal; the "WELCOME TO THE WORLD" graduation gift from my parents.

I had never kept a journal. But now with this first trip abroad, I felt an urgency to do so. I had continued to stare at the white blank page to begin my first entry. But what to write? Where to begin?

From my deck chair, looking out at the endless sea for inspiration, I finally realized I must begin at the beginning.

Every story has a beginning . . .

With hesitation I decided to scribble some notes about my past . . . that got me to this present point in time. My first words looked harsh on the empty page.

"MY LIFE UNTIL NOW HAS BEEN ORDINARY."

They seemed to cry out: "Your life is dull. It is not full; you have done nothing."

But, no, my life was not dull. It just was not exceptional. Was this trip about to change that?

My ordinary life began growing up comfortably as an ordinary all-American boy in the Mid-west with a love of sports, girls and food. My ordinary world included strong family values and a good education. However, I was not a scholar, just an ordinary average student. My insatiable curiosity came later.

My parents were not ordinary. Well educated, they were both wise and smart. Most parents are good at warning their children about the "pitfalls" of life. My parents emphasized more the "possibilities." Excellence was encouraged. But "best effort" was what mattered most.

My father offered a solid, stable background so necessary for a strong foundation in life. He was our "Rock Of Gibraltar." His formidable physical stature reflected this. We affectionately called him "B.D." for "Big Dad."

My creative mother added another rare dimension: the poetry of life. Together they shared the gift of being infectiously positive and life-affirming.

They both had high humor and considered it the best equipment for navigating the rough rapids of life wisely and well. There was always much laughter in our house, which I shared with a younger brother and sister.

We lived close to nature on Hickory Island. It being an island, sailing was an important part of our lives. My father was a good sailor. He was also good, but merciless, at tennis. We branded him:

"INTOLERABLE IN VICTORY. INSUFFERABLE IN DEFEAT."

Hickory was a small island, located at the southern tip of a larger homogenous island-community of commuting professionals. Their residents were solid citizens: not only voting, but recycling, flossing, curbing their dogs, singing in the church choir; and returning their library books on time. It was a place of manicured lawns and micromanaged lives.

We were glad we were separated from the main island. Hickory was woodsy and free. It had a touch of wildness and magic. As kids we were allowed to roam and explore. We did. The view from our front lawn was an endless expanse of Great Lakes open water. The only land in sight was Canada. Its moods and storms were high drama to us. Hickory was a place "for all seasons." We would skate there in the winter; swim and boat in the summer.

Like most kids I resented my parents' tireless efforts to "broaden my horizons." The height of cruelty in this otherwise happy existence, was being exposed to cultural events: trips to concerts, museums, art exhibitions, and the theatre.

"My horizons" and enthusiasm was reserved, not for art retrospectives and chamber orchestras, but for major-league baseball, professional basketball, football and especially hockey. Michelangelo? . . . Shakespeare?. . . Beethoven? . . .My hero was the Red Wings' Gordie Howe, #9!

When the "cultural cruelty" got too much sometimes, I can hear my mother's voice patiently reminding me: "Scott, I understand cultural events may not be your favorite thing to do right now. But in addition to sports, the more things of interest you're exposed to, the more enthusiasms you have, the richer life becomes."

So the seeds had been planted . . . And nurtured . . . But it took the rich fertilizer of time plus an inexplicable "X" factor. Perhaps a delayed chemistry kicked in finally from some stagnant gene pool? . . . to make this "late bloomer" become a "BIG BLOOMER." The only "blooming" I had done thus far was to grow to be 6' 2" tall, and a healthy185 pounds by my senior year of high school.

And so it was onward and upward . . . my curiosity exploded, as did my passion to travel. I wanted to become an explorer, of not only what was over the next hill, but of people, places, ideas, and of myself as well. It was a life transforming transition on many levels. A miraculous metamorphosis!

The first destination along the way to exposure to the wider world was going East to college in Boston. Education was a top priority in our family. College was non-negotiable. I welcomed my new freedom in this fascinating forum of ethnicity, diversity and opportunity. It is here I first fell in love in the enchanting Boston Gardens by the swan boats in Spring. And it is here where I started learning things. In a hurry. Not only the importance of book smarts but street smarts as well.

During my senior year of college, in anticipation of my travels, the walls of my room were covered not with pin-ups, but maps, spectacular global travel photos, and one large over-sized poster with a quote from "Auntie Mame:"

"THE WORLD IS A BANQUET
AND MOST POOR BASTARDS
ARE STARVING TO DEATH."

I was gluttonous in my insatiable appetite to see, sample and savor the world "banquet" first hand. By graduation time my travel books were piled high, on the front of my desk, dog-eared and underscored. My textbooks undisturbed gathering dust in the rear.

I was pulling "all nighters," not cramming for tests, but devouring my travel books of exotic global destinations. It was amazing that I got through final exams.

It is said: "Anticipation is greater than realization." But this first trip aboard the magnificent Queen Elizabeth 2 Luxury Liner, surpassed all its expectations.

WELCOME ABOARD! WELCOME TO THE WORLD!

I soon discovered my "Shipboard Scribblings" would evolve into something more, much more . . . my highly valued "JOURNAL." It would record my insatiable thirst and curiosity for the world and life.

First Port of Call: LONDON!

Chapter 3

BON VOYAGE!
FIRST PORT OF CALL: LONDON

I stood at the bank of the Thames in London. Overhead I heard the powerful, unmistakable, sound of Big Ben . . . Gong, Gong, Gong, Gong. Four o'clock.

Ah yes! "For Whom The Bell Tolls" . . . I wanted to believe it was tolling for me, beckoning me to continue to explore the world. My mind was torn with two conflicting moods: one of sadness because I was scheduled to fly back to the States soon, after a brief stay in Paris; the other of exhilaration, enthralled by the magic of the past five days.

I looked about across the dark river down to the Tower of London. I saw no one. This immense cosmopolitan city so hustle and bustle, so dynamic with its rich history, tradition and culture, now so still and sleeping. It felt surreal. I felt a shiver run through me despite the warm evening.

I had been walking the quiet streets now for several hours . . . I wanted to experience my last night in London as it slept. I had no intentions of sleeping this night.

As I wandered, the extraordinary images followed me: the British Museum, Westminster Abby, the National Gallery of Art, the Tate Gallery, Buckingham Palace; and stately Hyde Park and Kensington Gardens. I was having trouble recording it all in my Journal. "Imagine," I wrote, "the incomparable British Museum boasts over two miles of galleries, including the Rosetta Stone, Egyptian mummies and the Magna Carta." I had been especially impressed with the Great Dome of St. Paul's cathedral, the 17th century architectural masterpiece of Christopher Wren. And the Tower of London, built in the 11th century by William The Conqueror, containing the Crown Jewels.

But in addition to these celebrated landmarks, a surprising source of fascination and enjoyment was the excitement of the city itself and just jumping on and off the red double decker busses and looking down on the city. Or ride the "tube" and coming up in a whole new different area, almost like another country. One such colorful area was the West End Theater district with some forty theatres. It was a dizzying, dazzling city of contrasts and diversity of peoples of all shapes, sizes, colors, languages and customs. So different from my homogenous white suburban Midwest upbringing.

It was here, my first days in London, I tasted my first bit of curry. It was here that I heard spirited conversations in foreign languages. It was here that I first witnessed a heated protest march, and experienced an all night party and dancing in a London disco. And where I saw Arab men in long, white robes. It was here in London I noticed fashion and style. And began to really look at paintings.

There is a saying: "When a man is tired of London, he is tired of Life."

I emphatically was not tired of London. And as for life . . . my brief time in London seemed to fill me with a sense of wonderment. I felt my sensibilities exploding with a passion for living. I felt compelled to explore and discover the world. And myself.

Walking through Trafalgar Square, with dozens of dozing pigeons, I passed a newsstand with magazines from around-the-world. I wasn't looking for anything in particular, but what jumped out at me was a map of Europe. Putting the required coins in the can, I did not hesitate to buy it. Sitting with my bare feet dangling in the cool water of the fountain, I spread the map of Europe out in front of me. The early morning light was just starting to break. Looking at the map from north to south . . . the islands off Scotland looked lonely. Who lives there?

Norway resembled a turkey leg. Austria and tiny Switzerland shaded in deep brown for rugged mountains. Italy shaped like a boot. And so many Greek Islands. What did these places hold? What would it be like to travel to these strange destinations? If my mind was so stimulated with the new sights and sounds and curiosity after five days, what would it be like to travel to other countries? Or around-the-world?

I was torn. An interior debate commenced. The mind can play tricks. I drew up a mental list of "pros" and "cons." To travel on or not to travel on? That is the question.

* I was only 22. I could go later. But I probably wouldn't.
* There is plenty of time, right?
* But will you ever be as free again?
* I "should" probably be getting serious about my career and start work.
* I "should" be grateful and satisfied for this travel opportunity. Not expect more.
* The "shoulds," "oughts," and "musts" of life will only increase with age and increased responsibility. Is now the time?

I wrestled with myself. But the heart and the gut do not lie, if we have the courage to listen to them. Who knows what the future would hold? I am here now. I now have the time, energy and spirit to travel on. I have my whole life to work. I was glad I had five days left in Paris before returning home.

Time enough to make the right decision.

Chapter 4

LAST NIGHT IN PARIS

PARIS . . . C'EST MAGNIFIQUE!

My Journal entry began:

"I SOON LEARNED NOTHING YOU READ OR HEAR ABOUT THE GLORIES OF PARIS IS OVERSTATED."

This includes its heroic history and high culture; its grand architecture; magnificent museums; and incomparable beauty. It is also a sensual city with a passion for food and wine, fashion and joie de vivre.

But no description of this remarkable city would be complete without stating: Paris is the celebrated "CITY OF ROMANCE." It is this Paris that I longed to experience for my memorable last night in Paris. I had a plan . . .

A slight breeze was beginning to stir on this otherwise sweltering July evening. This is where I wished to be: the Square du Vert Galant, this the most western edge of the Île de la Cité which juts out below the Pont Neuf, the main bridge crossing the Seine. It was my favorite spot in Paris.

From my perch, the river sparkled in the fading sunlight. Strands of orange and pink were starting to appear in the sky. It would be an outrageous sunset, perfect for what I had planned. Reaching in my knap sack, I checked that all was there in readiness: a bottle of wine and a rose.

I had a streak of the hopeless romantic in me. Everywhere I saw lovers embracing. I ached to meet a girl, not any girl, but a French girl, a pretty French girl and sit with her on the Vert Galant, to share a bottle of wine, the sunset and hopefully a kiss.

As the bateaux mouches glided by with their waving passengers, I pulled myself up, grabbed my bag and bounded up the steps of the Pont Neuf, leaving the Vert Galant below. But hopefully to return.

The Pont Neuf, spanned the Seine at its most scenic location with a stunning view of the Notre Dame Cathedral. It also provided a superb position for girl watching. The sidewalk was wide here, and I could easily view four to five women walking abreast. The timing was right; the work day had ended and pedestrian traffic was heavy.

The choice of women was staggering: blonde sweeping hair, raven black cut short, frizzy red, stunning faces, ordinary faces, miniskirts with long legs, tank tops filled with full bouncing boobs, small tits with erect nipples, short shorts of luscious tight asses. There were fat asses also, but these could only belong to others. After all, it was universally agreed that Paris had slender women only. This spectacle was a true kaleidoscope of the female form.

I was not looking for the woman of my dreams that would be forever. No, I was just searching for a lovely face in the crowd that touched my heart to share this memorable moment with.

The sky was beginning to get more vivid in its coloring of crimson and oranges. This was my last night in Paris, I must strike now. Reaching in my bag I pulled out the bottle of Bordeaux and the red rose, and watched and waited for the perfect moment.

I felt nervous and uneasy. I was still reserved and self-conscious when it came to meeting girls. In college I had never been one to "pick up" girls, but rather to have a steady girlfriend. But here in Paris I felt such an urgency knowing these were my final hours, and tomorrow I would be leaving Paris. Only solution: I will throw caution to the wind!

The people on the sidewalk seemed to come in waves. There would be a crowded rush as dozens of girls would be heading for my "viewing stand," then quiet down as only two or three girls would walk by. I had to move NOW!

I then saw her, amidst the throng, a tall, exquisite raven haired beauty. Because of her height and vivid red blouse she easily stood out among the others. She held her head high, her eyes focused straight ahead and walked at a good clip, wedged between several others eager to get home. She was twenty yards away . . . ten yards away . . . I smiled at her from my position, on the railing, but she paid no notice. Leaving my position, I chose to approach from the back.

As I jostled with others, I came up her left flank. I was now walking even with her. She was even more ravishing close up, with a voluptuous form, porcelain skin and luscious lips. She was almost too beautiful. I felt a pang of shyness, she intimidated me. I thought of letting her go . . . but instead kept stride with her, hoping she would acknowledge my presence. For a short time we walked abreast straight forward. Soon we would have crossed the bridge to the Left Bank.

"Excusez-moi," I said.

She responded with a slight head turn and even smiled. I could sense she knew I was an American, as my accent was quite pronounced. But she kept smiling giving me encouragement to ramble on with my proposal, as we continued to walk in tandem. "This is my last night in Paris, and I would be . . ." And just like that she seemed to put her step into another gear and pulled ahead. She was waving wildly, smiling broadly, as she skipped into the arms of her lover. Just like you see in the movies.

I felt disappointed, but not dejected, though rejected. I've got to get out of my small town mentality, I scolded myself. In fact this first "pick up" attempt seemed to give me a surge of confidence. I developed a "who cares" attitude. No one knows or cares who I am. I felt liberated with a sense of daring. I have everything to gain and nothing to lose, I cheered myself on. What harm was I doing? I had a wine and a rose. What girl would not be touched and appreciate such a gesture?

The Paris sky was now erupting in flaming orange with long streaks of purple. I paused to marvel at the splendor of the scene. However, now was not the time to be distracted. Time was getting short. I had hoped to be on the Vert Galant by now. I had to move quickly, as soon it would be dark.

I had only about twenty minutes to accomplish my mission; my four objectives: girl, Vert Galant, sunset, kiss. I no longer rested on the railing, waiting for girls to pass by. Instead I paced the bridge briskly, from end to end and crossing back and forth from one side to the other, dodging the busy traffic.

The clock was ticking . . . of necessity I became less discerning in my hunt. During all this time, I had stopped four girls: one totally brushing me off with a "Get lost, buster, look;" one shaking her head with an emphatic "NO," as if to escape a sexual pervert. But the other two were nice. Taken back a bit by my unorthodox overture, one girl said she had a steady boyfriend. And the other one said she was sorry but had an appointment to get to. Maybe they were excuses, but I did not care. I was having fun.

The bridge was becoming less crowded. The sky was starting to lose its intensity of color. Time was running out. I felt a pang of sadness, of disappointment. I slowed my stalking and returned to my "viewing stand." I was now resigned to the fact that perhaps I would not have a romantic last night in Paris. But that would not diminish my appreciation of the exquisite evening in this my favorite place in Paris.

On the other side of the bridge, walking all alone appeared a very pretty young girl. Average height, slender, shoulder length brunette hair, she walked with a casual ease, as if she had no specific destination. I watched her as if in slow motion cross the last half of the bridge. A large buss passed blocking my view. She seemed to disappear. Where did she go?

Racing across the street, nearly getting hit by a taxi, I ran the length of the bridge to the far side by the Right Bank. Where was she? I looked past the bridge, nowhere in sight. Looking down below, walking along the embankment I spotted her. Being on the embankment alone with night approaching, I was sensitive not to approach her from the back. So I casually walked past her; stopped and paused looking out across the Seine to the Pont Neuf.

As she approached me, I casually looked at her and said: "Bonsoir, beautiful evening."

"Yes, it is. You are American, correct?" She was adorable with a sweet, expressive face.

"Was not my 'Bonsoir' spoken correctly?" I laughed. She smiled.

"Is this better?" I joked, repeating "BONSOIR! BONSOIR!" in a loud, heavy, deep, phony French accent. She began to laugh. And together we very naturally continued walking together.

Her name was Camille. She was a university student, at the Sorbonne, perhaps nineteen or twenty years old. I did not ask her age. I wanted very much to be with her.

Without further talk, I looked at her and said, "Do you see that spot over there?"

"Yes, of course, the Vert Galant," she replied.

"I love that spot," I exclaimed.

"This is my last night in Paris. I want to do something memorable."

With that I ceremoniously presented Camille with the now wilted rose and warm bottle of wine. I could see she was tuned in to my well meaning-overtures. Boldly, I looked into her dark eyes and said,

"Camille, you probably think I am crazy, but you are so lovely, it would give me great pleasure to spend my last hours in Paris with you sharing wine. Would you like this too?" From her warm smile I could sense that I touched her.

She replied with a soft-spoken "oui." Camille tenderly took my hand, whispered "enchante," and together we strolled along the embankment back over the bridge to my favorite perch under the Pont Neuf.

The atmosphere seemed magical. Paris, the "City of Romance," was choreographing the perfect setting. As the last muted colors faded from the sky, the bridge lanterns with their warm amber glow came on. But the best lighting was that of an almost full moon shimmering across the river. Snuggling closely, with her head on my shoulder, we gazed at it in silence.

Camille spoke: "We must make a wish on the moon." I agreed, but added: "But we can't tell our wish, or it will not come true." At that moment I knew exactly what my wish was . . . that I would have the privilege and the pleasure to keep traveling and have that moon shining down on me from many places in the world.

Camille felt we should not keep our wish on the moon a secret, but that we should share it instead. And even with her playful teasing and tickling me and even twisting my arm, I would not tell it. I could not risk it, because I wished so much for it to come true.

"Lovers do not keep secrets," she scolded me. "I shared my wish," she said. "Now it it is your turn."

This seemed to really matter to her. She was getting increasingly insistent. So I finally told her I could tell my secret wish, if it would make her happy. (Her wish had been that she would one day visit the U.S.A.).

"My wish," I said (with my fingers crossed) was that I could kiss you in the moonlight."

Silence.

Camille continued to look at the moon, then said: "I will now make your wish come true . . ."

It was a delicious, romantic kiss and long embrace, well worth planning and waiting for. It gave me a warm glow and sense of commitment to live life to the fullest in Paris or wherever I might be. "Travel on! Travel on!" I wished again on the moon. Did you only wish for one kiss in the moonlight?" Camille asked. "More is better, I think."

And with that said she started giggling and wildly kissing my cheeks, my eyes, my nose, my ears, and my neck. We were shameless.

And right there in plain sight, with the full moon shining down on us watching our every move.

A perfect ending for a last night in "Romantic Paris."

Chapter 5

MOVING ON . . . NO RETURN DATE

Sharing that last night in Paris with Camille in that romantic setting on the Seine was a transformative moment. It filled me with an "all things are possible" attitude and thirst to live life to the full; which meant exploring more of the world to see what was out there. I decided I would make my wish on that glowing almost full moon come true: I WOULD TRAVEL ON!

It was after 2 a.m. when I returned to my hotel room, but I was not tired. I was excited and energized by my decision to keep traveling. I spread my map of Europe on the floor. It covered almost half the size of my tiny Left Bank hotel room.

My travel plan was to follow the sun. After France I would head north to Scandinavia as fast and inexpensively as possible, and work my way south, as the warmer months of summer gave way to autumn.

I checked the map closely. My first destination would be Oostende, Belgium. It looked about 170 miles away. It was on the Belgian coast. From there I would take the ferry to Denmark, and on to Norway.

I was sky high and ready for blast off. It was exhilarating! Just looking at my map, wildly stirred my imagination.

But before getting too carried away with the romance of the "open road," the grim financial realities of the cost of travel came rushing in. I got out a pad and pen to record the cold, hard facts:

Fact 1 - Very important. My parents had just financed my college education. And now had my sister and brother to educate. With my commitment to continue traveling, was also my commitment to fund it myself.

Fact 2 – Back home I had $914 in my savings account. I would phone my parents to wire it to me at American Express in Paris.

Fact 3 – Cash on hand: $79 left. That gave me a total of $993.

Fact 4 – I would travel as far as my money would take me, which could hopefully be a good distance if I lived lean and traveled smart. "Smart" meant analyzing my three major expenses: 1) food 2) sleep and 3) transportation.

Fact 5 – I would need to supplement my "nest egg."

It meant earning more money. It meant WORK as I traveled.

It meant cutting expenses: Sleeping outdoors in my sleeping bag; working for room and meals. And to avoid the big expense of transportation (public busses, trains and planes), I would be forced to hitchhike for the first time in my life.

This practical information was important to share with mom and dad, so they could feel reassured I had thought this out and knew what I was doing.

When I phoned my parents collect long distance, my mom was thrilled and let loose with an emotional scream of happiness. Dad, however, was not pleased with hearing this news, feeling that I should get the jump on the good jobs offered right now following my graduation. So for about ten minutes, despite the cost of the call, my parents confronted each other, on the "pros" and "cons" of my traveling on. It was mom's "broadening of horizons" versus dad's "time to get the nose to the grindstone."

Fortunately mom and travel won out, and I was pleased to receive my dad's blessing.

In talking to my parents about my financial need to work, mom reminded me that I was no stranger to work. "You have had many odd jobs," she said.

"Some more odd than others." I was pleased that my father was getting into the swing of my travel adventure when he added:

"You're young and healthy, you have the time and energy, it will build good character. It's summer, farms need extra hired hands. Crops need to be harvested. Apples need to be picked."

I purposely didn't mention "hitchhiking;" as I knew they would worry about it. To be honest, I was somewhat anxious about hitching myself and how this would work out, but I had no other choice.

I didn't know how far my money and hard work would take me. But I did know, I didn't want just three months of "seeing the world." I wanted a <u>GLOBAL ODYSSEY</u>!!

They were sad-glad tears, when I finally hung up the phone. It had meant so much to get their support, though I was not surprised. My parents, especially my adventuresome mother, had always been champions of personal growth and expanding oneself.

Well, it was time to "expand" . . . The next morning bounding out of bed, I was the first one in line to get my wired money, when the American Express doors opened.

Yes, I was "moving on" . . . and had no return date.

Paris: the morning after making the decision to travel on.

CHALLENGE: HOW TO PAY FOR A PRICELESS GLOBAL ODYSSEY? (Work/Hitchiking)

Chapter 6

AU REVOIR PARIS! HELLO HITCHHIKING !

With backpack on I stood in front of the clerk at the American Express office in Paris. He studied my passport closely, and slowly counted the $914 my parents had wired me, changing most of it into travelers checks, at my request.

I felt giddy as I stuffed my life savings into my money belt. YES! The global odyssey begins today! But this euphoria was kept in check, as a heavy dose of reality hit me. HOW LONG COULD I MAKE THIS MONEY LAST?

It became pressingly and painfully apparent to me that if I wanted to make tracks on this travel adventure, I had to save money by hitchhiking. I had been seriously studying my maps (Europe and Metro Paris) as to how to hitchhike to Oostende, Belgium to get the ferry to Denmark. However, the Metro Paris map looked like a spider web. I felt confused. How do I begin? Where does one start hitching? This was all new to me. I needed help. (TRAVEL LESSON #1: ALWAYS ASK!)

I looked around the office hoping to discuss my concerns with one of the American Express consultants, of which there were many; all looking like L.L. Bean Catalog models: attractive in a safe, conservative, "buttoned-up" corporate way. They seemed so involved in discussing big ticket travel concerns with well-heeled clients: luxury cruises, Caribbean vacations, packaged tours.

What would they know about hitchhiking? How could they possibly help me?

But at a desk over in the corner of the office was a young man, probably in his early twenties. His dress was more casual, looking a bit rumpled in an open shirt and sweater, his dark hair somewhat shaggy. But he had an uncommon intelligent look about him, plus he manned a desk with an impressive name plate reading:

"STUDENT TRAVEL"

Yes, this was the consultant I would ask for help. I introduced myself. His name was Thierry. Winning smile. Strong handshake.

"Where are you headed, Scott?" he asked, with direct eye contact and earnest, sincere interest, as if he really cared. I said that I wanted to hitch-hike to Oostende, but was confused. My map looked like I had to go to Lille first, but I could not tell which road to take and where to pick it up.

His warm, genuine quality made me open up, as I confessed: "I have never hitchhiked in my life, and to be honest I feel a little nervous." Thierry was not only kind and informative, clarifying directions as he brought out the subway map of Paris and explained the subway stop I needed to get on the road that led to Lille, but he was a seasoned hitchhiker himself. He had a natural enthusiasm for travel, as he shared some of his favorite places in Europe that he had traveled.

"Do you have any tips for a rookie hitcher?" I asked, feeling comfortable in doing so. Thierry let out a small sentimental sigh, as if drawing on a deep history of memories of the open road.

"Scott, I give you three tips. First, you must make a good appearance; second, try to make your backpack look small, keep it behind your leg when hitching; and lastly, but most important, you must stay positive. There will be times that are difficult, long waits, frustrating. But you must think of the money you are saving. And also, the people you meet, who pick you up. The contact with others can sometimes result in special experiences."

Spending this brief time with Thierry had made such a difference for me. I had my directions to get to Lille, but also had a better feeling about the idea of hitching. I got up and thanked him again. But before leaving, he said, "I have something to send you on your way." He started rummaging around in his cluttered cabinet behind his desk.

With the help of a step stool, he uncovered on the top shelf a piece of white cardboard, about a square foot in size. He printed in big, bold, black letters: **"LILLE."** In the left upper corner in smaller letters, he printed: **"Student"**

"Your destination sign is important", he said. "And the word 'student' is respected across Europe and helps," he explained.

He handed it to me grinning: "This is for you, Scott. Bon chance!"

I embraced him saying: "Merci, merci beaucoup my French friend. This will bring me luck!" We both laughed, as I waved his hand-made sign high in the air, and my "hitching" thumb even higher, cheering:

"AU REVOIR PARIS! HELLO HITCHHIKING!"

All too soon it was SHOWTIME: PACK ON . . . THUMB OUT . . .

I stood on the entrance ramp to the highway. It was 12:05 p.m. I was filled with churning mixed emotions: I was in both high spirits and high anxiety to hit the open road with my backpack on. Yes, my true travel adventure was beginning today. I had my sign. I was ready to go. However, despite Thierry's earlier encouraging words, I felt unsure, awkward and tense. Was I doing the right thing?

"Face facts," I reminded myself: hitching was a financial necessity, a means to an end. I would have to adapt. GET OVER IT!

Part of my discomfort was because hitchhiking was so totally foreign to me. I had never even been in a car that picked up a hitcher. As a youngster I could recall my father passing those with their thumb out and saying: "very dangerous thing to do." My mind raced about the dire possible consequences of a strange person picking me up: maybe a criminal on the run, a pervert, or a serial killer . . . The news headlines flashed before me:

"AMERICAN BACPAKER SLAUGHTERED HITCHHIKING."

So many unanswered questions . . . What about my facial expression and what it conveyed? How long do I stand in the same spot without results? How should I be dressed? Are my khaki shorts and navy blue t-shirt okay? Should I have worn long pants? Am I too casual, too American looking? What about sun glasses? Where was the book HITCHING FOR DUMMIES when you really needed it? Help!! I was a bundle of nerves as I took to the road.

Even the process getting to the highway itself to begin the hitch was much more complicated and time-consuming a task than I expected. This was Saturday, the traffic was probably not as brisk as during the week, but still a fairly steady flow of cars came rolling toward the entrance where I stood.

It was now going on two o'clock. The sun was very direct, the air heavy, humid. I had been waiting for two hours. Up until now I had given the drivers a friendly little smile, as the car approached me. I changed this with a big, broad toothy grin. But I soon gave this up, feeling like a total dork, a clown. Nothing seemed to work. I went to the opposite extreme: reserved, cool, no smile. But the cars continued to whiz by with the drivers displaying a look of total indifference. I was feeling increasingly discouraged, questioning if I would ever get a ride, when a car stopped.

It was a beat-up, rusted-out, orange colored Ford Fairlane. It was a dump. But to me it was a Rolls Royce! I felt ecstatic and so relieved that this car had stopped. My first hitched ride ever, yeah! And yet despite being overjoyed in getting a ride, I approached the car with a cautious eye, checked the license plate number, while my father's words of warning clanged in my ears.

Oh no! There it was! I noticed a shovel and rope half-hidden in the back seat, tossed among some newspapers. My over-active mind caused me hesitation if I should get in.

However, the driver, a young guy, about twenty-five with a broad beaming face and wavy reddish hair, pushed the car door wide open and warmly greeted me. His name was Maurice.

He spoke good English. He was a mechanic, going to visit his sister. But in truth he was more like a loveable comedian, who had me laughing non-stop.

About forty-five minutes into the ride, he notified me that he would be turning off at the next exit. I thanked him again for picking me up. I told him he was a fantastic hitchhiking ride. You are my "first," I announced. That really amused him. He let out one of his thunderous laughs and said he was delighted to be my "first," and wished me many more good rides.

Too soon we arrived at our exit. As the dilapidated vehicle sputtered away, I gave one last enthusiastic wave. Maurice responded in kind, as his hand shot out the window. Yes, I was no longer a virgin. I had taken my first hitchhiking ride, and not only lived to tell the story, but actually enjoyed it.

Three rides, and two hours later I would arrive in Lille. Yes, I was hitching; my world global odyssey had truly begun.

It would be another 532 hitched rides, from sleek sports cars to lumbering ox carts that would get me around the world. And yes, there were plenty of incredibly trying times, with brutal long waits. Several were endurance tests of over eight hours in length, including an eleven hour marathon in the pouring rain outside of Norrkoping, Sweden. The worst wait ever was the thirteen hour agonizing ordeal trying to get out of a sun-baked Saragossa, Spain.

Other challenging rides included assorted "colorful" characters: from an aggressive groper; to a man who liked to bark like a dog; to those ranting about the Bible, others ranting on about their hate of American politics, or whatever. I called them "hate-ranters." Also to be despised as most hitchers have sadly experienced, were those mean-spirited people throwing garbage at you as they stop, and take off laughing, leaving you on the road in their dust.

However, like life itself, hitchhiking embraced not only suffering and the bad, but the good and rewarding as well. In addition to the obvious savings in money that allowed me the rare privilege to travel the world, was the enriching contact with the people, the locals who would give me deeper insight into the area; rides that sometimes resulted in a delicious home-cooked meal in a warm family setting; or a restful place to sleep, but also employment and a couple times even romance.

Looking back at the hitchhiking experience . . . it is essential not to overlook or underestimate the life lessons learned. ONE HELLUVA WAY TO BUILD CHARACTER!

And not one axe murder!

Chapter 7

PORTUGAL
THE "MAGIC MESSAGE:" LOST IN TRANSLATION

I have never been facile at foreign languages. In fact I struggled mightily with high school Spanish. But early in my travels, I soon discovered the power of language; and how important it was in connecting with the people.

Determined to make the vital "connection," if I could not be a linguist, I was committed to a short-cut system of instant communication. I drew up a well-practiced list of select words and phrases that I delivered with confidence and enthusiasm.

So no I did not speak their language. But yes, I did "speak" pivotal phrases that had emotional impact and that would resonate "loud and clear" with the local people (be it food, landscape, beauty, love, history or the arts).

So in every country I traveled, every border I crossed, I made sure I could speak fluently the following.

* I love to travel your country
* Beautiful landscape
* Stomach very happy
* Your face is pretty
* My favorite artist (from your country) is
* My favorite writer (from your country) is

And of course all the common courtesies:

"hello," "how are you?" "thank you," "good-bye,"
    "please," "I'm sorry," "good luck!"

But of all the phrases, there was none that was so important, so valuable to me as a traveler as . . .

"I am an American student traveling your country. I would like to work on your farm in return for food and sleep."

However, despite my most earnest efforts to say these two sentences, be it to the farmer in the field or the person greeting me from my knock at the door; I was most often met with a look of consternation: "What?" And a shaking of the head: "No understand." It was then that I would be compelled to reach into my pocket to unveil a small piece of folded paper: "THE MAGIC MESSAGE," as I called it. On this paper was written what I was attempting to "say," and written in the country's respective native language: who I was and what I wanted.

If fire or the wheel is considered man's greatest invention; well for me, "THE MAGIC MESSAGE" was the single greatest invention for me as a world traveler. This simple phrase, now that it was written down in their language, was understood and served as my calling card. The MAGIC MESSAGE was simply my saving grace, my life line that allowed me to travel on for such an extended period of time on such little money. The MAGIC MESSAGE provided much more than savings; it provided me with terrific quality contact with the people I stayed with, delicious home-cooked farm food and a restful sleep. The MAGIC MESSAGE would be written ahead of time by a native of the country who understood English, usually it was a student. I found the students, many who had traveled themselves, especially pleased to do this.

Here are a few examples:

French - "Je suis un etudiant Americain en voyage. Je voudrais travailler dans votre ferme et, en echange, vous m'offrez nourriture et logement gratuits?

Norwgian - "Jeg er en Amerikansk student som reiser rundt I Norge. Er det mulig a fa jobbe pa garden din mot kost og losj?

Spanish - "Soy un Americano que viaja a su pais, me gustaria. Trabajar en su gran ja a cambio de comida y albergue.

With the above languages, as well as Italian, Greek and even Serbian, the
MAGIC MESSAGE had successfully played itself across the European continent.

In Asia the message was a big hit in India, being translated into both Hindi and Tamil.

Certainly not every farm would welcome me in, following their reading of the MAGIC MESSAGE. In fact the percentage was about one out of three farms would take me in. The key point was that these people "understood" my request. And if they did not care to accept my service, there were always other farms down the road; so I was confident that I could always find a farm to take me in.

However, there was an exception . . . Portugal. I was in the village of Resende, located about twenty miles southeast of Porto when I approached the little green farmhouse in a lovely setting. Just the type of place I hoped to work for two or three days. The MAGIC MESSAGE was translated into Portuguese by a young male student I met five days prior in Lisbon.

I did not see anyone in the fields, so I approached the house and knocked on the worn weathered door. After a short wait, a mature farm woman, plump with a ruddy complexion answered. "Boa tarde," I greeted her with a smile (the customary Portuguese expression for "good afternoon").

I handed her the "MAGIC MESSAGE," hoping that the response would be warm and welcoming. And that it would be only a matter of minutes before I would be seated with the family chowing down on some hearty home-cooking.

She smiled in a cautious, guarded way, as she unfolded the paper and studied it. Suddenly her face became contorted in an anguished expression. She let out a horrified shriek, screaming at me and shaking her fists with heated intensity, and slamming the door, after throwing the message in my face.

She seemed, obviously, not interested in my services. I made a quick escape, as I found her bizarre reaction unnerving. I was shaken. I had been refused before with doors slammed in my face, but nothing like this with such hostility and sense of terror.

What caused this reaction, or over-reaction? Still shaken and confused, I questioned if it were perhaps the message itself. I intended to find out.

The next day I encountered an elderly Portuguese priest browsing in the local book store. Surely, I could trust his translation. The "Magic Message" was written as . . .

"Eu sou um Manericano solto d pervetido, pronto pra me divetir. Aonde esta sua filha?"

At my request, the Holy Father wrote out the translation for me. Without comment he made a hasty exit for the door.

The translation said:

"I AM AN AMERICAN PERVERT OUT TO HAVE A GOOD TIME. WHERE IS YOUR DAUGHTER?"

You would have thought I would have picked up on that word "pervetido."

Thinking back on the student I had translate the "Magic Message" for me in Lisbon, I should have picked up on his sly smile and weird laugh, as he wrote the message for me…the joke was on me. The "MAGIC MESSAGE" was not so "magic" that day. Language matters.

Chapter 8

VERY MUCH ALIVE IN A SWEDISH CEMETERY

The silver Saab raced across the border into Sweden. Sitting in the passenger seat of my ten minute hitched ride, I turned and looked over my shoulder as Norway faded away. I was now leaving this country behind.

But the images of its staggering landscape would never leave me: from the spectacular fjords Sognefjord and Geirangerfjord, to the quieter breathtaking gems Naeroyfjord, Fjaerlandfjord and Hjorundfjord. All of them majestic with their narrow deep inlets, set off by towering walls of granite, rising straight out of glass-like still water, accented by cascading waterfalls. I was filled with a sense of wonder and awe.

But I also was filled with a sense of traveler's pride. I had traveled Norway for thirty-seven days, this arguably the most expensive country in Europe, and had only spent forty-one dollars. I accomplished this by working on farms, usually for two to three days each.

My jobs on these farms ranged from: picking apples, digging for potatoes, painting a barn, wiring fences, and even babysitting. It was of course a good way to save money, but also to eat well and make good contact with the Norwegian people, who were kind and simple.

It was now mid-November. The weather was turning mean.

Darkness would arrive by three o'clock. I had been traveling now over four months. As much as I relished the constant movement of travel, I found it beginning to wear on me somewhat. I now was hoping to set my pack down and stay in one place for awhile to find a job, sleep in the same bed, kick back and recharge my batteries.

I had my sights on a specific destination to accomplish this, and that was the university city of Uppsala, Sweden. I must be honest. I had an ulterior motive. The reason I sought gainful employment in Uppsala was for one reason, the women.

As I traveled, the young male travelers I would come across and befriend our conversations would cover various topics from favorite European cities, delicious tasting beers, clean inexpensive hostels, best beaches. But sooner or later the topic would always get to women, European women, and which country had the most beautiful women. Well, I did not keep an official count, for I did not have to, that was how wide the margin of victory was. To my fellow male backpackers, Swedish women were it. (Most of the guys I spoke with had met Swedish women not in Sweden, but while the Swedish women were outside their country on vacation).

With this key piece of information in mind, I thought that sounds pretty good. I am going to go to the source, Sweden itself, and check it out. My initial thought was to try to find work in Stockholm. However, no, what would probably be more fun and offer better access to Swedish girls for me would be a big university, and that of course meant Uppsala.

Uppsala is the fourth largest city in Sweden. The university, which was established in 1477, is the second largest in Europe with over 20,000 students. The city is lovely, very green, running along a river and with an impressive red stone castle overlooking the city.

After a day of just walking around doing nothing but looking at tall long-legged blonde women, I acknowledged that my fellow male travelers were correct. Sweden was amazing; the women were stunning. However, I had to pull my racing hormones to a halt and get focused. Any thoughts of good times with Nordic beauties would have to wait.

The job at hand was to find employment. The first two days were discouraging. I tried several restaurants, either as a dish washer or busboy; the university as a custodian. I spoke with garbage collectors. I even went to a dog pound to be a catcher of stray dogs. But nothing.

I was also disappointed that I did not get any leads really from the people I spoke with (and in Uppsala, most everyone I talked to spoke some English). I would ask repeatedly, "Have you heard of anything?" Or: "do you know anyone I could talk to?" But the response was always cool, and they could not help.

There was a hostel in Uppsala, but at fifty kroner ($10), this was too expensive for my meager budget. So each night I would roll out my sleeping bag and crash on the floor of the train station.

The station, unlike Uppsala itself, was dingy and dank, with some rather undesirable characters roaming about.

There was one man, named Arvo, of Finnish origin, whom I will not forget. At first meeting he struck me as your typical hopeless drunk. A man of average height, about fifty, unshaven, tattered clothes, smelling of body odor and of way too much liquor.

He upon seeing me nestled down in the corner of the station in my sleeping bag, waddled over, his bottle waving back and forth like a track conductor's lantern.

"Do you hate the Swedes?" he slurred out, as he plopped himself down against the wall about a foot or two of my bag. I felt a little uneasy, but I had slept in several train stations before and had never had any serious problems with the colorful characters that often milled about. Just be cool, cautious and civil to those who approach you.

I told him that I had just arrived and the Swedes seemed okay to me.

"They're arrogant assholes, I tell you, and you know what else, they are stupid too."

"You are not a Swede, I take it," I asking the obvious.

"Hell no, I am a Finn. My name is Arvo. Let's drink to Finland!"

It was now about eleven o'clock, I was tired. But I was also wound up being anxious and concerned about the job prospects in Uppsala.

The man in front of me though a drunk, had something about him. His eyes had a knowing light, and one that I felt comfortable with. And though normally not being a drinker of hard liquor, at this time I wanted to partake and see what this man was about.

By one o'clock we were still talking and drinking. Though he did far more drinking of the vodka than I did I still could feel its effect. I brought out some Fontina cheese with dark bread to share with Arvo, and to keep me from getting too wasted.

In the couple hours we shared I learned about his life. He to my surprise was only forty years old. His weathered face looked much older. He was a student of the famed classical music academy in Helsinki, where he studied composing and violin.

"Do you like Sibelius?" he asked me.

I told him I did not know who or what that was, "Was it a food?"

He shook his head in disbelief, telling me he was Finland's greatest classical composer. I told him that unfortunately my understanding of classical music was limited.

With unexpected reverence, Arvo put his bottle down and his face became serious and at times impassioned. He told me about the life of Jean Sibelius: his genius, his repertoire of works, ranging from his seven symphonies, to shorter works such as *Finlandia*, and the *Swan of Tuonela*, and his *Violin Concerto*.

And how despite his success as a composer, he was a tormented soul addicted to drink and dark moods, retiring early in life to live as a recluse in Finland's deep central forest.

"To all Finns he is our hero," adding that he passed away in 1957 at the age of ninety-one.

Quiet passed between us. No talk, no movement for a good minute. Arvo looked lost in thought. He reached into his dark soiled rucksack. I expected to see another bottle of vodka. But instead he pulled out a cassette player and showed me the tape "Sibelius – Symphony #5," performed by the Helsinki Philharmonic, conducted by Paavo Berglund.

"Listen to this. Of the seven symphonies this is my favorite. It is an amazingly original piece of work."

So for thirty-five minutes we sat on the train station floor as we listened to the Sibelius symphony. Throughout the piece Arvo often with eyes closed would move his hands slightly as if conducting, or nudge me when some especially beautiful or moving passage was to happen.

Damn, I love this moment! Two hours ago I am on the floor of a train station accosted by a drunken Finn. And now I am enveloped in this enthralling music, and learning so much from this shaggy dirty man, for whom I feel such warmth and a sense of wonderment.

The piece was now in the final movement and Arvo said, "Listen we are coming near the climax," and with that he turned up the volume. By now we had four or five onlookers watching us with bewilderment, but also seeming to enjoy the music.

Arvo was correct, the closing was moving and explosive, as the music would soar, pull back, and when the music seemed to come to a climax, it would stop, to total silence for a second or two. Power again, silence, until ending in a sensational crescendo of a thundering drum.

"Oh, that was fantastic, and the power at the end with the drum," I explained.

"We call that Thor's Hammer," Arvo said.

"Could you play the final movement one more time, Arvo?" I requested.

And once more I took in the final movement, this time swaying and moving about to the noble music.

It was now nearing 3a.m. We walked outside in the very brisk cold night air. I offered Arvo a cigarette. I do not smoke, but I carry a pack just for a friendship gesture in such situations as these.

I asked him about his career as a violinist and he told me that he played for two years with Turko Philharmonic, Finland's oldest orchestra, but had a bad marriage, got divorced, had a mean quick temper and drank too much. It affected his playing and he was fired. He said that drinking was a real problem with many Finns.

That was some fourteen years ago. He never really made a go of it again, but instead spent several years traveling the world with the merchant marine. He has lived in the States working for a lumber company up in the Seattle area for a couple of years; and had now been let go from a job in Sundsvall, working on a factory line.

He seemed reflective and almost "what if" as he spoke. He was making his way back home, hitching across Sweden to get back to Finland.

"I would like to play again, but I need help first. I don't have the discipline to play and the strength to stay off liquor."

I felt much compassion for him. With opened arms, I gave him a big hug and wished him to seek help, and pursue his passion of music one day again.

I made a gesture with my hands that I needed get to sleep and added that, "I am job hunting tomorrow." He wished me good luck, and said, "The money was good but the Swedes are cold, stuck-up people. You won't want to stay too long."

I walked back into the station and slipped into my sleeping bag and slept deliciously with the notes of Sibelius' last movement dancing in my head, until the station became crowded with no-nonsense morning commuters.

Sporting a bit of a hang-over from the vodka fest shared with Arvo, I crawled out of my sleeping bag in the midst of scurrying legs. It was seven o'clock. I had slept maybe three hours. I felt tired and my eyes burned, but I had no time to lounge around. Today was the day I had to find work, or I would consider moving south down toward Austria and the ski resorts.

I went to the men's room and shaved, washed my hair and generally tried to make myself look as clean and respectable as possible. I was off, biting down on the last pieces of my cheese and bread, which I shared with Arvo the night before.

Today I looked very hard and was more aggressive in my searching. I went to the main campus student union area and almost everyone I spoke with seemed genuinely sincere in wanting to help. Several students gave me ideas of places to visit and some with phone numbers and "use my name."

These possible positions ranged from working at a bicycle shop, to a flower shop, to a grocery store, to a bowling alley, to posing as a nude model at the Uppsala Art Institute.

But despite the contacts and going to all these places in person, there still was nothing open. The flower shop would take me, but that was only two days a week. That would not do, I needed to make some money.

By now it was nearing two o'clock and the light in the sky was already beginning to darken. Just as I was starting to feel dejected regarding the job situation in Uppsala, and already planning my hitchhiking strategy for tomorrow, I looked over to my right. There about fifty yards away in the midst of the campus were two men raking leaves. Leaf raking, I can do that, and without hesitation I headed over to the closest raker.

The fellow was about thirty, very dark, looked mid-eastern and said, "No English." I made a gesture with me raking leaves. I am not sure he understood me, but he immediately motioned for me to follow him.

His name was Ismet, and he was from Turkey. I followed Ismet slowly through the graveyard as it was now almost dark. He pointed to certain rocks and big roots to avoid so I would not trip.

Soon I was face to face with a nebbish looking little man with big glasses, he reminded me of a Swedish Woody Allen. His name was Jaska. I introduced myself to him and explained my situation.

"I am a student from the States, traveling Europe and am seeking work here in Uppsala." I noticed how carefully he was listening to me. I went on to tell him that this is my fourth day of looking and I can't find anything.

When I attempted to speak Swedish asking him, "What part of Sweden are you from?" He looked at me and said flatly, "I am Finnish. A Swede would never rake leaves." This is certainly my good karma time with Finns, I thought.

He went on to say that my timing might be good, as one of the rakers recently had to go home to take care of his mother in Morocco, and they need another person.

Jaska excused himself for a couple minutes as he disappeared into a near-by shed. He came out shortly and handed me a piece of paper with the particulars of my official leaf-raking interview written on it.

It said Mr. Sven Anderson (the "Bob Smith" of common names in Sweden) wants you to meet him in his office at 9:12a.m. Jaska pointing to a little brownish house at the end of the graveyard about 300 yards away.

Alright, 9:12 am, not 9:15, but 9:12a.m. I tried joking with Jaska, "9:12, I guess he wants me to be on time."

Jaska gave no response, just turned and walked away, his little wiry body disappearing soon amongst the trees and darkness of the graveyard. On first impression Jaska seemed like the serious, quiet type.

I felt elated. You would have thought I had just landed the dream job interview. But for me at this time, right now in my life, it was. Oh how I yearned to put down my bag for awhile, rest up, make some good money, and be in the beautiful babe heaven of Sweden.

That evening I splurged and stayed at the youth hostel. It was an expense I normally would not have indulged myself. But it was worth the extra money, I wanted to make sure I would get a good sleep, and have a shower in the morning. Importantly to receive a wake-up call in time for the official 9:12 a.m. meeting.

I woke fresh and ready to go. For the meeting I brought out (this being the first time I would wear these clothes) a white shirt, tie and gray slacks. These I thought would only be used for special events like getting into a club or to impress a date, but never had I envisioned they would be for a graveyard job interview.

The DTK, "Dress to Kill," outfit I called it, was buried deep in the bottom of my backpack. The clothes unfortunately were badly wrinkled. I had a most anxious moment frantically borrowing an iron from the hostel and trying to navigate the iron over the clothes. No matter what I did the iron did not seem to work correctly. How pathetic, I could not even iron clothes.

In spite of being embarrassed, I did not hesitate to tell Kristin, the Swedish girl behind the desk, about my pressing (pardon the pun) situation; and ask if someone could please help me. She called one of her able assistants who did the entire ironing. Thank you! Thank you! Looking sharp! I scarcely recognized myself.

Well, I made it on time. Actually I arrived at the little brown house where the interview was to take place, at 9:06, and waited behind a tree for five minutes. With my cheap Timex watch I studied the second hand exactly as it hit 9:11, I set off to walk, and just as the second hand hit 9:12, I knocked on the door.

Behind the immaculately uncluttered desk, with only a pencil holder in the top right hand corner with several very sharp pencils sat Mr. Sven Anderson. He looked pasty and severely constipated. My appraisal on first impression was correct. This man was a nerd and all business.

On my approach to him I extended my hand and greeted him in Swedish. He did not smile or rise from his seat. He just gave me his hand, not a shake, just sort of handed me his hand. It was limp and unwelcoming.

Without any small talk Mr. Anderson got right to it, "Why do you think your background is right for this job?"

You would swear I was interviewing for a top position at IBM. I felt like saying: "Look, anyone can rake leaves." But I knew this flippant response would not go over well, so I stated:

"Mr. Anderson, I grew up in the Midwest, in the state of Michigan."

This seemed to trigger a small spark in Anderson as he said, "Many Swedes in Michigan."

"Yes," I replied, not as many as Minnesota, but we have our share." Feeling a little more confidence, I continued: "Being the eldest in our family, it was my responsibility, (deliberately using this word 'responsibility' instead of 'job,') to rake the leaves off our large lawn."

So here I am telling Anderson this half-assed, totally full of shit story about leaf raking and he has his head down writing notes as fast as he can about my "experience." I knew I had him now, and I was heading for the slam dunk.

This next phrase I knew would lock the deal. Anderson's face came up from his fervent note taking. I paused and looked him straight in the eyes and said in the most earnest voice possible, (though I had to do everything to keep from laughing).

"Mr. Anderson, would you like to see my stroke?"

He nodded and without hesitation I launched into four consecutive, powerful but smooth raking movements. You'd think he would say, "Sit down you wise-ass, hot dog, you got the job." But instead, he looked at me carefully and in the most appreciative tone said: "impressive."

That's what he actually said: "impressive." And he was nodding his head back and forth with approval as if he had discovered some amazing young talent, as if he were a scout for a minor league baseball team.

After my exhibition of my stroke, and telling him my rich background, Anderson did loosen up and said: "We would be pleased to have you as a raker. You would be a good addition."

"Good addition," I love it.

He explained to me the hours; 9a.m.-3p.m. six days a week; Sunday off; and pay of twenty-five kroner an hour. When he said that, I almost jumped out of my chair into Anderson's arms. That was $5 an hour for this leaf raking gig. And on top of this he told me, thinking this would be bad news for me that I could only stay on for six weeks. But it was perfect, the ideal time period I was hoping for. I was ecstatic.

First day on the job I reported bright and early and had been hard at work until almost lunchtime. Scarcely conscious of my change in pace or direction I found myself raking a huge mountain of leaves. I could not resist. I got a big running start and jumped into them with abandon with a booming squeal of exhilaration. (Just like a kid back home).

I lay there awhile, the sky so open above me and those autumn leaves in their brilliant sun-lit golds and crimsons floating down on me.

Sven Anderson would never understand. But my toiling Turkish fellow rakers near-by seemed to get it. Soon we were having a rollicking leaf fight. We gathered up big armfuls of leaves, chasing and hurling them at each other, laughing hard and shouting, all of us jumping together in my huge leaf pile. We had become leaf men, covered head to toe with leaves. Our hair like leaf helmets.

I was in a celebratory mood: I was celebrating autumn in all its splendor. I was celebrating freedom and fun in any language. I was celebrating hope and success. I had aced my first interview. I had landed my first job out of college: "Official Leaf Raker." I could now afford the delicious luxury of purchasing a Swedish pastry. Not much of an accomplishment most would agree. But my father would always say: "There is nobility in all work."

So my first day on the job, I was feeling "noble." I was feeling silly and crazy. I was feeling very much "ALIVE" in a Swedish cemetery.

Chapter 9

AUVERGNE: TOILING THE FIELDS OF FRANCE

I took one last look. I walked. I did not want a ride. The landscape that I was leaving was unlike any I had ever seen . . . a sea of extinct volcanoes, one after the other, as far as I could see. Treeless, barren, it was savage and raw.

The sky was dark, the wind biting. Far off in the distance I could see fractured rays of light breaking through. The weather, so ominous, just added to the surreal allure of the wild terrain.

I was in the Auvergne. More specifically, I was in Auvergne's Puy Mountains, taking in the grandeur of the eerily, other worldly landscape of the "Chaine des Puys." This consists of eighty extinct volcanoes, made up of various sizes and shapes of cinder cones and lava domes. Legend has it that this area is "the child of the marriage of ice and fire" and was formed by the collision of the continents of Africa and Europe. This area was a center of extreme volcanic activity twenty- five million years ago. For two days I would wander alone in this remote, desolate landscape. It was bliss.

The Auvergne, situated directly in the center of the country, is recognized as the poorest and least populated of the twenty-six provinces of France. It is slow and simple. It possesses a "far from the madding crowd" feel about it.

Totally un-chic, its anti-Riviera earthiness is it's unique charm. I found it interesting when I would speak with the French of where they would most like to vacation in their country; their choice was the Auvergne more than any other province. There seemed to be a mystique about it.

But it was more than the rugged bucolic pleasures that attracted me to the Auvergne. It was also the lure of FOOD. In my backpack I carried a picture from a French food magazine showing a dish called "wild boar." Not just a boar, mind you, but "wild" boar. This stirred my imagination and appetite for some adventurous eating. As did Auvergne's celebrated cheeses, the trio: St. Nectaire, Cantal, and Blue d'Auvergne. All were held in high esteem in the pantheon of French cheeses.

I continued to walk, relishing the cold bone-chilling wind and brooding dark sky. I would wave away one car after another and walk on, the unrelenting bleakness just adding to the mood. I felt so alive. But also ravenous, as the past two nights, enjoying the night sky from my sleeping bag, I was reduced to a dinner of canned spaghetti cooked over my sterno can. I was overdue for French home cooking!

What I was really in the mood for was to stay on a farm, to find work and eat farm cooking. The Auvergne, being the most rural and least developed area of France, had no shortage of farms.

Where I was walking was along an isolated road. Although it offered dramatic landscape, it was uninhabited. I had been walking over two hours now. It was time to get serious, to start hitchhiking, and get to an area that had farms.

Out came the sign . . . A cardboard sign I had created expressly for France, as this country had a bad reputation among fellow backpackers for hitching. It had proven to be a magnet in France, amusing drivers and attracting rides. The sign simply read:

"UN GARCON TRÈS GENTIL" ("a very nice boy").

In five minutes I had gotten a ride. I could see the man behind the wheel of the red Peugot laughing at the sign, as the car slowly approached and stopped. He was headed for Aurillac. I would travel with him until farms began to appear. It was a short ride, perhaps ten minutes, as I got off outside the village of Murat.

As I got out of the car, I began to walk along the rural gravel road. Yes, I was in prime farm area now. It was a cornucopia of farms being offered. However, I was seeking out the "ideal" farmhouse and none of them were it. I can't describe exactly what it was that I was seeking in this farm . . . I suppose the setting, rural charm, seeing the people out in the field. I just felt that when I saw it, I would know.

The narrow road began to rise steadily. Directly on my left was the facing of a steep hill.

For about twenty minutes I walked up, up, up. Reaching the top where the road evened out, I rounded a bend and down below nestled in a green valley was a lone farmhouse. It was even red in color, rare for France.

I continued to walk slowly on the dirt road which ran about 200 yards above the valley floor. Looking at the farmhouse below I could make out the images of three men standing around a tractor, two young children wrestling with a puppy, and a woman hanging up laundry. Yes, it was the French version of a Norman Rockwell family portrait. Yes, this was "it." I had found my farm.

I could not really make out where the main entrance led to the farm, so I navigated slowly down the hill toward the farm. I could still see the people, but it had seemed as if they had not noticed my presence. (One rule of thumb in approaching farms: it seems much easier when people are outside, versus knocking on a closed door. I found that if people saw you approaching it made them more comfortable in sizing you up).

I had now reached the valley floor. I was no more than thirty yards from a wire fence that needed to be crossed to get to the farm. It appeared now that the three men standing by the tractor had seen me, for as I walked toward the fence they began to wave at me frantically and yelling something to me. My gosh, what a wonderful reception, I thought. Who said the French were standoffish? As I drew closer to the fence, they started to run towards me. Their enthusiasm at my presence was amazing . . . then it happened.

Placing both hands squarely on the wire fence to pull myself over, a surge of electricity ran through me. THUMP . . . It was as if I could hear my heart explode. Down I fell. I was out. Yes, an electric fence. If I had looked at the sign posts supporting the wired fence, even though written in French, one could clearly make out the lethal looking lightning bolt with three exclamation marks that followed. That meant "don't touch" in any language!

Talk about a graceful entrance . . . I am still not sure how long I was unconscious. When I came to, standing over me were the people I had recognized earlier from the road: the three men who stood by the tractor; the woman with the laundry; and the two little children with their puppy.

As I lay there looking up at these caring, concerned foreign French faces, hearing faintly the exclamations of "C'est terrible!" I thought of the scene from the Wizard of Oz, when Dorothy awakes from her dream in Kansas . . . Even the French version of Toto, the little puppy was there taking licks at my face.

At least my timing for my encounter with the electrical fence "HAUTE TENSION NE TOUCHER PAS" (HIGH VOLTAGE DO NOT TOUCH) was good, as it was time for the midday meal! About thirty minutes later, I was sitting at a long wooden table, being overly pampered and gorging myself on hearty French farmhouse food.

Is there a correlation between being electrocuted and a big appetite? Has there been an official study? I don't know. But I can still clearly see the look of amazement on the three strapping men sitting at the table, and the petite woman working the stove, as I wolfed down an embarrassing amount of food. "J'ai faim!" (I knew how to say "I am hungry" in any language).

And what food it was! Classic of the region, earthy and delicious: pork loin, mashed potatoes with a hint of garlic, a huge mushroom (which I later learned was called Portobello), white wine, apple pie and, yes, cheese. The cheeses presented were two of Auvergne's classics: St. Nectaire, creamy and rich; and Cantal, hard and slightly sharp.

Between shoveling food in my eager mouth, I tried to explain in my limited French what I wanted. My goal was to work on their farm for two days in return for food and sleep. "Travail pour deux jours" (work for two days), "manger" (to eat), "dormir" (to sleep). As I mangled their beautiful language, to demonstrate each word: acting as if pitching hay; then I switched to an eating motion; and closing with the tender gesture of sleeping with hands folded under my chin, head cocked to the side and eyes closed. They all seemed to understand, as they all laughed.

But to confirm there was nothing lost in translation; I brought out a piece of folded paper and placed it in the middle of the table. This is what I called the "Magic Message." It stated exactly what I wanted (to work for food and sleep) and it was written in French.

The oldest man, the father of the house was only about 5' 6" but had arms as thick as my thighs. He looked at the piece of paper and let loose with a definitive: "Oui! Oui!" His name was Henri. His wife, the petite woman, was named Claire. His sons Gerard and Jacques were a year apart, sixteen and seventeen; and built as if they could suit up and play linebacker for a Division 1-A college football team.

Well, my hoped for two-day stay went to three days, then four . . . and it was not until the morning of the sixth day that I finally said my poignant goodbye. If I wanted to stay for a month I am sure they would have let me. And what a time it was . . . these people so kind and generous, providing me with such good insight into life in rural France. During the day my work consisted of: lugging baled hay, digging a ditch and helping paint a barn. The work was hard, but it was fun working with Henri and his sons; and of course being rewarded with delicious mountains of food three times a day. It was a very satisfying situation.

No, I never had the wild boar dish as it was not the season, but we walked in the woods where the wild beasts ran about. November was apparently the time for boar hunting, and I was strongly encouraged to come back for this. However, Claire was a wizard in the kitchen, and seemed impassioned to make my stomach and heart sing. With the French country classic dishes such as Coq au Vin, Beouf Bourguigon, and Leg of Mutton, she also prepared the Regional Auvergne specialties: La Potee Auvergne, "Auvergne Hot Pot," a hearty dish of cabbages, potatoes, pork and sausage; and a delicious country meat loaf with herbs and prunes; and a constant nibbling of the famous Auvergne cured ham.

At night, a couple of evenings, I would join the sons and go into Murat, the largest village in the area, where there were two local bars that we would run back and forth between. Gerard and Jacques in their matching leather coats, muscular physiques and brooding good looks were like magnets attracting girls. But they had an air of indifference about them; and preferred to concentrate on watching soccer on TV, playing foosball, or throwing darts.

But what I enjoyed even more than the village visits with the sons, and they seemed to go in every night, were the evenings I would stay at home being with Henri and Claire. We would sit in their small living room around the fieldstone fireplace, laugh and chat (best we could) while drinking red wine and munching on what seemed an endless supply of Cantal cheese and bread. It seemed the more we drank, the better we understood each other.

I soon understood many things. Things that mattered. These days of hard work on the farm had produced some rich rewards. There were the obvious rewards of feeling healthy: "early to bed, early to rise," all that fresh air, the energizing physicality of large muscle activity, the honest sweat under the summer sun, and the nutritious, absolutely delicious home cooked meals.

But these caring, wholesome people had nourished me in not just food for the body, but in a joyous, simple "way of life," nourishing the spirit as well.

I liked how Henri would look at Claire when he came in tired from the fields. I liked her reassuring pats on his back, and their obvious pleasure in coming together. And the spontaneous, easy warm hugs all the family would exchange. The respect and devotion of these sons for their parents was unshakable. They could not work hard enough from dawn to dusk to demonstrate their deep caring.

It is said that the emotional barometer of the home is the mother. Claire filled it with laughter and gladness. She would bring her immense pleasure in pleasing others to every meal: the fresh wild flowers adorning the table; the home-baked bread hot from the oven, ready to be sliced; and always more wine ready to be poured. I liked the tempo of their days . . . with time to enjoy life.

And for family closeness, while also reaching out to others to make a difference; like to me the hired hand, privileged to share their family table.

Another rich reward, in addition to their inspiration and nourishment on many levels, was an invaluable education in learning more about French Cuisine. I was the most enthusiastic of students; and they were the most knowledgeable and enthusiastic of instructors.

I would spread out my map of France on the bare, wooden floor and kneel over, pointing to different regions I was planning to visit, or some of those that I wasn't; and they would nod their heads, knowingly, and call out the food of the region I must try:

Dordogne … Duck Confit
Aude … Cassoulet
Marseilles … Bouillabaisse
Brittany … Galette
Alsace … Choucroute

They were so genuine in their interest for me to understand their cuisine. They would actually get down on the floor with me and point to certain areas that were "superb" for a special food. And Claire would pull down books on French cuisine from her kitchen shelf, lavishly illustrated with food photos and emphatically point out and exclaim: "Très bon!" "Très delicieux!"

Henri pointed out on the map the town of Sarlat in the Dordogne region where his sister lived with her family. He went on to say that this is one of France's most prized regions for cuisine, and I must visit them. Within minutes Henri was on the phone to his sister explaining that they had a young American staying with them, and I had a "very big appreciation of the French Cuisine," and asking if I could stay with them for a couple of days.

Well of course I took Henri up on this. And as a result of this contact of meeting Henri and Claire began in essence a delicious domino effect. Going from their farmhouse to his sister's in Sarlat, then from her home in the Dordogne, to her brother-in-law in the Pyrenees, and …

This circle of hospitality took me all the way around France. In total I stayed with seven families in France. Some of the contacts were just for dinner and the night, others longer in length. But in each instance it was meeting such generous, warm people and sharing their local regional food, prepared and presented with such love . . . Viva la France!

Chapter 10

AUSTRIA: SNOW SHOVELING CZAR

Having made my dramatic escape from the tyranny of the Hotel Evergreen (Chapter 26), I made my way down the icy dark road to the village of Igls.

It was cold out, but I felt terrific, as I was free and moving on. It was mid-winter. I was in the mood for sunshine and heat. I would be hitching and traveling as fast as possible. My destination goal: Morocco.

The Igls village illuminated clock said 11:15 p.m., no busses running this late. My immediate concern was getting to Innsbruck to sleep in the train station. The village was still as I took one last sentimental look and began the ten mile trek down the mountain road to Innsbruck. This journey was one I was not looking forward to as it was icy and dark, and I had to be cautious in navigating my footing.

But in spite of this I felt energized and hopeful. Especially when I saw the red tail lights of the car pulling out from one of the restaurants. Was this an auspicious sign perhaps? As it approached, it slowed and stopped. The car window came down. "Innsbruck?" the driver asked. "Yes, danke," I replied gratefully. The man was a Yugoslavian dishwasher, who spoke little English.

We bonded at once on our shared professions. Twenty minutes later, I was at the train station.

The next morning, I wanted to hitch out. Standing on the exit ramp which fed to the main highway, it was blustery cold and snowing heavily. It made me all the more eager to head south to warmth and sunshine. Morocco here I come!

However, after about an hour of attempting to get out of Innsbruck, the snow began to get very heavy. The wind was kicking up with strong gusts blowing into my face. My face stung as I tried to make out cars, virtually impossible as they approached. After another thirty minutes, it was blizzard conditions.

I felt it was useless as there seemed to be no cars traveling, and I was turning into an ice cube.

It looked for certain that I was not going to be able to hitch out of Innsbruck today. This was disappointing as I wanted to get going. But as a traveler, sometimes you just have to accept the situation, adapt, and make the best of it. Roll with it, when things don't go your way. And always remember the three "P's" of the road: Patience, Perspective, Persistence.

I reminded myself of this, as I started walking back towards the center of town, thinking about the day and where I would stay tonight. This was unclear, but that is nothing surprising, as seldom do I know where I will rest my head at the end of the day. The one thing that was clear was that I was drenched from the wet snow, and I needed to get inside. I soon saw a cafe, but hesitated. I did not want just any cafe. I wanted "The Central," Innsbruck's oldest and most famous.

Although it took extra time getting there, as I had to walk through the slippery, narrow side streets of Old Innsbruck, an extra fifteen minutes in the blizzard would not make a difference. I was beyond wet. I wanted some-place special. I remember reading that the Central was built in 1868 and had a Viennese style. I had not been to Vienna, but it sounded inviting.

The warmth of the cafe engulfed me immediately, as the smell of roasted coffee filled the air, and the distinct hissing of cappuccino being made felt comforting. The Central bespoke of another era with ornate lighting fixtures, spacious high ceilings, beveled mirrors and marble top tables. Also impressive were its many select magazines and international newspapers for its literate patrons.

Sitting in the back of this renowned coffee house, I ordered a Cafe Viennese and Sachertorte. The Sachertorte is a cake of dense chocolate with a thin layer of apricot jam on top and coated with dark chocolate icing on all sides. It is so beloved by Austrians that they have a National Day to celebrate it every year, on December 5th. Although I had been in Austria almost three weeks, this was my first taste of the luscious dessert.

I knew this house specialty was expensive, but I didn't care, I was in the mood for spoiling myself. Sitting back in the fine upholstered chair, I felt enriched absorbing the gracious atmosphere of another time and place.

And all the people who had come before to share in the timeless spirit of the Central. It was just as I had imagined.

My clothes began to dry. I was feeling comfortable and cozy. It was nasty out and I was in no rush to leave. As I bit into the decadent dessert and sipped my frothy, hot Cafe Viennese, I caught up on my Journal.

I knew eventually I would have to go out in the snow again. I had hoped it would let up. But the waitress reported that the blizzard conditions were expected all day and tomorrow, up to half a meter (19 inches) of snow. If the snow continued at this rate, it would be unlikely to hitchhike out of here tomorrow.

It was now about three o'clock. I had been there almost two hours. Leaving the luxurious warmth of the cafe, I cautiously made the slow, slippery frigid walk to the local Youth Hostel. Visibility was poor; the snow was now mixed with pelting sleet. I could only walk with my head down, and at times turning my back against the strong wind and walking backwards. As I walked backwards I bumped into something, it was a trash can.

In the trash can, most of it covered by snow was a snow shovel with a broken handle. I had a grim vision of all the shoveling I would be doing if still imprisoned at the wretched Evergreen Hotel for slave wages. But it gave me an idea, a big enterprising, entrepreneurial idea. I looked around, reached in and took the snow shovel with dollar signs dancing in my head.

Could the snow and shoveling be turned into BIG BUCKS?

Almost an hour later, looking like a snowman, I finally arrived at the hostel.

Upon my entrance I was greeted with an enthusiastic "Hello" in a strong Austrian accent. It was Siegfried, the guy in charge of the hostel reception desk.

He remembered me from the last time I stayed here.

After exchanging greetings and "catch up," he asked looking bewildered: "So what's with the shovel?"

I answered his question with a question: "So Siegfried, what do you think the chances would be that I could make some money shoveling sidewalks?"

Siegfried looked encouraging: "That could work, especially if you go after the right clientele."

I had thought of going into the old town and offering to shovel in front of stores.

He dismissed this idea, saying they had a team of professionals doing it.

"Your target market," he said, "is the elderly, especially those that have some money." I nodded in agreement. "Yes, that makes sense." I was getting excited about my new business venture.

Siegfried unfolded a map of greater Innsbruck out on the table. He outlined the area with a red marker. "Your target market is here," referring to an affluent area just outside of Innsbruck. He explained, "It is settled, older. These are the people who need your service."

We discussed price and settled on 60 AS. ($3.60) Doing some quick math in my head, estimating the time for each walk, I figured this job prospect could be financially promising.

I thanked Siegfried sincerely for all his help. "One last request, please, would you write in German my magic message stating: I am an American student traveling Austria and will shovel the snow off your walk for 60 AS."

He was glad to do so and offered, "Scott, if you want some practice you can shovel the Youth Hostel's walk, and I will give you a free night's lodging."

"Good deal I'm glad to," I accepted.

I got another idea, which I immediately shared with Siegfried: "Why not advertise my service with a sign that can be read from a distance? So while shoveling one walk, I could hustle more business from passersby?"

"Scott, you're on fire!" Siegfried provided a big oversized cardboard and was kind enough to translate "Sidewalk Shoveled for 60 Schilling" into German and print boldly in JUMBO letters with the marker:

"GEHSTEIG GESCHAUFELT FUER 60 SCHILLING"

The next morning, I was off early to begin my new-found shoveling business.

It took about fifteen minutes on the trolley and a short walk to reach my destination.

I stood in the middle of the street and took it all in. Well established homes flanked both sides of the tree-lined street. From my first impression, I liked what I saw. Yes, perhaps this would be my shoveling goldmine.

It was a sea of white as far as you could see. The street had been plowed, but everywhere else were high drifts covering the cars. It was so quiet, no one could be seen, nor any sound detected, not even that of a bird chirping. It was somewhat other worldly. I checked my watch. It was nine o'clock. Was I too early? Wanting to make my first snow shoveling attempt a successful one, I navigated my way slowly down the center of the street, the shovel in my right hand, my sign, advertising my services, dangling on my back.

I could imagine the locals peering out from behind lace curtains, as they watched this stranger ambling down the street. I felt like a gun slinger coming into town to do my job and move on.

I wanted a friendly looking house, one that looked inviting. I felt instinctively I would know the house when I saw it. There was a loveliness to the stillness of the early morning. I felt lost in this dreamlike silent world.

However, my tranquility was shaken, when I heard coming from behind me the sound of a shovel on cement. What!? Yes, behind me about two hundred yards was someone shoveling snow. I felt like protesting: "Hey, what are you doing? That is my job!"

The hell with seeking the friendliest house on the block, I had to get into action. Let's go, time to start 'shovelin'! Turning an immediate right, I was faced with a two-story wooden white house with black shutters and a big pine wreath with a red ribbon on the door. It had the classic "winter in New England look." It brought back memories of a Hallmark card, and yes, it certainly had a friendly look.

I headed toward the house, up what I thought was the sidewalk. The snow was up to my knees. It was an effort just to move and maintain balance as I maneuvered carefully to the door. I noticed a light on the second floor. I touched the bell. It made a jarring buzz, not in keeping with the look of the house. I waited about fifteen more seconds and buzzed again. Yikes! What a sound. I felt embarrassed, perhaps it was too early, and I was waking someone up. I started to walk away when I heard the sound of the door opening. There stood a tiny old woman, easily under five feet with thick glasses. She wore a bathrobe and her face showed a perplexed combination of annoyance and confusion.

I should have left and not returned. But instead I trudged back through the snow and speaking as I went, forgetting for a moment that I was in Austria, "Hello, sorry to bother". Switching then awkwardly to German: "Guten morgen!"

"Arbeit." And I made a couple gestures of shoveling.

She had no idea what I was speaking about. She looked terrified.

Reaching into my pocket, fumbling to get the "magic message" (the message written in German which Siegfried wrote the night before, explaining exactly who I was and what I wanted). Just a nice student wanting to shovel, ah yes, this would put her at ease. But instead, she began screaming: "Nein, Nein, Nein!!" slamming the door in my face. Perhaps she thought I was reaching for a gun. Not a good start to my shoveling business. However, I drew solace from recent experience of working on farms across Europe. So being refused sometimes was to be expected.

However, I did find her reaction extreme and felt a bit unnerved by it.

One thing was certain and that was to move quickly away from this house, "the friendly house," remember? And move down the block, way down the block, out of viewing distance. I could just imagine her on the phone calling her neighbors warning them of a strange man with a shovel. Sounds like a film doesn't it: "Strange Man with a Shovel."

Further down the block, I could see a man out by his car which looked like an igloo, as it was completely covered with snow. From the road, I let out with a "guten morgen." He waived back enthusiastically.

I continued to approach him as I spoke, and he is walking toward me also, two big men, strangers trudging slowly toward each other in the deep snow and exchanging handshakes and introductions.

"My name is Scott."

"I am Dieter."

He was a man I would say in his mid-fifties, bald, but very healthy looking with high coloring, broad shoulders, and clear direct blue eyes. He looked, unfortunately, very fit and that he would have no trouble shoveling his own sidewalk.

"Dieter, you speak good English."

"Oh, I don't know, but as a young man I went to school for two years at Marquette University in Milwaukee."

"Yes, of course, good school. Are you a basketball fan?"

"Absolutely. Love basketball. The Warriors!" he exclaimed.

Being a big fan of college basketball, I mentioned the 1973 season with Al McGuire and their NCAA championship. His face gleamed with satisfaction. Wanting to share in his enthusiasm I raised my hand to give him a high five. He returned my five with such power that in the deep snow I lost my balance. He reached out and I pulled him over on top of me. We both started laughing at how ridiculous it was. He was such an enjoyable person and had such a good energy; I almost forgot that I had business to discuss.

However, before I could mention this, he said, "Come in for coffee or tea." Time was important, as I wanted to get in as many shoveling jobs as possible. My goal was eight sidewalks and make 500AS.

I decided it would be rude to just break into my shoveling sales pitch after having such a nice personal bond. This could wait till after.

In his home, comfortable and warm, he introduced me to his wife, Helga. She was pleasant enough, but did not have the dynamic presence of Dieter. He wanted to know what I was doing. I explained that I had just graduated from college. And that I was travelling around Europe, working as I go, picking up odd jobs, such as today I am offering my services to shovel sidewalks and driveways.

Dieter, let go with a hearty laugh, "Ingenious." "So Dieter, can I shovel your walk? You would be my very first client."

"How much?" he asked.

"Oh, I don't know, say 60 AS."

He looked concerned, and said, "I don't like that price, how about 80 AS?" Before I could even get out my thanks, he said: "Scott, if you can help me get my car out of the driveway, I will give you 100 AS."

"Absolutely, let's go," I said, enthusiastically, trying to force the issue to get to work, as I noticed on my watch it was already 10:30, and I wanted to get in as much shoveling as the day would allow.

Fortunately, Dieter seemed to read my thoughts, as he said "I have some important business to attend to, so please make yourself comfortable and start the shoveling when you want." As soon as Dieter left the room I finished my coffee quickly, thanking Helga, and made my way out to begin the shoveling.

The snow though deep was soft and powdery, not overly heavy, and it took less time to complete the job than I expected.

Just as I was finishing I looked up and Dieter's glowing face was beaming down on me. "Scott, very good, you are a natural. Come in I'll pay you, and I have some exciting news for you." Dieter patted me on the back with affection and handed me my money, and said, "Good news for you, Scott. I have two more customers for you."

I wanted to burst in with a big "thank you," but Dieter rambled on as if he had just won some big negotiating contract for his own business. "I spoke to Wolfgang and Fritz, good friends of mine and I already got the deal cut for you. They each will pay 80 AS. Their walks are about the same size as mine."

"Dieter, thank you so very much."

He interrupted me and was waiving his hands about, "Scott, I will drive you; they are both close to each other, about two miles from here."

As we started out, I said my "goodbye" to Helga. He stopped and said: "Wait I know another person who could use your service." He disappeared into the kitchen and began talking on the phone in rapid, highly animated German. In thirty seconds he returned. Yes, I had yet another customer. I don't know what Dieter said on the phone, but it worked. This guy was amazing!

I felt so touched by what Dieter had done. Thanking him repeatedly as I got out of his Audi, he said: "When I was young in the States, I met so many kind people, it's the least I can do."

A heart-felt digression: It is meeting people like Dieter who reach out and make a difference, who go out of their way to help, that made my travel experience richer and more rewarding. I would meet other unforgettable Dieter "types," as I traveled. And even if the time was brief, their impact was significant and the memory remained part of me.

If I had a wish to come true, it would be to bring together all the kind, remarkable people who "lent me a helping hand" during my travels; and have a BIG BASH, a celebration in their honor to embrace and thank them and wish them well. And to pledge a champagne toast: "HERE'S TO MY BELOVED CHAMPIONS. MAY YOUR GOOD DEEDS BE REWARDED!"

I felt giddy with joy at the thought of such a reunion! But now back to the project at hand, Dieter's two friends, Wolfgang and Fritz, lived next door to each other. They were older gentlemen and had known each other since the age of five. I made quick work of both their driveway and sidewalk. As I was shoveling I had three people walk by and comment on my sign: "SIDEWALK SHOVELED FOR 60 AS," and added each of them to my "satisfied customer" list as well. Those three, plus Wolfgang, Fritz, Dieter and his other friend Manfred, and his business associate Gerhard.

By the time I had finished my last shovel, it was around four o'clock and the winter light was fading. The snow had stopped, and the sky was clear. I felt absolutely buoyant about what I had accomplished in my first day as a professional snow shoveler. I had made 600 AS in eight jobs! This could be lucrative. But the weather had to cooperate. Meaning it had to snow again and snow BIG TIME!

Yes, I would indeed pray to the snow gods tonight. But I was in the mood to celebrate my windfall now. The person I wanted to celebrate with was Siegfried at the Youth Hostel. However, when I got to the hostel I was surprised and disappointed to learn from the desk clerk that Siegfried had the week-end off and would be out of town. Damn, I really wanted to share my enthusiasm and appreciation with him. After all, he was the caring choreographer of my snow shoveling success.

Despite no Siegfried, I was still in the mood to have some fun! It was Thursday night and I doubted that Innsbruck had much going on in the way of nightlife. But when I asked the young guy at the desk, Wilhelm, he assured me that Thursday is big with the University students. He wrote the address of a bar down for me, saying that he really was not sure of the name, just location. "It's sort of hidden, very authentic, no tourists, lots of university girls," he said.

I was ready for that. I was in one of my "crazy" moods. Crazy in a good way that I felt tonight was going to be terrific, and I wanted to get a little wild. So for some crazy reason, I decided to take the snow shoveling "message" with me. Why, I don't know. It just seemed it had brought me a lot of good luck today; maybe it could bring me some luck tonight.

The bar reminded me of a favorite place I used to frequent as a student in college. As you enter you descend down steep stairs into a small, dimly-lit room with a low, beamed ceiling and dark wooden booths. Both posters of Rock Stars and Mozart graced the walls. Though only a little after nine o'clock, it was already crowded, with lots of smoke and throbbing, hard driving music from the seventies.

I sat at the bar taking in my second pint of the local beer. I am pretty much a light weight when it comes to drinking. I do not drink to get drunk. But I do enjoy a nice mellow "glow." I had that feeling now. Just the right "glow" that puts you into that pleasant comfort zone of being your most authentic, best self: warm, open and free to reach out, and in high spirits, full of good talk, good laughter, good cheer. In fact the whole world could use a bit of a "glow."

The dance floor was packed with good looking fit Austrians shaking about.

Everyone seemed to be of a student age and dressed casually in jeans and pullover sweaters. Only the sound of the German language being spoken made me aware that I was not back on my college campus.

The music of Donna Summer was blasting: *Love To Love You Baby.* I felt compelled to get up and move. Leaving my stool, I craned my neck in all directions surveying the "scene." I slowly began to amble about, bumping into people, due to the crowding. Unfortunately, it seemed most of the girls were being hovered over by young robust Austrian men, most looking straight from the slopes; or just having stepped out of a slick ad in a ski magazine.

Across the bar in the big over-sized corner booth, I noticed six girls, laughing very loud, pouring drinks from two huge pitchers of beer. I was especially attracted to the very pretty girl with long dark hair and a radiant smile, sitting on the end closest to the wall. When she looked up I started dancing to the music, doing the frug by myself. When I had her attention, I reached in my pocket and brought out my sign: "WILL SHOVEL WALK FOR 60 AS," holding the sign against my chest, while swaying my hips to the music.

She gave me a confused look on seeing the sign, and I could see she was nudging her girlfriends as if to say, "Look at this odd one." As I approached their table, I focused my eyes only on her. She was now smiling at me, and seemed to be both amused and confused as she spoke to me in German. Although I had no idea what she said, it made me feel good that she spoke to me in German, and that I did not appear to be an obvious American tourist.

"I don't speak German." I had to shout to be heard over the pounding sounds of the Rolling Stones' *I Can't Get No Satisfaction*.

"What do you mean by that sign?" she asked with an inquisitive but smiling, inviting face. Within minutes, after explaining my business venture, they all insisted I join them and share their beer.

They were delightful. They all introduced themselves. They were all students and all spoke English with that unmistakable strong Austrian accent. "Sit in the middle here," the lovely dark haired girl said. Her name was Gretchen, an Architecture student. Her friends were attractive as well and could not have been more warm or welcoming. They were eager to know about my travels, where I had been, and where I was headed.

I interrupted our lively conversation with a question from out of nowhere:

"Do you want to see my shoveling stroke?"

I boasted. "Oh yes, please," they cheered me on. I stood up to my full height, with my captive audience looking up as I made my powerful stroke, with their bright eyes fixated on me, squealing and applauding.

A couple of pitchers of beer later, our booth now getting raucous, I led the girls to the dance floor, dancing with two, three, four of them at once, as I introduced them to my new dance: "THE SHOVEL;" jiving to the music, dipping way down in shoveling form, and lifting way up. Soon those on the dance floor were all watching us. The usually conservative Austrians were now caught up in the new dance craze: "THE SHOVEL."

I heard a couple of the girls call out to others in German: "It is called DAS SHOVEL!" Now almost the entire dance floor was wildly grooving to the latest dance craze: "THE SHOVEL." We were rocking! We were SHOVELING! We were "glowing!"

Dripping with sweat, following the frenetic dancing, I squeezed back into the booth with the others, kissing Gretchen on the cheek. But regretfully, my blissful evening like Cinderella's, was about to come to an abrupt end; as it was almost 11:30 p.m. I had to get to the hostel by midnight, as they lock the front gate.

I broke the news and there was a collective groan of disappointment. To my surprise, without me even thinking about it, one of them said,

"Do you want to shovel my parents' walk tomorrow?" And before I could answer with a big nod, others chimed in: "Yes, shovel our walk."

"Please shovel my walk, Scott."

With time getting short, they quickly wrote down their phone numbers and insisted I call early tomorrow morning.

All the girls, except one named Sonia, lived with their parents. They mentioned again that it was important to phone early, as they would be in classes by 9AM. I got up to leave with just time enough to hug each one. Holding Gretchen especially close I said, "I would like to see you again." She returned my hug and said, "Call me."

"YOU DON'T MIND BEING SEEN WITH A SNOW SHOVELER?"

I asked humbly. With that alluring smile she exclaimed: "I love that you are a shoveler!" And I love your stroke and want to see it more!" Wow! What a high note to leave on.

Racing back to the hostel, I made it by two minutes, got into my bed, grinning as I first checked that my trusty shovel was below on the floor. My head was buzzing from the beer, and with thoughts of Gretchen's pretty face, I felt giddy about tomorrow. I said one more prayer for more snow and dropped into a delicious deep sleep.

My prayer for snow was answered, as during the night another fresh eleven inches fell. WHEE! Terrific! Up at the crack of dawn, I immediately went to the front desk, and with Wilhelm's kind permission, made six quick phone calls to the girls.

As I began to dial Gretchen's number, I became concerned about the logistics, where each home was located, and if this would be time efficient. Suppose the girls were located inconveniently far from each other . . . No problem! Those girls were amazing, figuring out all the details. Not only did they each talk to their parents and get their permission to shovel, but they planned out precisely which order to do it in to be most productive.

Gretchen assured me that the distances were not far apart, and that one of the parents of each girl would drive me to the next shoveling location. Gretchen told me she would be home at around three o'clock, when I was scheduled to shovel her walk. And added, ominously, that there was something she needed to talk to me about.

The snow shoveling went like clock-work. The parents of all the girls could not have been nicer. Each seemed pleased with my services. And all invited me in for a coffee, hot chocolate, a sandwich, or a pastry, before transporting me to my next location. I shovel, I eat, I smile, get paid, get hugged, and get moved to my next snow-covered sidewalk. Good deal.

Shortly after three o'clock, I arrived at Gretchen's, the last of the six sidewalks. I was eagerly looking forward to seeing her. When I spoke to her earlier in the day, and she said: "There is something I want to talk to you about."

It had a much more serious tone, then at last night's "I can't wait to see more of your stroke!" Finishing my job, we sat on her sofa as her mother introduced herself. She was an older just as pretty version of Gretchen. After chatting a bit, she excused herself and disappeared upstairs.

I noticed that Gretchen was somewhat guarded, uneasy. She seemed to sit further away than seemed natural. She made a polite joke about my shoveling ability. I made a sincere effort to thank her and her friends for arranging all the snow shoveling business. "It really has helped me out. And it is extra good fortune meeting you last evening." I started to put my hand out to take hers, but thought otherwise.

"Scott that is what I want to talk to you about." She looked at me with earnest, troubled eyes, much different from the laughing, carefree eyes of the night before. She almost did not seem like the same person.

I just kept staring at her, trying to look as easy and relaxed as possible.

"I had so much fun with you last night," she said. "You are so funny and engaging, Scott, I could easily see myself want to be close to you."

I smiled and replied, "That makes me happy. I feel the same way about you. Perhaps we can go out tonight."

"Scott, that's the point, I can't. I have a boyfriend in Geneva. He is going to the Hotel School there, and although things have been a little rocky with him being away, I am still his girlfriend and want to remain faithful. Going out with you would make it even more difficult."

This is what I expected was coming. As one believing in strong relationships, I certainly did not want to get in the way of breaking anyone up, and told her this.

Holding her hand smiling I said, "I understand completely. Don't be concerned about it."

She returned my smile but looked sad and thoughtful.

An awkward silence.

I wanted to leave her laughing like last night. I loved her laugh! So I added:

"Well, I guess that means you won't see more of my stroke." She looked confused, and remembering last night, she broke into her signature laugh, nodding, and saying: "Too much beer!"

We exchanged addresses. I sincerely wished her the best of luck and so moved on, regretting I could not have gotten to know her better.

Heading back on the trolley to the hostel, shifting gears, I gloated, adding up in my mind the money I had made today. Three of the jobs today paid the requested 60 AS; two paid 70 AS. I continued my calculations: Gretchen's parents paid a full 100, despite their driveway being the smallest.

Total for the day 420 AS. FANTASTIC! The GRAND TOTAL for two days of snow shoveling was 1,020 AS ($63) I'm rich!! In two days had made more than half of what I made in the full month of working at the Hotel Evergreen.

I felt rich in other ways as well. "Lesson of the road," the priceless value of reaching out and connecting with the people during your travels. I had learned valuable entrepreneurial skills, promoting and selling my services, meeting and greeting my customers. And oh yes, the power of advertising! And the rewards of hustle and best effort, earning money for a vital cause: let the world adventure continue . . .

What a financial success! No, it wasn't an MBA degree from prestigious Wharton or Harvard School of Business. But . . . it was a start!

I was the SNOW SHOVELING CZAR of Innsbruck!

Chapter 11

HUNGER'S DRIVE TO DESPERATE DEEDS: I WAS SHAMELESS

In my on-going efforts to save money to prolong my travels, by working and hitchhiking; I hesitate to mention another source I resorted to in desperation.

I was shameless. No, I did not become a male stripper or rob any banks to raise money. I became a restaurant voyeur of children's plates. Let me explain.

One needs energy to travel and to maintain good health. That means eating, which I could not afford. I traveled hard, was always on the move. The energy expended was immense. I was always hungry, as never before in my life.

Eating in the rural areas was not a problem, as I would make my way around knocking on farmhouse doors and working in return for delicious home-cooked meals with generous second and third helpings.

Also, while hitching, time and again, thanks to my "go to" line:

"I love traveling your country, but I am not eating well," would consistently result in a warm invitation to the proud driver's home for their regional food specialty; and to meet the family.

But cities proved more difficult for me to eat well on my miniscule budget. I was consumed by saving money, so because of the cost I would rarely go to a restaurant. Instead I would opt for a single slice of pizza, or just cheese and bread; or perhaps a can of baked beans cooked over my sterno can. Even the occasional hamburger or fish and chips left me hungry and unsatisfied.

It was a rainy night in Newcastle, England where I first found "enlightenment." I am not referring to an otherworldly, out-of-body religious experience, but instead a process whereby I could savor and be nourished by the finest food of quality restaurants, and not pay big bucks ($$$$). In fact pay no bucks at all!

As the rain continued to pound down, I pressed my face against the window of the Newcastle restaurant. It looked so cozy and inviting, as I witnessed heaping plates of hot food, being carried by the waiters to their expectant guests. The thought of returning to my wet tent, and eating out of a can, made me sad and nauseous.

The welcoming, warmly-lit restaurant with its delectable display of food beckoned to me. I had a weak moment. I broke down. I could not resist. I entered the dining room and splurged on pork chops and mashed potatoes. The food tasted so flavorful, so filling, so satisfying, so comforting. BRING IT ON! There was nary a crust left in the bread basket.

But even more important than the food, was the "enlightenment" I suddenly received. This "enlightenment" came in the form of looking around at the patrons in the restaurant and realizing that a good portion of the tables were families, many with young children. And what jumped out at me was the amount of food that most of the children left on their plates. The waiter would clean the table and take away the leftovers. It was then that the light bulb started flashing in my head.

From that time on, I would go into a restaurant, slowly cruising the place to position myself close to a table that had young children. I would order something inexpensive, such as a small side green salad or just french fries.

I would eat very slowly, nibbling on my salad or fries, and sipping my glass of water. This gave me time to ingratiate myself to the parents and amuse and admire their children. I would be very upbeat telling them of my travels, the enjoyment I had traveling in their country; and my desire to continue to travel, as long as I could financially do so.

Timing was the key. When I felt the necessary "comfortable bond" was established, and at the same time eyeing the respective child's plate, making sure that the kid looked "finished," yet being cautious that the waiter not take away the food too soon . . . I would confide: "I AM ON A TIGHT BUDGET AND NEED TO BE CAREFUL OF MY EXPENSES. COULD I PLEASE HAVE YOUR CHILD'S LEFT-OVER FOOD, INSTEAD OF WASTING IT?"

This question: "if I could have the child's food," always caused an initial startled look, a question they had never been asked before. However, after the first look of bewilderment, they were eager to donate their child's leftover food to help me.

I was amazed at the success of this process. So brazen would I become, and so sure that I could end up with a child's food, that when entering a restaurant I would leisurely linger awhile to check out and assess the quality of the food, especially what the kids were eating. If I did not like what I saw, I would move on to another restaurant.

There were often times when I was situated between two tables with children, and the other adults overhearing would say: "OH, YOU CAN HAVE OUR FOOD AS WELL. PLEASE HELP YOUSELF." I did.

This gig of being "a restaurant voyeur of children's plates" was so helpful, and so incredibly gratifying for me in eating well and saving money, so the world journey could continue . . . I give thanks to all those families, especially in England, Germany and Spain, who supported my hunger quest.

Much later in my global travels in a city in Morocco, this "restaurant scene" took a much different, darker turn . . . The Moroccan waiter had just served me. Suddenly a shabby little girl rushed up to my table and stole food from my plate; then scurried out the side door.

She did not have the luxury to ask, as I did. A different level of hunger. A different degree of desperation. I understood. I was shattered. And no longer hungry.

BREAKING BREAD AROUND THE WORLD

Chapter 12

CASSOULET NIRVANA IN CASTELNAUDARY

The Citroen, old and rusted, with its unmistakable oversized head lights rounded the bend on a rural country road outside of Toulouse. As it inched its way up the hill, it began to shake and sputter. It stopped, or seemed to break down about ten feet in front of me. The grizzled man behind the wheel looking about the same age as the car, say forty, kicked the passenger door open. I got in and off we went.

After exchanging my repertoire of basic French phrases, my "bonjour, comment sa va, tout va bien" soon exhausting my French vocabulary, I eased into English, speaking of my travels, the places I'd been, and where I was headed. The talk then turned serious, to food.

His name was Claude, a farmer visiting his sister in Toulouse, though he himself was from Bazas a village outside of Bordeaux. We talked of cheeses and pâtes from different regions of France. He was especially fond of the goose liver from the Dordogne region. I mentioned to him that I had just spent two days working on a small farm in Seynac. "La ville très belle." Yes, it certainly was a beautiful village.

I mentioned a new food I had discovered. Cassoulet. His face beamed. "One of the country's gastronomique treasures," he said. "Where did you have this dish, in a restaurant, or at a home? Did someone prepare it for you?" he asked.

"Well no, actually I ate it out of a can, cooking it on my gas sterno before sleeping in my tent."

He looked at me in disbelief; "merde" (shit), he shouted. The Citroen swerved and stopped. Claude had deliberately stopped the car. He looked shaken. He ranted in rapid impassioned French. I had no idea what he was saying; however, certainly I understood that I had offended and upset him in some way.

"Claude, what is wrong? The cassoulet was good. I have an extra can in my backpack. Would you like to try some?"

He shook his head in disgust. "You typical American. You like the quick food; yes, you and your McDonald's and KFC."

"But the can is convenient," I tried to explain.

"You my friend, if you are serious about eating the foods of France you have to eat them the right way." Claude inched closer and with a reverence reserved for a pious setting said in a solemn voice: "Scott, especially in this area, the region of Aude, most famous for cassoulet in all of France, please for your sake, do not let anyone know you eat cassoulet out of the can."

Claude was super serious about this. I found his fervor exciting. And he cautioned me, "If you are sincere about tasting authentic cassoulet, you should go to the town of Castelnaudary. This is the place where cassoulet was born."

Claude indeed seemed like a man who had eaten a good deal of cassoulet in his time. This is just what I had hoped for in my attempts to eat my way through France, knowing people like Claude who would take the time to guide me and explain firsthand the regional delicacies that I should be sampling and savoring.

And Claude was not alone in his over-the-top enthusiasms for a specific dish or food item. All through my travels in France I was fortunate to meet Claude types, those who would become impassioned not just over celebrated regional dishes, but over the most simple food item: be it the coloring of a snail; the texture of a mussel; the smell of a baguette; or the way an aged camembert should run. But this is France, need I say more? Food is their thing. God, I love this country! Claude, indeed, was my own personal "cassoulet guru." Feeling a good deal of respect for him, I asked, "Claude, what is in cassoulet? What makes it so special?"

His response had the poignancy and power of a Shakespearean soliloquy.

I swear it looked like he had tears in his eyes, as he described in detail the ingredients and the need for slow simmering of them in their own juices.

"Do you hear that, Scott, S – L – O – W? You Americans do not understand the concept of slow. Remember, Scott, anything worth doing is worth doing <u>slowly</u>, whether it is lovemaking, sipping wine or cooking cassoulet." I told him I appreciated what he was saying.

"I understand, Claude, and it does sound delicious. No more cans for me, I promise."

Claude nodded in approval as if discussing the facts of life with a young son. I asked him where Castelnaudary was located. With that Claude got out his map from above the visor and explained that we were now about 20 kilometers from Toulouse where he would be stopping. He pointed to a road heading southeast of Toulouse about 60 kilometers.

I had planned to take the road going north to Albe. Castelnaudary would be out of my way, but I did not waste a moment in making my decision. Yes, I would make a pilgrimage to the home of cassoulet.

I had one request of Claude. Despite feeling confident that I could speak enough French to communicate my cassoulet mission to others, I had Claude write on a piece of paper the following message in French: "I am an American traveling in your country and seeking delicious cassoulet. Can you recommend a restaurant please?" The "magic message," yes, just in case I need help.

Claude started up the Citroen again. It made its same unusual belching sound, as we traversed the bucolic French countryside, soon arriving in Toulouse where Claude let me off. Thanking him again for enlightening me in the ways of cassoulet. Two hitched rides later I arrived at the outskirts of Castelnaudary about four o'clock. I requested that the driver stop outside the town, when I saw a pretty stream by a wood where I could set up my tent for the night.

The walk into the village of Castelnaudary was quite scenic, as the famed Canal du Midi (a 150-mile waterway that empties into the Mediterranean) runs beside it. The town of 11,000 had a colorful small market and a lovely small square. I decided not to go to just any restaurant and have cassoulet, but instead would take my time and find out which restaurant was best for this dish. I had made the pilgrimage to the home of cassoulet, you bet I wanted to eat the best cassoulet possible!

I did this by asking the locals. I would stop people, all types, but was especially interested in those who were older and had a fullness of form, those who were obviously experienced cassoulet eaters. It was as if I was conducting my own Harris Poll.

Within an hour, word had spread that there was a crazed young American roaming the streets looking for the cassoulet of his dreams.

The early poll results were in. I had probably spoken to over twenty people. There were four restaurants recommended. Two of them were in the majority, each having the same number of votes.

However, there was a dark horse emerging. Inching one vote ahead for serving Castelnaudary's most delicious cassoulet was not a restaurant, but a couple named the Rondiers living on a farm just outside town. They had only one more vote than the leading restaurant, but it was the ardent intensity of the respective voters. Those in the Rondier camp would say things like "Oh, the Rodiers, their cassoulet is made for the gods." Or: "Their cassoulet is a thing of legend." Whereas with the restaurants, the voter response was less impassioned, such as, "I guess I would say Le Refuge."

It was nearing six o'clock and my presence was causing quite a commotion in the little town square. There were probably twenty-five people hovering about in heated discussion about where to send the young American to eat his cassoulet. Can you spell PRIDE? I envisioned in my mind what would happen to me if I pulled out a can of cassoulet now.

One of the most vocal supporters of the Rondier's cassoulet was a man named Jacques. A short but powerfully built man, he wore a jaunty black beret, white sleeveless T-shirt and red- checkered scarf tied at the neck. He really looked the part! He commanded attention. Jacques stood up on the bench where I was seated, pulling me up with him saying: "We want our American friend Scott to have the best cassoulet in Castelnaudary. To me this means the Rondiers." No official hand count was required, as the crowd now nearing probably forty people broke into loud cheering. Yes, a definitive decision regarding where I would eat my cassoulet had been reached.

And with that Jacques gestured for me to follow him. About seven others joined us. It was a real cast of characters including: two nuns easily in their seventies; one young-looking punk rocker with orange hair; his big-breasted, tongue-pierced girlfriend; a Jean-Paul Belmondo look alike; and a tall gangly teenage boy with a motorbike. Together we began the approximately one-mile walk down a dirt path out of the town to the farm-house of the Rondiers to make the introduction.

Passing wild flowers and ancient trees, we came to the dark grey stone farmhouse. Nearby was Madame Rondier, a dark-haired, ruddy-cheeked woman of about fifty digging in the garden. "Bonjours" were exchanged and Jacques launched into his request to have her cook cassoulet for me, the American traveler. I felt a bit uneasy; understandably, as he implied that she should drop everything and cook this guy one of her super duper-duper cassoulets.

However, the woman beamed with pride. Jacques said: "Madame Rondier would be pleased to cook you a cassoulet for tomorrow's lunch. Say one o'clock. Is this good for you?" I thanked Madame Rondier profuse-ly and told her how much I was looking forward to her famous cassoulet.

That evening, back at my tent, I settled cozily in my sleeping bag and munched on pate, apples and a stale baguette. A can of cassoulet was in view in my open backpack. I thought of Claude and smiled. He would be proud. Sleeping was difficult. My anticipation of Madame Rondier's cassoulet was like a child tossing and turning the night before Christmas, anticipating the arrival of Santa Claus.

At noon the next day, walking with a brisk step, I made my way to the Rondiers. It took about forty-five minutes to reach their farmhouse. As I approached, I could see there was a gathering of about twenty people out on the lawn, some whom I recognized from yesterday.

I heard a loud, "SCOTT." It was Jacques, the one who was the driving force in this gastronomic adventure. I waved and let loose with a jovial "bonjour, bonjour" to him and all those present. There was some whoop-ing and clapping, as I came forward. It was like a reception that a lost beloved family member might receive.

Monsieur and Madame came out of their farmhouse. Madame said "manger" (eat) and gestured to come inside. I gave the Monsieur a hand-shake, which he returned with a hearty slap on the back. I hugged Madame Rondier, kissing her on both cheeks and saying "merci beaucoup."

The large wooden table, which was set for nine, was positioned in the center of the small dark stone dining room. On the table were simple white dinner plates, silverware, three bottles of red wine, and a lovely arrangement of delicate wildflowers in the middle.

I was instructed by Madame Rodier to sit at the head of the table. The other diners included: the Rondiers, and their two teenage children, Maurice and Catherine, both of whom seemed a little shy at first by all this fuss, but later warmed up and were very kind. Jacques was joined by his wife, Nancy, a vivacious redhead of big proportions and big laughter. She was a pastry chef at one of the hotels in town and spoke fluent English. For much of the lunch she served as the translator.

The others invited were two of the people I recognized from yesterday, the Jean-Paul Belmondo look-a-like, who today was dressed in a long classic blue and white striped sweater. His name was Yves and he was the brother of Madame Rondier. Despite his rather tough look, he appeared very gracious and fun, though he spoke little English. The other diner was the teenage kid with the motorbike. His name was Stephan. He was the boyfriend of Catherine. He was quiet, but seemed very bright, spoke good English and wanted to get involved with film production. He quizzed me right away on which was my favorite Truffaut movie . I replied *The 400 Blows*. He nodded, seeming to accept my response.

Even before the food came, I said "thank you" to everyone at the table, in my best broken French, with special focus on both Jacques, and of course Madame Rondier. She appeared carrying an individual cast iron pot and placed it in front of me. "Merci, merci." I got out of my chair to embrace her once again.

The cassoulet sat before me. It had a brown crusted glaze. I looked around the table. All eyes were on me, and though everyone had their cassoulet in front of them, no one lifted a fork. They were waiting for me. Even those that did not have seats at the table were gathered standing around the table to observe the young American who made his special trip to Castelnaudary to taste his first cassoulet. (Total viewing crowd was about thirty).

With so many eyes on me, I felt a little nervous as I remembered the drill: pick up fork, put fork in food, bring up food and put in mouth. The combination of the pork, garlic sausage, duck confit and white beans exploded in a powerful delicious flavor. Delicious was not a strong enough word. I had reached gastronomic Nirvana! I let loose with a wildly enthusiastic: "Très bien, très bien!"

The cassoulet was accompanied by a very spirited and festive group of dining companions, as the red Languedoc wine flowed freely. Most of the conversation I was pleased was in French and among the other guests, which I preferred, with no obligation to speak English and keep me entertained. This was much more natural and allowed me to truly savor my cassoulet. God, the melody of meats for a carnivore like me was heaven. The garlic sausage so succulent, and the duck confit, and the pork shank fantastic!

I told the story of Claude and his disdain for my canned cassoulet. This brought out howls of laughter, as Nancy translated the tale. I asked a simple question which set off a heated discussion:

"I have heard there are variations on cassoulet, different ingredients to use. Is this true?"

Nancy, translated my question, the entire table jumped in. Jacques speaking in English and French simultaneously, as he wanted everyone at the table to join in, began what was almost an oration on the dish.

"Scott, you need to understand that cassoulet is in some ways like a religion. People worship, but have their own beliefs in how it is prepared. Cassoulet dates back some eight hundred years, created here in Castelnaudary. And even here in this town there is discussion on what is the right way or the preferred way."

Nancy chimed in, "Some say all the meat and sausage must be pork-based, usually a combination of slab bacon, pork rind and garlic sausage; while others insist on lamb. The poultry used most of the time is duck, but can be goose, and sometimes chicken.

I looked at Madame Rondier, who was quiet and just seemed to take it all in as she sipped her wine. "What do you think are the classic ingredients?" I asked her. This was not even translated when she began to speak.

Nancy translated her response. "You ask ten chefs they all say that you MUST have this and that, but to me I like to change it sometimes.

"What Nancy said is true, but sometimes I prefer to add goose instead of duck confit. I would never use chicken, and the lamb, which I like to use, is debated. Also I am very strict on the using of breadcrumbs mixed in the dish."

"She is the master," praised Jacques, and I raised my glass in a toast: "A votre santé, Madame Rodier;" and everyone cried out "a votre santé." We had been at the table for over two hours.

It was now after three o'clock. I felt deeply satisfied, my stomach singing with gladness. I had such a warm glow from both the wine and meeting these kind, charming people. I embraced everyone and kissed Madame Rondier on both cheeks one more time.

Later that day as I grabbed my belongings and threw on my backpack, I looked with loathing at the can of cassoulet. As I passed the nearest trash bin, I said: "Au revoir!" . . . I could almost feel Claude's approval.

Chapter 13

PHILIPPINE PIG ROAST! PRAISE THE LORD!

As I sat on the hot, unshaded dirty public beach of Puerto Princesca, the unspoiled palm tree-lined beaches of northern Palawan felt like paradise very far removed.

Puerto Princesca was the largest city on the Philippine island of Palawan. Despite the remarkable natural wonders and magnificent beaches covering the island, this one was like any other city beach . . . trashy, crowded and noisy. But one thing seemed to be missing: where were the usual vendors serving up an array of food, be it not very good food, but some nosh of some kind?

I had been at the beach for about an hour. It was now going on one o'clock, and I was getting hungry. However, much to my surprise I could not find a stall or a vendor selling food anywhere. I began to walk up and down the beach, which appeared to run at least a mile. It was swarming with people, with lots of families eating picnic style from an assortment of tantalizing foods spread out.

Yes, there seemed to be food, lots of it. But none for sale. None for me. By now it was two o'clock, and my stomach was growling. With all these families around, I was sure I could figure out a way of getting some food from them. I would walk slowly by a large group chowing down and speak in the national language, Tagalog, "mabuhay" (hello), and smile and say pleasantly, "masarap" (delicious). I was sure one of these families would be won over by my friendliness and invite me to picnic with them. After all I was a foreigner, a rarity in this part of the world. Very few tourists get to Palawan. But to my disappointment there was no such luck.

I would continue this painful, slow process of going by picnickers and hovering for a handout. I became more assertive with my desire to obtain food. I would actually go up to families and say: "I am looking for a place to eat, but there seems to be no restaurants. Could I buy some food from you?" I was hoping to hear a generous-hearted, "Please join us;" or at least someone saying, "Here I will sell you this lumpia for twenty pesos." But all I heard was an indifferent: "No, our food is not for sale."

Wow! What was going on? I had been traveling the Philippines for over a month, two full weeks on Palawan alone. And the Filipino hospitality was as warm as any I had ever encountered. This was a strange and unwelcome turn of events.

It was now well past lunchtime. My hunger pains were increasing, and being surrounded by all this tempting food made it even more unbearable. I envisioned getting a running start and swooping down on an unsuspecting family, then running away with a big chicken leg, as I dashed down the beach gnawing on it. Yes, that was a thought, but I resisted the urge.

I now had reached the end of the beach, which actually ran longer than I expected. I noticed above the beach, on a grassy knoll, a large gathering of people standing under some shady palm trees. This was an ideal setting, as the beach had no shade from the unrelenting sun.

The delectable aroma drew me. I walked closer slowly. There was a group of people, dressed rather formally in flowing white robes, roasting an entire pig. A pig with an apple in its mouth, being turned slowly over an open pit.

This was just brutal punishment for me to witness. Not that I am a vegetarian speaking out for animal rights. No! It was because the roasted pig, the "lechon," is considered the Philippines' greatest culinary delicacy. I had read about it. I had heard about it. I had seen the photos in glossy gourmet magazines, but I had never witnessed it first hand. Now I had, but it was doubtful I would be invited to join in.

This was too much to take. It was an opportunity that could not be ignored. I started to walk briskly toward the group. I was sure one of these people I could befriend for a little nibble of the piglet. But I stopped short, even though my stomach was calling. The people gathered about the pig looked solemnly in prayer, holding hands and chanting. It was a much too serious occasion for my crass, primitive behavior. So I restrained myself and respected their piety.

Hungry, tired and despondent, I sat down about halfway between the roasted pig and the shoreline, not sure what my next move might be. Probably I'd head back to town, although the bus was not scheduled for another two hours.

Hearing the rollicking laughter of children behind me, I turned and saw two young kids, a boy and a girl, both about the ages of seven or eight. They were hugging their mother, and running with abundant joy toward the water. Immediately, several other kids came running to join them. They came from the shaded area where the pig fest was going on.

Then a light went off in my head. The mind is cunning. Cute kids splashing enjoying the surf. A nice scene, yes, but I had an alternative motive. It looked as if the parents had no intention of extending an invitation to the pig roast to "outsiders." But perhaps, yes, just perhaps, by befriending the children (splashing in the ocean), I might be able to win their affection, resulting in an invitation to the pig feast.

I had to be cautious how I approached these young children. I did not want to come across as some overly friendly child molester. I could see the NEW YORK POST headline now: "AMERICAN VACATIONER BUSTED ON PHILIPPINE BEACH FOR GETTING COZY WITH KIDS."

Luckily, I did not have to go out of my way to approach them. For as soon as the kids (probably a dozen from the pig-fest group splashing about) caught a glimpse of the tall, white-skinned foreigner, I was greeted by a chorus of squeals: "Hello Misters" and "What is your name?"

Yes, things were working out. The kids had found a new friend and were amused by me. I made like Frankenstein and started to walk towards them with arms stretched out straight in front of me. In a very deep and other worldly voice, I said: "My name is Scott." The kids would giggle and scream and form a big circle around me, splashing me. Soon more from the shore came running and joined the fun.

Yes, I had won over the kids. They were having a wonderful time. And yes, it amused me, too, for about a minute. But after twenty minutes of keeping this up, I was getting tired and bored, and starving. Hey, where were the parents? Didn't they care that a grown, strange man was splashing about with their children? Please, mom or dad, come down to the shore and check out if your child is cavorting in the water with a potential pervert.

I could see some of the parents now standing and observing the scene from where they were gathered, about fifty yards from the water. Then finally hallelujah! A father in the billowy dress code "du jour," came down to the water's edge and eyed his child standing a few yards away from me. I immediately shifted my attention away from the mom with the group of other youngsters, toward this child. About ten years old, he screeched and ran towards the shore. I continued to walk towards him, still doing my Frankenstein shtick. The child laughed, hugging his father, and I immediately came out of the water to greet the father.

"The kids seem to like you," the dark, handsome man of about thirty-five said. I dropped the Frankenstein gig, at once, and got serious. The pig roast occupying my mind with every spoken word. "I am Scott Stone. I love traveling Palawan. It is my favorite island in the Philippines."

His name was Roberto. About five minutes after exchanging the usual introductory "openers;" where I was from; what I did for a living; and where had I traveled, he looked me in the eyes and asked: "ARE YOU A CHRISTIAN?" Oh! Good God! Why could he not have asked: "Are you hungry?"

Well, without going into details on my conflicted feelings about organized religion, I weighed two choices:

1) Tell him my true reservations about the religion question and risk a riot, or a crucifixion, or worse, banishment from the pig feast. Certainly I could in no way share with him one wise man's definition of religion:

"ORGANIZED RELIGION IS THE BUREAUCRACY THAT GETS IN THE WAY OF TRUE SPIRITUALITY."

or:

2) Become a religious enthusiast for the day, and bask in his new friendship, which I predicted would guarantee an instant invitation to the pig roast.

The decision was not difficult. Choice #2: Food over Faith.

Actually, if required, walking and talking in churchly ways was no stretch for me: baptism and confirmation, Sunday School, Youth Fellowship, formal church services, and the Christmas Eve candlelight service were all a part of my upbringing.

I confess, we were seasonal church goers. Once school was out for the summer and sailing season began, our family was out on the water, not in a church.

So I was prepared to play a pious, "churchly" role today. I was prepared to answer his question. With a beatific smile, I responded: "Yes, Roberto, I am a Christian. Are you?"

"Yes," he answered with pride, I am a 'born again,' and I'm here with friends of our church celebrating the Lord." But Roberto would not leave it at that. He continued talking about Christ and religion and had non-stop questions: about if I loved Jesus; about my religious background; and about the state of Christianity in the USA today. As the Jesus talk marathon rambled on, the aroma of the pig roast was getting stronger, and I was getting weaker, being seriously hungry.

I felt like screaming:

"LOOK, ROBERTO, I ANSWERED THE QUESTION RIGHT: I LOVE JESUS. NOW FEED ME FOR CHRIST'S SAKE!"

Roberto and I had stood there on that beach far too long. He had done a lot of talking. I had done a lot of polite listening only, just so I wouldn't ruin my chances for the pig roast. But there is much of importance I would have liked to have said.

Decision time: no strategy had worked . . .

Time to move on. There was no food in my future here.

"I must go now, Roberto," I said.

Putting his arm around my shoulder, he said, "I'm glad we had this talk, Scott."

Roberto was a fine man. We embraced and were about to say our final farewell, when I decided in desperation to give it a last try and boldly asked: "ARE YOU COOKING SOMETHING UP THERE? THAT IS A DELICIOUS AROMA!"

"Yes," said Roberto simply. "Would you like to join us?"

Spontaneously, unexpectedly from the bowels of my being, I heard myself SHOUTING: "PRAISE THE LORD! Thank you, Roberto, I'd love to." Where did that come from? He laughed.

Roberto joined me in another L-O-U-D:

"PRAISE THE LORD!"

Our shouting and even louder laughter attracted the others nearby. Within minutes I was surrounded by Roberto's fellow church members. He introduced me as: "MR. SCOTT, THE CHRISTIAN FROM AMERICA." "Praise The Lord! Praise The Lord!" they sang out in unison.

I found it interesting why they all dressed the same in white, as if they were a sports team in search of a cricket match.

The members were extremely kind, and so profoundly interested in my feelings about Jesus Christ, and if I had been "born again." "I AM BORN AGAIN WITH EACH NEW DAWN," I assured them, grinning cheerily. That seemed to satisfy them for the moment.

Just when I began to feel a little comfortable and mellow, Roberto made the gracious gesture requesting that I do them the honor of saying "Grace" before the pig feast began. "Scott, you were delivered to us for a reason today, we feel. You know how Jesus walked by the Sea of Galilee. Today you walked by the sea and found us," he said persuasively.

When I finally and reluctantly offered my prayer, it was brief, simple and sincere:

"Let us give thanks for our many blessings today: the food, the fellowship, our families, and the beauty that surrounds us. But most of all for the gift of LIFE, which we celebrate today. I thank you for your kindness in sharing this great feast with me. AMEN."

There was silence . . . And then applause and a unanimous request that the "Christian from America" be first in line to be served for the Pig Roast.

As I was gluttonously chowing down, I had no doubt that the Pig Roast was well worth waiting for; it was so succulently delicious and roasted to perfection. I could not have enjoyed it more.

I enjoyed, too, that none of the other church members continued to badger me: "If I had been 'born again'." I had. Not in churchly ways, not in their ways, but in other ways impossible for me to comprehend or articulate.

I could feel Roberto's powerful "presence" now beside me, to say "good-bye and to wish me well." We expressed how we wished our paths might cross again. At a future "coming together," I hoped perhaps we could share not only food, but nourishing "food for thought" as well.

After all, as my old Sunday School Bible verse reminded me: (which I didn't understand at the time):

"MAN DOES NOT LIVE BY BREAD ALONE."

Chapter 14

THAI FAMILY DINNER WITH ALL THE TRIMMINGS (DAUGHTER FOR DESSERT)

I had found the ideal spot. Situated about fifty yards off the rural roadway, were a cluster of palm trees creating almost a perfect protective circle. The grass was extra soft and fertile here, ideal for spreading out my sleeping bag for the night.

It was dusk. The light was fading and the sunset's colors played lovely on the high verdant hills of Laos across the Mekong River. Although I was in Thailand, I felt worlds removed from the hectic hustle, heat and noise of Bangkok. This solitary place was like a blessed escape. I felt at peace here. This is what I needed.

My recent six months in India, though incredibly fascinating, punished me health-wise. I had come down with dysentery (not uncommon for anyone traveling hard in India). My weight had dropped now to an emaciated, stick-like 127 pounds. Arriving in Bangkok from India, I checked into a hospital and received medication. But the doctor's best prescription was to rest and make sure I ate at least six peanut butter sandwiches a day.

Being a good patient, I was just biting into my fifth of the day when I heard a voice and saw out on the roadway a cart pulled by a water buffalo. This was a welcomed sight and sound, as meeting local Thais, spontaneously, during these five days of walking and traveling slowly down the Mekong River region in northeastern Thailand, has been filled with amazing hospitality.

He waved towards me to come over to him. I greeted him with folded hands and the common greeting in Thailand of "sawadika." He was an elderly man, lithe and dark, with a welcoming grin with three or four teeth missing. He motioned to me, shaking his head in a "NO!" gesture, objecting that I sleep on the ground. With his hands, he made the eating gesture.

Yes, that was the inviting gesture I loved to see; and one that would certainly improve on my scheduled two peanut butter sandwiches to come.

The cart ride home took about an hour. It was slow and tranquil, almost surreal: stretched out in the back, lying against my backpack; hearing only the rhythmic, comforting clomp of the water buffalo; and feeling the soft night breeze, as darkness slowly crept in. Here and there the stars started to make their reassuring nightly appearance. I took in some deep breaths of country air.

Embracing this night was a delight.

I didn't care where we were going, or if we ever got there. So after turning left on to a smaller side road, I was almost sorry when the cart came to a final stop.

His small humble house was nestled in a grove of bamboo trees by a narrow stream. His name was Nat. In Thai he introduced me to a younger man and woman, who greeted us as we pulled up.

Pointing to the man, he said the word "son." The son, in turn, introduced the woman as "wife." We seemed to sawadika and shake hands for a time, as we exchanged greetings. They led me inside to a mat on the floor. The wife gestured the eating motion, and down I sat. Dinner was to be served, as the three of them joined me, all sitting cross legged on the floor.

It was then that a young girl came out. She was very pretty, petite, with playful dark eyes and long silky hair. I began to stand up for her, but all gestured for me to stay put.

The father said: "Daughter name Phalin." She could not have been more than seventeen years old. And although I tried to be subtle, I could not keep my eyes off her.

The dinner as I was hoping featured classic Isaan cooking (food of northeastern Thailand) which is much more akin to the cuisine of Laos than other parts of Thailand; consisting of green papaya salad, known as Somtam and the Kai yang, chicken marinated in herbs and honey and grilled over an open fire, and Sai Krok Isaan. This is a very large sized sausage and unique in its sour, pungent taste. The taste sensations were varied, unusual and delicious!

There was not much said, as we sat on the floor and ate. As we waited for dessert to be served, the father looked at me and said something in Thai that I did not understand. The family spoke only a few basic words of English. He repeated it again louder, and I said in Thai: "Do not understand."

Then came a shocking turn of events that even the impeccable Emily Post would not have been prepared for in her definitive etiquette book on proper table manners.

No, it was not "finger bowls . . ."

It was "finger play."

A few seconds of silence passed. The father tapped my knee to get my attention, and made the universal, unmistakable gesture of forming a circle with his left hand, and with his center finger of his right hand moved it, faster and faster, in and out. He pointed to his daughter.

Phalin was giggling, as young girls do. Nat, the grandfather seemed turned on by this, and now he was repeating the motion with his old gnarled hands, being sure I got the message.

Well, yes, he had gotten my attention. And, yes, I got the message. Through this gesture, the father was giving me permission to have sex with his daughter. I don't remember reading this chapter in my guidebook. . . We have not even gotten to dessert, and he is offering this up to me. Phalin seemed oblivious to the gesture, which I know she clearly saw and understood. She just gave me a slight approving smile.

My first thought was that he was trying to make money off his daughter. I had heard that many of the young girls that partake in the sex bars of Bangkok are from small villages in the northeast, and are recruited heavily.

I felt uncomfortable and awkward. I knew I had to handle the situation tactfully, as I said, "Thank you but no money," gesturing with the loose baht I had in my pocket. This seemed to insult and enrage the father, as he barked at me shouting: "No Baht. No Baht!"

The grandfather was still continuing with his "finger play." The wife whispered something, got up and returned shortly, with the Thai-English Dictionary. Handing it to her husband, he began to flip through it. All during this time Phalin remained quiet, but now was blushing a bit and seemed slightly embarrassed.

With the dictionary opened, the father pointed to a word. It said: "CUSTOM." I repeated the word "custom," and the Thai word. The mother and father repeated the word extra loud with emphasis: "CUSTOM!" They nodded in affirmation and pointed proudly at their daughter.

I wanted to be perfectly clear about this: So I guess what this meant was, that it was my duty as the guest to honor this tradition or "custom" and sleep with the daughter, as the host's ultimate act of hospitality to me. I felt strangely ambivalent.

The gracious host was getting "pissed." I already had insulted him once. I could not refuse his generous hospitality again. So I gestured with slow, cautious movements to confirm that I understood: first, pointing to the daughter; then gesturing holding the daughter; and sleeping with the daughter.

I must admit, it turned me on. And it was certainly good for my ego, as I thought the way I looked, so skinny and bleak, no attractive woman would have interest in me. But then again . . . there wasn't much traffic on that old water buffalo trail, maybe anyone would look good.

It had been a very long time since I had been close to a woman. I ached to hold a pretty girl, and Phalin was just so very pretty.

As if we had been discussing the weather, we passed around some fresh fruit as dessert and ate in silence. I again graciously thanked my hosts for the meal, smiling and saying "aroi mak mak" (delicious) several times and rubbing my stomach happily in satisfaction.

When the plates were cleared, the parents motioned for me to follow them through the small house and pointed to a narrow, cot-like bed in the back of the house. It was only separated by a hanging white sheet. Yes, this would be a most intimate family experience.

The parents and grandfather seemed to conveniently vanish, and it was just Phalin and I left. She led me back to the bedroom by the hand. If I couldn't refuse the host's hospitality, I could perhaps compromise. I decided I was going to be content just to hold Phalin and have the pleasure of her soft, warm body beside me. And spare her the "duty" of being further involved with me. I was beginning to feel sorry for this sweet young thing. My feelings were more of tenderness than lust.

But this is not what she wanted. Lighting a candle, she seductively and artfully removed her clothes, as she helped me with my belt. She was very smooth and practiced at this quaint "custom." I certainly was not the first dinner guest to grace her bed. Yes, she knew all the right moves. She was "hot to trot."

No, this was not an innocent sweet, young thing. So . . . with my "brains between-my-legs" mentality, I soon willingly allowed myself to get swept away by this teenage tigress, and determined to enjoy the night to its fullest.

However, as we began to get more intimate, my mind began to spin. Fortunately I had not lost all rational reasoning. My conflicting, uncomfortable concerns began overtaking the carnal passion and pleasures. There had to be a catch to this, I thought.

What will happen tomorrow? Do I just get up and leave? After all having a USA husband, even one with little money like me, might play well for the family, and the locals, and was to be encouraged.

I didn't want to be looking up any words in the English-Thai Dictionary in the morning. Such as: marriage, pregnancy, shot gun, prison. With these alarmist, troublesome thoughts racing through my head, I was "cooling down," before "heating up." I was kissing and caressing her, but went no further. She was getting irritated. Old American traveler custom says:

"WHEN IN DOUBT, DON'T!"

And I didn't. Instead I became consumed with how to make a graceful exit, before it was too late.

So suddenly I started faking being stricken with a gastronomical attack. Bent over in pain, grabbing my stomach, gesticulating wildly, and making vile gagging sounds, as if violently vomiting; I pleaded where the toilet was. She pointed outside.

Fortunately, my back pack was next to the door. As I headed supposedly for the toilet, I grabbed my pack on the way out, bolted for the door, and disappeared into the night. The fresh air of freedom felt exhilarating!

I in no way wished to dishonor my host's hospitality. But this was just too high a price to pay for dinner and dessert.

And . . . "WHEN A GUY'S GOTTA GO, HE'S GOTTA GO!"

Chapter 15

BRITTANY BELLY BUSTER

With bloated stomach, I wobbled cautiously down the steep dimly-lit stairs following Pierre, Monsieur Rosseau's eleven year old son, to what led to a rec room.

Pierre, tall and lanky, with straight black bangs and wearing a Bruce Springsteen T-shirt, flicked on the light and pointed to a La-Z-Boy recliner in chocolate faux leather, sitting in the center of the room. Everything seemed to radiate from "the chair," a pool table, a small bar, a dart board, and a television set.

American pop culture adorned the walls: Madonna, Sylvester Stallone as "Rocky," and Marilyn Monroe with her skirt being blown about. Except for the small picture of the 1974 French World Cup team, and what seemed to be the French version of "The Price is Right" on TV, this could be "anywhere rec room USA."

But I did not care what was on the walls, or how it seemed to be a tad tacky, or that there were no posters of French icons like: Catherine Deneuve, Jean-Paul Sartre, Truffaut, or even the ubiquitous map of France displaying proudly its 400 plus cheeses. All that I cared about was my stomach, and how satisfied it was, after an absolutely delectable dinner, prepared lovingly by Madame Rosseau.

I had a vision of my father getting such enjoyment from the La-Z-Boy chair. A vision that never happened, as my mother would not allow "that chair", which she called "tasteless" to enter our home. Tasteless, perhaps, but for me at this moment, as I pulled on the side lever and felt the sensation of the chair inching down and up and out all at once. It was bliss.

Loosening my belt I wallowed in the sensation of my satisfied overstuffed sated self.

As soon as I had "landed" in my ideal La-Z-Boy position, appearing out of nowhere was Nathalie, the Rosseau's precocious nine-year old.

"Pour vous," she smiled.

"What is this?" I asked.

"Charlottes," she exclaimed.

I felt so full. I wanted no part of it. But my manners being intact, I took a small bite out of the lady-finger shaped chocolate charlotte in appreciation. The chocolate was so rich dipped in liquor with the inside filled with chocolate mousse.

Wow!! From one small bite, I gobbled down the other three remaining on my plate. I looked at Nathalie and let out with a: "Très, très bien delicieux, merci beacoup."

Nathalie broke out with giggles, jumped up and down several times, and dashed up the stairs calling out to her mother with unbridled joy.

Now it was the father's turn, as he stood before me holding an unmarked bottle. In my "chair," I felt like a reclining king as his servants, or in this case one member of the Rosseau family after another presented me with yet another tasty morsel to sample and savor.

"This is called Pommeau," he announced. "It is famous in Brittany, a combination of sweet cider and apple brandy. We make it locally in the town," said the beaming James.

Handing me the cognac-shaped glass, I took a sip. It had a distinct sweet taste, a little too sweet for me. But being aware of James' probing eyes, eager for my reaction, I appreciatively nodded my head slowly up and down, savoring every drop: "Très bien, oui, merci." James said that he had to go upstairs to help Madame Rosseau for about half an hour, and I could just relax here, if that was fine with me. Yes, it was.

So now alone with my La-Z-Boy I drank down the remaining brandy and placed the plate and glass on the floor. Ah, yes, such a satisfied feeling. I shut my eyes as I fondly played back the past eight hours. I reflected on my meeting with James, his kindness, and the "magic phrase" that once again worked wonders, resulting in strong family contact and delicious home cooked French food.

It was a truck stop off the main road that headed west towards Brest, Brittany's largest city, that I met James. Truck stops are a gold mine for hitchhikers. I especially like to take advantage of eating in the cafeteria.

Not because the food is that good, for it is usually mediocre and over-priced. But because it allows me the opportunity to sit by someone, strike up a conversation, and make good contact.

It was 12.32 p.m. and the cafeteria was buzzing. It was packed with travelers. For lunch I decided on a rather uninspired filet of tuna. This was the least expensive of the entrees on the menu. I stood holding my tray looking for just the right place to position myself by a potential "patron." This is what I secretly liked to call the people I would meet in my travels, who were kind in bringing me greater enrichment wherever I was. Be it with a ride, sharing of information, a home-cooked meal, or a warm bed.

Over in the far corner I noticed a group of young boys all dressed in the same matching green warm ups, most likely a youth soccer team. Soon, the entire team, about fifteen boys started to vacate the table. The long table now was left with only five people scattered about. One man about forty years old, with a receding hairline, rather on the chubby side wearing a bright orange wind- breaker, sat alone with three empty chairs between him and the end of the table. Yes, this was perfect.

I approached and nodded to him, as I sat down. Not wanting to waste any time in hoping that he would talk to me, I launched right in after sitting for all of fifteen seconds. In my most American Midwest accent asked: "Do you know what time it is?" (This despite the fact that there was a gigantic clock positioned on the wall behind me). He turned his wrist toward me showing the time, which I notice many Europeans do, said: "12:42." He became inquisitive, asking me the basic introductory questions: "Where are you from? Are you a student?

His name was James. He spoke broken but recognizable English. His soft voice did not match his rather course features. James was eating steak and frites. His steak looked much more appetizing than my wilting tuna. I noticed that he still had a good portion of his food left on his plate, so we had time to talk.

I could see outside the rain beginning to fall. This seemed the norm for Brittany. Looking at James, watching his stubby hands quickly maneuver the steak knife, my hope was not just for a ride but a home cooked meal and another opportunity to savor the wonders of French cuisine. In my quest for continued gastronomic joy on little money, yes, perhaps James the man sitting here would be my next benevolent "patron."

He then asked it, the question I was hoping for. The question which I longed and loved to hear: "So how are you enjoying your travels?" Like a seasoned thespian, I knew my line of response. I had recited and delivered it many times. But always I delivered the line sounding so natural as if stated fresh for the first time.

"There is much I have enjoyed about my travels. The Brittany coast is magnificent. I especially enjoyed hiking the pink granite coast around Cap Frehel, and the unusual rock formations of the Carnac Stones." James nodded, pleased to hear that my experience had been a good one.

Pausing, I looked straight at him and said quietly, but firmly (with conviction) and shaking my head slightly: "I have not eaten very well."

This caused an immediate perplexing: "pourquoi," as if you are in France how could this be possible?

James leaned toward me. I elaborated. "It's just that I am not eating the dishes that I hoped to eat in Brittany. Before coming on this trip I read from American food magazines about French cuisine and how each region has its specialties that they are famous for. And here in Brittany the food I read about, the dishes I had dreamed to taste, such as Cotriade Bretanne, (the fisherman stew), Coquilles St. Jacques (cream scallops served in their shell), and Giot d' Agneau (leg of lamb), I have not tasted."

"Yes, those are some of our best regional dishes. I am impressed you know about our cuisine. But why have you not tried them? You can eat these dishes at our local restaurants." My answer (call me shameless if you want, but my stomach was calling out): "I must be honest, I just can't afford to eat at those restaurants. I don't have the money. I want to travel France to explore, to learn all I can, but I have to do it on the cheap. I travel with a backpack. I hitchhike. I sleep outside. All to save money."

My soliloquy was having its effect on James, as it had already on several kind people that I had met in northern France. It was a prideful thing, the food of France, and more specifically, the regional food. I was a traveler, unhappy that I could not sample what Brittany was famous for. People would take this as a challenge to present me with their regional dishes that I had ached for.

To me the analogy might be: if some young French traveler intrigued by baseball, the famous American sport, dreams of going to Yankee Stadium but can't afford it. Yes, you bet I would make his dream come true.

James asked what direction I was headed. "To Brest." He was quiet, as if in deep contemplation, and said: "Wait here. I must call my wife. I will be right back." I felt a surge rush through me. I could feel that possibly I'd have a new "patron" in James. He returned saying the words that were music to my ears: "Scott, if you like you could stay with us tonight and have dinner. My wife is a very good cook. She will cook you special Brittany dishes.

When I hear those words "staying the night, my wife will cook for you," it is almost a "high" that I get. Sure it is good to save money this way, but it is so very much more. It feeds the soul, nourishes the spirit. For me, this is the essence of travel: the contact of a family in a foreign land; to see the inside of their home, to meet their children, to see how they interact. To be involved with their pleasure in eating, their laughter, their talk, their vibrancy. Even to see what they watch on TV. Yes, to me this is the most meaningful part of travel, the contact. Many people travel, but few connect with the people, regretfully.

And what a dinner it was! Sitting at their simple wooden dinner table in the small two bedroom home in the village of Gouesnou, a suburb of Brest, I was absolutely famished. I had worked up an appetite by playing soccer with Pierre and his friends, and giving Nathalie one piggy-back ride after another.

Madame was bustling about in the kitchen. I was in high anticipation of this dining experience, as James over the squabbling voices of Nathalie and Pierre, proudly announced:

"Scott, tonight you are in for a treat. The dish that Evelyn has cooked is called Homard a' l'Americaine (lobster in a spicy tomato broth). It is considered one of Brittany's most famous and loved dishes."

As if on cue, out came Evelyn; she was a woman of average size with blondish, curly hair, and a much bigger than average smile. She radiated with happiness, as she carried the mammoth steaming kettle, to the table.

The meal was outrageously delicious, filled with such joyousness and an abundance of laughter and pure passion for food. The lobster dish was accompanied by a choice Muscadet wine from the neighboring Loire Valley, just the right distinctive, clean bracing taste. What a memorable meal it was! An incomparable Brittany Belly Buster!

I could hear the sheets of rain pound against the window. Feeling so content and comfy I dug down deeper in the La-Z-Boy and drank the rest of the brandy, which gave me a pleasant glow. Tomorrow I would be leaving northern France and heading south. My time travelling in Normandy and Brittany was filled with kind, generous people, and fabulous home cooking lovingly prepared.

Feeling so very satisfied and sentimental, I closed my eyes and drifted off . . . I was not counting sheep. I was counting unforgettable French foods parading in sweet dreams: sauces, soups, breads, cheeses, crepes, and quiches. And the unforgettable French families who prepared and shared them with a hungry, grateful traveler from America.

Tout va bien!

WHAT'S A GUY LIKE YOU . . . DOING IN A PLACE LIKE THIS?

Chapter 16

SWITZERLAND: SWINGING, JET SETTING ST. MORITZ

After the dreary experience of working at the Hotel Evergreen in the village of Igls, Austria (Chapter 26), with its achingly boring nightlife, catering to family-package skiers, I was in the mood for someplace that had some "action." That meant St. Moritz, Switzerland. Yes, swinging, jet setting St. Moritz!

It took me two rides to get to St. Moritz, the first from a young German who drove recklessly fast, passing cars on mountain turns. He had a severe Mohawk haircut and a sullen mood to match. It almost seemed as if he stole the car and was trying to get away from someone; or had a lethal death wish. I felt relieved that the ride was only about eight miles. He turned off just before reaching the Swiss border.

From the Swiss border to St Moritz, I was picked up by a guy named Arnold, about thirty years old and a native of Madrid. He was head chef at a local hotel where he had worked the past five seasons. He loved the town for its picturesque setting, its partying atmosphere and terrific looking women. He seemed to know all the hot spots and informed me of the places I had to go. I took note, as I wrote them down. The drive to St. Moritz offered spectacular alpine scenery. But the snow was kicking up, and it made the driving around the mountain roads treacherous, taking almost three hours to go just fifty miles.

As Arnold let me out in the town's main intersection, I felt a sense of high anticipation. Immediately, I could feel the festive atmosphere as many attractive young skiers strolled about in their bright day glow ski outfits, so different from Igls. It was wonderful to be here. Time to have some fun!

The town of St. Moritz is quite small, cradled dramatically in a long valley of the Alps called the Engadine. Its "international playground for the rich" reputation is well documented and states explicitly it is not interested in catering to those on a budget, needless to say, those carrying a backpack. Not even bothering to check out hotels, as the price for one night's lodging would set me back about three weeks of funds, I immediately went directly to the train station. My plan was to store my stuff in a locker and return to sleep in the train station. One night in St. Moritz, that was my plan. I was going to party hard and make the most of it!

I had some time to kill, as it was only five o'clock. With the setting sun the white peaks had a pinkish glow. Sitting on a bench sipping a hot chocolate, it was fun to take in the passing parade of ski vacationers. Some looked like they had just raced down black double diamond runs; others I questioned if they had ever been, or had any intention to ski, but were more concerned with après ski, and how they looked.

Fur was everywhere! Massive full-length coats, not just on the women but men, too. Some of the women wore dazzling jewelry. Others I noted trying to navigate their footing on the snow-covered pavement in six-inch stiletto heels. Yes, St. Moritz had an unquestionably ostentatious feel about it. But it was a lark, so energized, so international, hearing Italian, German, French, and English. A strong Texas twang hung in the air. Russian was spoken the least; but those that did seemed to swagger with "attitude" the most.

Hungry, I grabbed an overpriced bratwurst, walked through the village gawking at the stunning window displays: huge diamonds, emeralds, rubies, pearls; designer shoes, designer everything; decadent chocolates, all lavishly presented. I strolled down by the frozen lake and enjoyed the "priceless" silence away from the street and the "madding crowd." The backdrop of the massive snowcapped peaks was fading now as dark descended on the "circus" below.

The weather was beginning to change as the light snow flurries gave way to full- sized flakes. The wind picked up and the snow was heavy and constant. As the weather became harsher, it was time to go inside. It was only about seven o'clock. I had at least three hours before hitting the bars.

I felt confident walking into an opulent hotel lobby. I had shaved and changed in the train station to my one and only presentable outfit, a handsome black cashmere turtleneck sweater and dark dress slacks. In this outfit I took on a different persona, from "backpacker" to: "I belong here."

I split this waiting time between the Kulm and Palace hotels. However at the Palace I was asked: "Can we help you?" I answered matter-of-factly that I was meeting my uncle, who was a guest and his flight was delayed. No questioning followed. The Palace, today known as Badutt's Palace Hotel, is unquestionably St. Moritz's most famous hotel. Built in the late 1890's, it has had the reputation of being the hotel for celebrities and royalty. Its incomparable setting on the lake boasts stunning views of the Alps in all directions.

It was while I was waiting in the lobby of the hotel that I had to use the men's room, located one floor below. The public bathroom was large and well appointed. But what made it especially unique was the spacious size of the stalls, all in Italian travertine marble. It was like a work of art, like an Egyptian tomb; at least ten feet deep and the walls ran ceiling to floor to offer total privacy. I had never seen anything like that before.

It was time for some nightlife. I arrived at the first bar which Arnold, the guy who picked me up hitching, had recommended, and it was pretty dead. I spoke to the hat check girl from California. She suggested the best place was called Afterglow. There was more life here as live rock music was blaring from the entrance. I had a good time dancing some, nursing my beer and meeting a young German girl named Renate. She had that classic German look; tall slender, blonde and blue eyed. She was from Stuttgart on a short vacation with her family and a girlfriend. She gave me her number and asked if I wanted to join her skiing the next day. My mind was saying "yes, I would love to," but I was concerned about the cost of renting skis and the day ticket, so I replied: "Could I call you tomorrow morning on that?"

From here I went walking about checking a few more places. It was fairly lively, but not as I expected. I thought it would be wilder. The snow by now had increased, as the wind was blowing hard, near blizzard conditions. I was also a little tired and decided to head back to the railway station and retire for the night.

When I got to the station, the door was locked. I was shocked. The trusty railway station, all through my travels, be it Gothenburg, Uppsala, Hamburg, Munich or Innsbruck. I could always count on it to be open at all hours of the night to give me shelter. But now, when I really needed it more than ever, it was closed! What was I to do?

Sure, I was tired, I wanted sleep; but more important I needed the station for protection, as it was brutally cold. It was probably near zero and I only had on my turtleneck sweater and a flimsy windbreaker. The conditions were dangerous. It was now near midnight. I walked about searching for a bus shelter but there was none. I felt envious as couples strolled by laughing, going back to their cozy hotels. I toyed with the idea of biting the bullet and getting a hotel room, which I could not afford. An outrageous cost I could not justify. But one thing was certain: I had to get out of this cold.

Across the lake I could see the majestic Palace Hotel glowing like a warm lantern. Oh I wish I could stay there. I remembered the public bathroom, the stall, the gigantic stall, big enough to lie down in, big enough to sleep in. Yes, that would be my destination.

As I approached the entrance of the landmark hotel, I could see someone "official" stopping people as they came in, checking to see if they were guests. Damn! I hovered around on the outside watching closely. As a group of boisterous Germans approached, I noticed that the doorman seemed to check only the head person. My German is limited, but I could make out the words: "we are together."

That was the key. I had to wait until a group approached and hopefully I could mix in. I heard a distant church bell ring once: one o'clock. The wind was getting fierce and I was freezing. I had to be careful t not to stand out in front of the hotel, as I would look like a vagrant and never make it through the door. So I hid behind a large pine tree about sixty yards down to the side. Although I was painfully cold and uncomfortable, I had to laugh at what an amusing Dickensian situation it was: "It was the best of times. It was the worst of times."

I was confident I could pull it off. I was positioned behind the tree, anxiously watching, waiting, hoping for a group of people. I saw a couple enter the hotel and the doorman nod, two single people strolled in. As each person entered I could hear in the respective language, "cold outside."

Yes, it was! I had been waiting almost an hour now. I couldn't remember ever being so cold. I needed a group of people, come on please, where are you?

Suddenly I hear coming from my right cackling laughter. From the words spoken, I discerned they were French, a group of seven or eight. I could not make out faces or ages, just body shapes bundled up and hurrying to reach the warmth of the hotel.

I could not wait. This might be my last chance. I had to move now. But I had to be cool and merge gracefully with the group. As they passed parallel with the tree, I came out. They did not see me. If they did it probably would have scared the hell out of them, seeing this guy just coming out of the woods.

Letting them get ahead of me by about twenty yards, I came up on their flank quickly. One of the women noticed me. I nodded and greeted her with a "bonsoir, trés froid." Thankfully, two of the men were tall, at least as tall as me 6'2". As luck would have it, they were positioned in the back. As we neared the steps of the hotel, I squeezed in between the two tall Frenchmen and sort of crouched over, they serving as my personal protective bookends.

"Good Evening, ladies and gentlemen, are you guests of the Palace? Never had I ever been so acutely aware of society's "have and have nots."

Four arms went up casually displaying room keys. "Merci," said the doorman, who turned right and walked away. I continued my somewhat hunched position making an immediate turn left, as I entered the hotel.

Now that I was in, I had to be cool. I had to recoup my bearings of where the stairs led down to the men's public bathroom. I felt as if I was in a James Bond thriller.

The stairs, unfortunately, were positioned on the other side of the reception desk. There was little chance that I could get by the two people at the desk without them seeing me. If I tried to dash across or sneak from potted plant to potted plant that would cause a lot of attention and alarm bells to "Who the hell is that?"

So I decided to just walk nonchalantly straight for the stairs by the reception desk. The young Swiss receptionist looked up, and I spoke first, "Good evening; sure is cold out."

"Yes, it is cold. Good night, sir," she responded with a smile, as I calmly disappeared down the stairs. . . .My bed was waiting.

That night I slept well. Using my windbreaker as a pillow I curled up on the hard marble stall floor. A blanket would have been more comfortable, but it was dark, warm and quiet. And I felt very thankful. Only twice did I hear people enter the bathroom; once during the night, and early in the morning when the washroom attendant knocked on the door.

"I'll be right out," I said. As I exited from my sleep tomb, my hair feeling very disheveled, the attendant who looked to be North African politely apologized. At the same time he looked confused, as to why is this guy using this bathroom so early. I greeted him as I normally would and headed upstairs.

Walking through the lobby I noticed a sign advertising a band in their bar. They had a bar? This interested me, and I inquired about it. The same desk clerk at the front desk from the night before mentioned that the bar stayed open until midnight, and you did not have to be a guest of the hotel to visit.

This was very key information, I thought, if I plan to stay in St. Moritz another night and need to use the grand stall as a crash pad again. I felt very encouraged by this news. As I exited the Palace I felt fantastic!

It was a gorgeous sunny, brilliant blue sky day and I was looking forward to seeing Renate and skiing. I was anxious about what the cost of the day on the slopes would cost. But as good fortune would have it on meeting Renate at ten-thirty she informed me that her brother injured his ankle yesterday and I could use his equipment and Day Ski Pass. The St. Moritz Gods were indeed looking over me.

The day on the slopes in St. Moritz was fabulous! My skiing experience growing up was limited mostly to a place near home which was really nothing more than a hill created from a garbage dump sodded over, with snow on top. Local ski enthusiasts described it endearingly as "MOUNT

TRASHMORE." I had never experienced anything like the winter wonderland of St. Moritz.

I explained my unimpressive ski background to Renate. She smiled and assured me she was just an intermediate. I would soon find out that she certainly was a better intermediate than I was. But she was understanding and patient with me, and we skied together all day. Blissfully so, with time outs to exchange embraces to keep us warm, and soft kisses on the rides up the mountain.

In St Moritz there are three main ski areas. From the start I was overwhelmed with the spectacular gondola ride to the top with the panoramic view of the surrounding snow covered Alps; the clear, cloudless blue sky, sparkling sunshine and white powder everywhere.

I shut my eyes and felt the warm sun hit my face, I thought back to how bitterly cold I was last night.... And now, oh life is good!

I was convinced it was these contrasts, the serendipitous "twists and turns" in life that helps us appreciate just how good it can be.

This was to be Renate's last evening in St. Moritz, as the family was heading back to Stuttgart late tomorrow morning. I told her I wanted very much to see her tonight, and if there was a chance we could be alone. We agreed to meet at the Afterglow at ten o'clock.

As I arrived at the Afterglow, there seemed to be more happening than the night before. They had a different band tonight that was playing more slow ballads, in addition to the usual blaring rock and roll. This was fine by me. I was fortunate to find space on a low couch that was close to the fireplace. Soon I saw Renate and waved her over.

In the back of my mind I was thinking of the stall. If I were to use the stall this evening I had to get to the Palace before midnight to avoid the hassle of trying to merge in again. Especially if I were planning to have Renate with me, this would be difficult to pull off. For by arriving before midnight I could say I was going to their bar. I would have to move fairly quickly with Renate.

We each had a drink, she a beer and me a scotch and began dancing. Although she seemed on the reserved side, she was a wild dancer, shaking her torso with very provocative movements. After too long a time of hard driving rock and roll, both of us drenched in sweat, a slow dance finally broke the pattern. Holding each other closely, she, looking in my eyes, made the first move and kissed me. Yes, she tasted very nice. Our kisses continued. Pulling her over in the corner our kisses grew deeper and more passionate.

"You are a terrific dancer and an even better kisser," I told her as we each ordered one more drink.

She laughed and said "I am having such a good time I don't want to leave you tomorrow."

"Let's make the most of tonight. "I want to be alone with you, would you like this too?"

"Yes. Can we go back to your hotel?" she asked.

I explained, taking her hand returning to our couch. The flames from the fire made her sweaty face look sexy.

"What hotel are you in?" she asked, looking eager with anticipation.

"I am at the Palace." "The Palace," she exclaimed, "that is the most expensive hotel in St. Moritz. I thought you were backpacking. How can you afford that?"

Taking her hand and giving her a soft kiss, I exclaimed. "I am going to tell you something that is pretty strange."

"Okay, what is it?"

"I am staying in the bathroom stall," I said.

"What, you are staying in a bathroom?" I explained in detail about last evening, how immaculately clean, spacious, and private the stall was, and how my sleep was totally uninterrupted.

She let out an amazing laugh and between kisses, I said, "Well, what do you think? Should we make our last evening a memorable one?"

Without hesitation she agreed: "Yes, I want that. What a wild, crazy night this will be!"

It was now close to eleven-thirty, I explained quickly about the time pressure with the bar situation, and it's closing at midnight.

"We have to move fast, Cinderella," I laughed.

She asked if there was time to run back to her hotel and get a blanket, which was a good idea. Not only did she bring a blanket, but a small bottle of champagne from the room's mini-bar. I added to the mood by providing a candle that I had purchased earlier at the hotel gift shop. Yes, for the last night in the stall, the romantic mood was going to be mellow and memorable.

Never was a bathroom stall put to better use. A "first" I am sure for the elegant posh Palace Hotel and "Swinging, Jet Setting St. Moritz."

So . . . what was "a guy like me doing in a place like this?" Merely having the time of his life.

Chapter 17

MOROCCO: BAT CAVE AT KNIFE POINT

I ached for Morocco . . . It was the travel destination that I dreamed of escaping to, while subjected ("doing time") to my dreadful job at the Austrian ski resort. Beyond the frigid winter, I longed to break away from the brutal owner, with his oversized ego, temper tantrums, and narrow mentality.

So intense was my passion for Morocco, that as I would go through the motions of dishwasher at the hotel each morning, I would dreamily gaze at the pictures of Morocco I posted on the sides of the dishwasher. On the left side a photo of a busy, buzzing bazaar in Fez; on the right side a tantalizing ocean view with a golden beach. Morocco consumed me . . . I wanted sun . . . I wanted heat . . . I wanted the exotic.

I got this. And a great deal more.

Morocco was a country of "Firsts" for me:

* First Muslim country
* Witnessing extreme poverty
* Disfigured beggars
* Women Completely Veiled
* Stabbed with a Knife
* Stabbed someone with a Knife
* Smoked Hashish
* Offered Big Money to Sell Hashish/and refused
* Seeing someone shoot up with Heroin
* Offered Money for Sex/refused money for sex
* Wiped Ass with Rock
* Riding on top of a Bus
* Traveler Steals from me
* And this was in the First week!!

It was also where I first learned of the expression: "Gringo Highway."

The "Gringo Highway" is not listed in Webster's Dictionary (yet), but basically it is referring to a specific destination. Usually it is a small village, almost always located in a "developing country," where every backpacker traveling in the respective country seems to migrate. Because the "Gringo Highway" destination is small, the backpackers arriving in hordes seemed to totally take over. Everything becomes "westernized" to please the whims of the packer: from food to music, to the outlook on cultural mores, such as drugs and sex. The local culture becomes virtually nonexistent.

In Morocco . . . the "Gringo Highway" led to Taghazout. It seemed every traveler I met in Morocco, be it in Fez, Meknes, Marrakech would say, "Man have you been to Taghazout?" Even if they had not been, all seemed to wax poetically about what a "paradise" it was and must not be missed.

Being an inquisitive traveler, I had to check out this undisputed "paradise." The village is located about fifty miles south of Agadir. The setting was lovely with little white thatched huts for travelers to share, located just steps from the beach and the Atlantic Ocean. Plus the delicious food, familiar "comfort food," such as, tacos, macaroni and cheese, and hamburgers. Yes, this part of it I did enjoy. However, after four days, observing the over abundance of heavy drug use and the non-stop partying began to wear on me.

I shared my small room with three travelers: two Austrians and one French guy. Each looked more strung out than the other and achingly thin. The two Austrians had been in Taghazout for two months. The French guy whom I had to witness "shooting up" each morning had been there for nearly a year. He claimed he had "zero money" and said he wanted to die in Taghazout.

The room was a drug dungeon. These "losers" were beyond wasted. I felt a strong sense of disgust. I tried not to be judgmental. I had to get away. But I seriously questioned what they were getting out of their travels. I hated the whole atmosphere, including their constant, pounding, mind-numbing music; and the queasy sense of distrust. One afternoon I came back to the room and caught one of the Austrians going through my pack.

The scene was just too much. I had to get away from these toxic characters. It might be contagious. Yes, Targhazout might have been a "paradise" for some. But for me it was sheer hell, a total "turnoff." I needed space. I needed quiet. I needed to be alone. I needed to create my own "paradise."

The morning of my fifth day I was gone. Taking to the road, thumb out hitching south; I had no specific destination in mind. Just to move, to be free. I felt joy and filled with lightness. I relished being on my own and blazing my own unknown trail.

After two hours riding in the back of a bone-jarring pickup truck, jammed among eight Moroccans, five chickens, two goats, and three big bags of grain, I arrived at a village. I did not know its name. I was not even sure where I was.

It was tiny and dusty. Three homeless, laid back dogs checked me out with calm, inquisitive eyes; instead of the usual snarling bark and bite gesture reserved for backpackers.

I stood up and stretched. I liked the way the locals moved quietly about. It seemed so different from the hustle of the big touristic Moroccan cities; and definitely a world away from the insane backpacker scene of Taghazout.

I made my way across the street where I found a little cafe. It appeared to be the only cafe on what seemed to be the village's main street. The cafe was about half full, and heads turned as I entered. I was not hustled by anyone asking if I wanted to "buy a rug," or "come to my shop."

As I sat at my single wooden table, a young boy about twelve approached me cautiously. He seemed to be taken back and surprised to see me. He had kind eyes and seemed shy.

I asked if he spoke English; he shook his head. I tried a little French, but this did not seem to help. He disappeared returning a few seconds later with another boy. This boy looked like him, but a slightly bigger more mature version. Probably about fifteen years old. "Brother," he said.

I shook his hand as I introduced myself. He said his name was Mohammed and his younger brother Aahil.

"Do you want some tea," he asked. I answered yes, and asked the name of the village. "Name of village is Mirleft."

I unfolded my map of Europe, which included Morocco. I did not see the name of the town. He leaned over pointing and asked, "Can I mark on map?"

"Yes, please do," I replied.

With a blue pen he put a little star right on the coast in the very south of Morocco, down close to the Spanish Sahara.

"Is the ocean close by?" I asked.

"Not far, about twenty minute walk, that way," he pointed. I took my time sipping my tea. They offered me more. They were very polite and respectful of my privacy.

I paid him my bill, including leaving a small tip on the table and walked out, thanking and waving as I did. I stood in the middle of the dusty road. It did not run far, perhaps a couple hundred yards in each direction. I liked the town's remoteness. It was just what I was seeking.

I started heading in the direction he had pointed out toward the beach. I had only walked about seventy yards when Mohammed came running out: "Mister, Mister, you left some money on the table." I explained that was a tip for him. He tried to give it back to me.

I refused, and he thanked me again. "Mohammed, you said the ocean is about a mile away, which direction is best?"

He began explaining, something about going straight and when hit the cliffs, you need to turn right and walk about 400 yards, and you will see a path. He emphasized that the cliffs were "very, very steep," as this is only route down.

As he was in the process of describing the bad condition of the path, and its dangers, he said, "I will show you where it is. Is this okay with you?"

I nodded and gave him a hearty "merci beaucoup." He said, "One moment, just need to tell my brother Aahil." He ran back and returned seconds later with something in his hand. "Here have an orange, very good for you." Peeling it as we walked, I bit hungrily into the orange, small in size, but big in flavor. So delicious! I was feeling better already.

I appreciated that Mohammed did not pester me with questions, which was so common in meeting locals in Morocco. He just was inquisitive to know where I was from and where I had last been in Morocco. I felt at ease with him, as we strolled. The weather was absolutely gorgeous, full of sunshine in a cloudless sky with a soft soothing breeze. After about a fifteen minute walk, I could look out and see the ocean. The Atlantic, the coloring stunning, in two shades of blue: one deep, the other in a contrasting clear, pale aqua.

After about another twenty minutes of walking, most of it in silence, we came to the cliff which presented a breathtaking view. The ocean spread out before me in a sweeping panorama. The sea with its surging rhythmic waves with white crests crashed upon a deserted, golden beach.

I paused and took it all in. "Very, very beautiful," I exclaimed to Mohammed. He nodded "yes," seeming to appreciate the view as much as me. We continued to walk five minutes more on the cliff's edge. I had to focus on not falling over the edge, as I was in such a transfixed state of being mesmerized by the overwhelming beauty and not really concentrating where I was going.

The cliffs were imposing, possibly three hundred feet straight up. It was a sheer drop. There is no way one could navigate getting down from here. If one were to fall, it would most likely be fatal. We had not gone far, when Mohammed showed me the path that led to the beach.

"This is the path, the safest path to the beach," he said. From what I could see it didn't look too steep or difficult from here. I began to thank Mohammed, and he cautioned me: "About halfway down it becomes more dangerous," making an angle with his hand for steep. "Here there is a rope, and you need to hang on to lower down."

I assured him I would be okay, shook his hand, and thanked him. "I am sure I will see you in town later," I said. As soon as he left, I started my descent down, which was not that difficult. The rope was thick and secured well to a metal stake. I grabbed hold and slowly repelled myself down. The drop probably covered about eighty feet. From here the path leveled out to the beach.

I was alone on the beach. Not a footprint in sight. The sand seemed to stretch for miles in a gradual curving formation. The jagged, reddish cliffs overhead looked powerful. I just stood still in astonishment, turning around slowly in all directions, taking in the wonderment of it all. And the surreal silence. This is what I wanted, to get away, from everyone. To me right now, I had found my "paradise."

As dusk set in, I sat on my sleeping bag preparing my uninspired dinner. This consisted of a can of beans and franks, cooked over my small sterno can, and washing it down with Moroccan lime soda pop. The beans tasted a little old, past their prime; and the soda was warm. Nevertheless, it could not dampen my spirits, as a raging orange and pink sunset, slowly faded away to a dazzling night sky, exploding with stars.

I felt small and humbled in the vastness of Nature. But I also felt huge, empowered and enriched, enveloped in its magnificence. By eight o'clock I was in a deep sleep.

For the next several days I continued my Robinson Crusoe existence. My idyllic days had a peaceful relaxed pattern: Arise early, walk the beach, body surf in the ocean, read, write in my journal, walk some more, swim some more. I would go into town sometimes to treat myself to a good meal of lamb tagine; as well as to stack up on food to take down to the beach. For the most part this included lots of oranges and bananas; but also some vegetables and chicken, which I would cook.

My stay on the deserted beach was most enjoyable. However, the days could be hot, and I had no protection. Even though it was January, the sun this far south in Morocco was penetrating and punishment for my fair skin. Unwelcomed too were evenings when it would rain, and I would be forced to dig myself deep into my sleeping bag.

But there was so much to relish. So much to love. The quiet. The being alone. The peace. I kept looking all around at the vastness of the beach and the high cliffs. I had to pinch myself; I was filled with such happiness. What a blessing to be here instead of the party-down atmosphere of Taghazout. My being here only confirmed what I had learned and would later adopt as my travel mantra: "If you don't like the 'Gringo Highway,' get off it, and create your own path."

It took about an hour to walk into the village. The only difficult part was towing up the rope on the steep cliff, not so much the pulling up, but the rope passed over an area where scorpions gathered. When I saw one, I had to maneuver over it, as I shimmied up the cliff.

In town I settled back in the cafe. Mohammed greeted me warmly. I appreciated that he did not pry and ask where I was sleeping, and what my plans were. I did not want anyone to know that I was sleeping on the beach. While in town, I got to know some of the local vendors, all very kind and friendly. And like Mohammed, relaxed and not pushy. It is from these vendors that I would purchase vegetables and fruit, and canned goods also.

It was on the seventh day that I made a discovery. Instead of just walking along the ocean shore for about a mile and turning back, which was my daily route, I decided to hike further, but walk along the way of the cliff instead of the beach.

As glorious as the view was from the beach level, with elevation, it was even more spectacular with the panoramic expanse of blue sky and water, and the rugged cliffs and distant rock formations.

After a couple of hours of walking, I saw another rope running down the cliff. This one was not as long as the other rope. I decided to go down to the beach. In this area the waves seemed more powerful. I loved its strength. As I walked further along the beach, I soon came to what appeared to be a cave. It was situated about 200 yards from the breaking surf.

I entered cautiously. It was dark and cool and spacious. Its dimensions were about: 50 feet high; 100 feet deep; and perhaps 60 feet wide. I had little experience with caves, except reading about them. They always fascinated me, from pirate stories of buried treasure, to *National Geographic* photographs.

I stepped out of the cave, inspecting it from different angles with all the concern, as if judging a potential purchase of a Manhattan co-op. Well, I certainly did not need a broker to decide that this cave was something special. It meant privacy, protection, comfort. And it meant this would be my new address. I was about to become a cave-dweller with a water view!

Another three days passed, and the cave proved to be abundantly more enjoyable and more comfortable. It was a welcome contrast to come in from the baking on the beach, and collapse on the cool sand of the cave, and look up and around at the dark walls. I would actually take long naps sometimes during the day, it was so inviting.

In my new cave home, I saw no people, none at all, whereas, at my prior location I would see locals on the beach occasionally. My food was almost completely gone. It was time to go back into the village and stock up. Being further away, the walk now took nearly two hours each way.

I was shopping at the small market, buying couscous grain, vegetables and fruits. By now I had gotten to know some of the sellers at the market. They were playful in their bargaining with me. The dogs were there as well. It seemed that this sleepy, little hamlet always moved the same, with the same characters, slow and easy.

But then, something did change. I heard the voice first. It was someone speaking English, asking to buy some bananas. I turned, looking over my right shoulder and saw a tall, slim guy, mid-twenties with reddish blonde hair. He was negotiating now in French regarding the bananas. I saw him nod and smile, as he handed his money to the fruit peddler. He gave him a congenial pat on the back, chuckled, and walked away.

He seemed pleasant from observing him, but I did not want to meet him. I wanted to leave without him seeing me. Do not be mistaken if I sound like such an anti-social, lone wolf; but the truth is, at this point in my travels, I did yearn to be alone. I had found my desired separate peace here in the hamlet of Mirleft. And in my cave I had found my home. I had visions of more backpackers coming, and my slice of heaven soon disappearing into the hedonistic, crazed Taghazout from which I had run.

I tried to leave quietly without him noticing me. He was no more than twenty feet behind me, but his back was to me. I tried to express a sense of urgency in getting my vegetables from the seller, but he went at his usual slow pace. When I finally got them, in my haste I stepped on a sleeping dog and tripped over him, sending me tumbling to the ground, knocking over some stacked cans of apricots. The dog, seeming so laid back before, let loose with wild barking. Heads turned, one of the heads that of the foreign backpacker.

As I lay sprawling on the ground, I heard "hey, you okay?" It was the packer.

"Yes, no, problem, thanks," I said. Composing myself, I started to walk away when he said, "What's your name, you been here long?"

He had a very open way about him. Before I could make my escape, I found myself attracted to his natural warmth and humor; and now here in my usual cafe, where we each had a tea.

Mohammed brought the tea in his usual friendly but reserved way. But this time he asked looking at the new traveler, "Who is this?"

I gave him a surprised look, as of course, I did not know who he was. "My name is Stephen." He shook hands with Mohammed.

"I am Scott, nice to meet you."

So there I sat with this traveler sharing a cup of tea, looking at him as an intruder on my cherished hideaway. But as much as I wanted to just finish my tea and move on alone back to my cave, I found that I enjoyed being with him. He seemed different from other packers in Morocco.

First he looked clean, and he was open and engaging. He also had been doing some impressive traveling. He was a native of Toronto, though he began his travels over a year ago in Australia. He had picked several challenging jobs to keep himself on the road.

Ironically, in many ways he reminded me of myself and how I traveled. I asked him if he had been to Taghazout; he groaned with a definitive: "Shit, what a crazy place."

He went on to say that he was there for a week and just could not handle the scene. "That's the way I felt as well," I exclaimed.

We just looked at each other sipping tea slowly and nodding in a common bond of "that" place. He looked at me and said, "Hey, how long you been here?"

When I told him about ten days, he asked, "Where you staying?"

And there it was; the question. Do I tell him the truth of my cave hideaway, or do I make something up?

I had enjoyed so much the solitary life, the quiet, the peace. But as much as I did, perhaps if I had the right traveler it would not be such a bad thing. Perhaps even a positive thing as some of the travelers that I had met on the road were fascinating people. I felt fortunate to have known them, and we would continue to stay in contact.

I still had not answered his question about where I was staying, as we were interrupted by Mohammed pouring us more tea. He said, "Hey, you got any books you want to trade?"

"Yes, I do," I asked with a hungry urgency "What about you, any books?"

"Hell, yes, a pile load." And out he pulled three novels, two of them huge: *The Drifters* by James Michener, which I was familiar with; *Atlas Shrugged,* by a woman named Ayn Rand, which I never heard of; and *Catch 22,* which I had read before.

That was it! On seeing those books my decision was made. I was starving for new literature to read.

"So you've been here ten days, where you staying?" I added that I had some Vonnegut, and Philip Roth books I could give him.

"Great!" he exclaimed.

And then I told him . . . I told him about how magnificent the ocean was, the high cliffs that ran above, and my secluded place. The cave was the perfect antidote from the decadent scene we both had escaped.

So I now had a cave mate. And I can say without hesitation that as far as cave mates go, he was the best. Stephen was positive. He had a good energy about him. He was a terrific story teller, quick witted and funny. We had many nights in the cave staying up late, sitting by the fire, sharing stories of the road.

He told me colorful, lively tales of places I had not been. I in turn, told him of places he had not been. We talked of those we shared in common. We had that right Traveler DNA that we just clicked. He, like me, also valued alone time and doing his own thing sometimes. Often we would not see each other during the day, but always meet back at the cave for sunset, followed by dinner.

Stephen also brought a special set of skills, which won me over immediately. He was a trained chef, being a graduate of a prestigious culinary school in Montreal. So dinner time was no longer my basic baked beans over the gas sterno can, but instead delicious home cooked meals, or should I say cave cooked meals, that at times bordered on the elaborate.

We would go into the village and buy chicken, mutton or fish, and roast it over our fire with our own handmade rotisserie. Also savored were the fresh vegetables, and fruit for dessert. I ate extremely well.

The time went by easy and smoothly. I had been in my cave for three weeks, but was not bored, or feel the need to get moving. I was not getting anxious or restless to leave. Once in awhile I would think perhaps I should be moving on, exploring more cultural, historical areas. But each morning awaking to that brilliant sunshine, sparkling blue sea and pounding surf, I felt so exhilarated, so relaxed.

Not a care in the world, just soaking in the beauty and the sheer joy of it all. Our surroundings were like a pleasurable sauna to the senses. Stephen seemed to feel the same. Every time we mentioned leaving, we would just start laughing and end up saying, "What for?"

As far as the locals, we got to know several of them. Many others we would recognize, and though not knowing their names, would wave and give a hearty "salam." There were four young Moroccan kids, about twelve to fifteen years old, who would be on the beach quite a bit, kicking the soccer ball around.

We would join in at times and became friendly. However, they knew nothing about our cave, or where we stayed. We told no one about the cave. Also we had our favorite vendors for shopping for food, and of course Mohammed. His cafe was our place to go for a cooked meal, tea, or to just hang out.

Being sort of "regulars," Mohammed would make sure we received extra big portions of food, be it couscous, tagine, or his famous spaghetti and meatballs.

No one ever pressed us as to what we were up to or where we were staying. It was relaxed and friendly. However, there were a few of the locals, we had not seen before, that seemed to view us with a critical, questioning eye.

There were three of them in the restaurant that would stare at us. They were older, and each sporting a long white beard. They never threatened us, never even said anything to us, but it was their look that seemed somewhat hostile, as if challenging "what we were doing here." But we just ignored it, and never spoke with them. When you travel as a packer in a foreign land, you often get weird looks. It's best just to be cool and not to be confrontational.

One day walking from town back to the cave, along the cliffs, I heard Stephen exclaim: "What is that?" And down below, splashing and cavorting about in the surf were three very white bodies. "Could it be?" I muttered. "Well they certainly don't look Moroccan do they?" Stephen stating the obvious.

We moved back from the path, not wanting to be seen, but stood above watching and listening. The loud screaming and shouting sounded German. Two of the bodies, who were girls, came out of the surf on to the beach and proceeded to run around in the sand playing some kind of tag game.

Their bodies looked ample, bordering on hefty. Then a very tall, skinny bearded guy joined them. They now were holding hands with each other, dancing in a circle and yelling something, which was not understandable. This phrase they repeated again as they circled around, as if some primal war cry.

We stood there on top of the cliff, and looked down in horrified fascination. The skinny guy broke free of the two girls, and as he ran he pulled off his clothes, prancing down the beach naked.

Seconds later, as if he were the Pied Piper, the two girls tossed off their tops, squirmed out of their bottoms, and with screams and laughter ran after him in hot pursuit.

We could not believe our eyes. "Well there goes the neighborhood," I jested. We felt stunned, frozen. Our idealized paradise had been interrupted. Not just interrupted by other "western travelers," but by those that prance around the beach naked in a Muslim country.

Muslim countries are dangerously strict in showing the flesh. Even a skimpy bathing suit on women is considered offensive. But to go completely in the buff, flaunting their nakedness, this was showing no respect for the country's culture and mores. Behavior like this can trigger a violent reaction from the locals. Not a smart thing to do.

As we walked slowly back along the cliffs to the cave, we kept pausing often turning around to look back at the trio of naked bodies, cavorting about the beach.

We witnessed in silence, their "fun and games": rolling about in the sand with the one person acting as a log and the other two rolling the log through the sand down into the surf; doing jumping jacks and running in place; laying out spread eagle; re-grouping into their dancing, handholding circle, complete with the same dancing and chants as before. However, we noticed now they would often meet in the center and rub their bodies against each other.

Wow . . . back at the cave we fell into silent reflection, deeply saddened that perhaps our paradise would be transformed into a "paradise lost." It could be ruined, violated by these mindless travelers, and all the careless, shallow travelers that might follow. It was the pureness of Mirleft that I cherished. An influx of packers, especially those coming from Taghazout would indeed change it.

We felt that if perhaps we kept a low profile, meaning staying close to the cave (the cave being a couple of miles from where we saw them); and being careful as we headed back into the village, that we could avoid them. And that proved workable for almost another week. It was as if we had almost forgotten them, and we just continued to live in our own little world, not even knowing or caring what "they" were up to.

Until . . . it was around 2 p.m. the height of the heat of the day, and we had taken shelter in the coolness of our cave, resting on our backpacks, doing some reading. I was immersed in Michener's *The Drifters*, and Stephen with Kurt Vonnegut's *Slaughter House Five*. Yes, all was well with the world again.

All of a sudden, as if just dropped down from out of nowhere, the three appeared on the surf in front of us. They were clothed this time, but still wildly jumping about and yelling, as in the state we had seen them before. We looked at each other pleadingly: "please pass, please move on." We could see them, but how we were positioned deep in the cave, they could not see us. But they certainly could see the cave from where they were.

We watched the dreaded three pass, as they walked and hopped about along the shore, moving further away, disappearing out of sight. We felt for the moment that we were safe. However, about fifteen minutes later, just when we started to relax that they were gone, the tall German bean pole appeared again. He yelled to the girls something like "hohle, hohle" which I suppose is the German word for "cave." We could see him clearly now pointing up to the cave. He waited for the two girls to catch up to him, and together they walked directly toward the cave right toward us.

Yes, they had discovered the cave . . . we were discovered. Upon finding us, they seemed somewhat surprised to see us. The two girls giggled and the emaciated guy nodded and said, "hey". We went through the motions of being friendly to them. There was no reason to make the situation worse by not being pleasant and polite. "Wow, some kind of cool cave here," he said, with a guttural German accent.

I would guess he was around our age. But looking at him closer, as the sun hit his face directly, there was a sickly pallor to it. His eyes looked vacant. He had that fried, exhausted look that comes from heavy drug usage. His matted hair was long and stringy. And his alarming weight could not have been more than 130 pounds, despite his height being probably about six foot four.

We got up from our backpacks and greeted them with our names and handshakes. The girls must have been flying on something, because they were so hyper, spinning in a circle with each other and laughing and laughing at seemingly nothing. The girls looked older than the guy, probably near thirty. But whereas he was bony, these girls were fleshy, with wild blonde stringy hair like his, but thicker and dirtier, almost like dreadlocks.

They both wore skimpy bikini bathing suits. The slightly taller one snapping open her bikini bottoms and saying: "hate the sand in my pussy." The other girl, who was convulsed with giggles, as if she were about eight years old, broadcasted matter-of- factly: "We are cousins. People say we look alike, but we also are alike because we both have lice. We come to Morocco to get rid of our lice. We are girls with lice." Lovely.

The German guy, who was more composed, said his name was Siegfried, and that they were all from Frankfurt, and had been traveling for six months, about four of the months in Morocco.

"We were in Taghazout for three months. Man, what a fucking cool place, drugs, drugs, music, drugs, sunshine." Stephen and I looked at each other with a disdainful "what a surprise."

Siegfried brazenly walked passed us, as he entered our cave uninvited alone. He moved over to the side of the cave to look at the "Miss Morocco 1976" poster, that we had taped up. This being our one interior decorating statement.

He seemed to stare at the poster for an unusually long time. He backed away from the poster and looked up at the height of the cave, did a little twirl around, and just plopped himself down in a lotus position, right in the center of the cave. Immediately, the lice cousins were sitting next to him in the same lotus position, as if he were their assigned shaman and must copy his every move.

I felt taken back by this, and I could tell that Stephen was bothered as well. I mean seeing them on the beach and greeting them was one thing, but now they invaded our private sanctum.

They said some weird words to each other, as if in tongues, and held hands for a few seconds. He reached into his small brownish soiled satchel and pulled out a bag of gunja and proceeded to roll a huge joint. "Man, this stuff is killer, will totally fuck you," and passed it on to the lice cousins, as they exchanged deep drags and continued their maddening giggling.

He just stared vacantly at us. Stephen and I were dumfounded by his arrogant invading of our space, as if the cave were his home, just rudely "lighting up" with no consideration of others.

"Here, want some of this, come take a drag." Stephen and I were not prudes about smoking grass, if someone wants to relax once in awhile and have a toke. But the absurd size of this joint, in the middle of the day, with these unsavory characters in our cave; we just declined politely.

I wanted them to leave. I wanted to shout: "Get your skinny ass out of here!" But I thought it smarter to play it cool, let them have their smoke and get on their way. After passing the joint around a few times, they got in a laughing jag. He collapsed on his back, and of course the girls immediately piled on top.

"Oh, this is so cool, being fucked up in a cave," giggled the taller lice cousin. They all started to laugh uncontrollably, gasping for air. They were seriously weird. I looked over at Stephen rolling his eyes.

Trying to establish some sanity, Stephen asked: "Where are you staying, and have you been here long?"

Siegfried in a very stoned way muttered. "Wow, I think five days, maybe six or seven. I can't remember."

After an eerie silence, the one girl said in a hushed, shaky voice: "We are far away, a long, long walk away." The other lice girl, (we never got their names) responded from another-worldly place: "This seems too far away, I am spinning. This cave creeps me. I got to get out of here!" She was freaking out dangerously agitated, bordering on hysteria.

Siegfried rubbed her head and slowly raised her up to her feet, as the other cousin moved in for a communal body hug and some reassuring comforting. We just stood there quietly taking it all in.

Siegfried broke the silence, "Man, we need to go."

Oh! I liked hearing those words. As he left he said: "If you want to visit, we have a tent. Some friends from Holland are coming in a day or so to bring some serious magic mushrooms. We are going to party non-stop."

Later that night after our fury had subsided, and our humor returned a bit, I asked Stephen jokingly: "What would the arbiter of good taste, Emily Post's advice on proper "cave etiquette" have been today?" It was good to hear him laugh again. I loved his big, rollicking, infectious laugh.

So our cave visitors were gone. We were shaken, but really believed they would not return. And that there would not be a problem continuing our peaceful, private life in the cave, as they were so far away from us.

However, over the next three consecutive nights, we had a string of very strange and bothersome things take place. The first disturbing episode happened in our cave late at night. We heard a shrill, mysterious crying noise. We both fumbled for our flashlights and we could make out something small flying about and darting and diving low just over our heads.

"Shit, what is that?" I barked out to Stephen from my sleeping bag.

He said, "I don't know, but Christ look out, here come more." And suddenly a whole squadron of them came swooping down with that same piercing, high pitched sound. We felt under attack!

We were both zipped up in our bags, cursing and conversing under cover. We both came to the conclusion that they were probably bats, mad as hell that we had invaded their cave. This "spooky" swishing about back and forth, of whatever it was, lasted for a good hour.

I never thought it would end, but finally it did. And we returned to a troubled sleep.

The following night, during the deepest of sleeps, I felt a cold rushing of water upon my feet. This was followed by an onslaught of stronger surf pounding into our cave. We quickly gathered all that we could, and though losing some clothes, nothing of real value (camera, journal, money-belt) was lost, as these items were deep inside my sleeping bag. However, the force of the water was indeed unsettling.

On the third night, I decided to sleep outside on the beach, as it was a warm, balmy evening. Stephen remained in the cave. Later that night, I was abruptly awakened by a gruff, angry voice demanding:

"WHAT IS YOUR NAME?" I thought it was a ghoulish nightmare at first. When I came to, after violent shaking, there was a grizzled older-looking Moroccan guy, kneeling over me.

"What is your name?" he demanded again. Still recovering from my deep sleep, I could now see, from the light of a full moon, that he had a knife he was holding right above my face. "Tell me name. Are you German?"

He was now even more insistent. I could see the sweat pouring down. I could hear his heavy breathing. I could feel the strength of his body straddling mine. But what terrorized me most was the cruel, vengeful look in his dark Moroccan eyes. I could feel the hate. My life meant nothing to him. He had a score to settle.

I answered, shouting a resounding: "NO! NO! I am not German! I am an American, my name is Scott Stone, American, not German!" I shouted again.

And that was it! He released his neck hold, got up off his knees, put back his knife, and disappeared into the darkness.

Obviously the vulgar, insensitive Germans' presence of frolicking around naked on the beach, and their offensive drug use was pissing off the locals. I was not surprised. Their country, their people, their customs, their religion and mores had not been respected. They were justly feeling violated.

126

I was shaken. I awakened Stephen immediately. I could not possibly wait until morning to tell him of this late night scare, and report all the grisly details of what had happened. In recalling my uninvited night visitor, from our brief, rough encounter, I was certain he resembled one of the bearded men in the cafe that were always giving us the "stink eye."

So it was there, late that night that we decided these Germans were bad news for us, and our future staying on in the cave. The past three nights: the bats, the flood, the knife-wielding attacker, were all ominous signs that it was bad karma. The decision was made for us: tomorrow we would leave the cave and Mirleft forever.

Early the next morning, the morning of our departure, the clock-work-like sunny skies which greeted us each day, were instead a blanket of heavy darkness, a metaphor for the mood we felt now our time in the cave (twenty-six days for me) was to end.

As we left our cave (taking our Miss Morocco 1976 poster with us) and walked along the cliffs for the last time, we spoke of what an extraordinary time the "cave" had been. We knew whatever challenges faced us, for better or worse, we could always look back on this uniquely beautiful time and place, and know we had shared something very special.

The cave had symbolically become a sanctuary, a refuge. It protected us from that "other world" now crowding in, and crowding us out: the destroyers of Paradise.

We lifted our spirits by recalling those days so filled to overflowing with the good vibes and easy laughter between us. And with eager talk of our travel plans. Stephen was going to head inland, across the Atlas Mountains. And I was going north back to Spain. We continued walking slowly, gulping it all in for the last time, determined to remember every detail with a photographic memory.

As we reached the place where the trail cuts across to the town, we stopped and gazed one last time at the awesome panorama of endless sky and golden beaches. And there down below to our revulsion was not just one tent, which Siegfried and the lice twins occupied, but four more tents, marring the natural beauty that surrounds them.

And there would continue to be more. It would be but a matter of time before this pristine paradise became another destination on the ugly "Gringo Highway."

Yes, man can create beauty, I reflected. He can value it, embrace it, and be inspired by it. But he can also destroy it. Our timing had been good. We had arrived in Nature's most pure natural form. Before toxic people, polluters of mind, body and spirit, could spoil it.

With difficulty Stephen and I embraced and said our final "good-byes." After we parted . . . I know big boys don't cry. But I did.

And so my "paradise" found became "paradise" lost. And although I knew that even a small slice of "paradise", so fragile and fleeting could not last; for a time, a very short time, I lived it, embraced it, and seized the day.

Would I ever find "paradise" again? Possibly. It might be in a different form from: the "Cave," and vast stretches of sand, sky, sea and silence. And vast stretches of time . . . to think, to read, to write in my Journal. Time to enjoy! Those barefoot days walking the beach; carefree days stretched out under the Moroccan sun; splashing in the surf each day; counting the constellations at night . . . this bit of "paradise" was not lost. It would be with me always.

Chapter 18

SINGAPORE SLING : BROTHEL GETS NASTY

"Cheers, prost, chin-chin!" As I clicked glasses with my two newly discovered traveling companions, whom I had met earlier today at the hostel, and proceeded to chug down my fourth Tiger. The ice cold brews brought some momentary relief from the stifling, oppressive humidity of Singapore.

It was nearing midnight and the Bugis Street "pretty boys" were out in force. These young men dressed as enticing young girls were out to play "tricks" on unsuspecting tourists looking for romance. Tired of this over-hyped scene, we instead opted for a more quiet side street and settled into a cramped food stall where we began to wolf down on a mountain of shrimp fried rice and succulent chicken and beef sate.

Yes, we were feeling no pain, as we toasted to "Singapore." We were all in agreement that the city in spite of its uptight, "rules and regulations" reputation, and a place where you had to obey those rules, was a welcomed respite from the rough rigors and chronic chaos of other sprawling grimy south Asian cities. Its cleanliness, its order, its sanity and its "No Beggars Allowed" policy; plus its delicious food was indeed the ideal cure for a drained traveler . . . In a sense a safe, secure, protected feeling like checking into a hospital.

However, it was hard not to rag on Singapore with its CLEAN, CONTROLLED, CONSERVATIVE image. We joked about the sign which sits on a major road as you enter the city: "Singapore Welcomes Bona fide Tourists, But NOT Hippies." Of course we all had heard the stories of being thrown in jail for three months for chewing gum in the subway; and being caned for violating any minor government infraction.

Brent, the Australian, a rather boisterous sort, short of stature, but displaying big bravado, who on first meeting let me know within minutes that he was a Black Belt, joked about how people in Singapore seemed scared to cross the street.

"I mean shit, there would be no cars as far as you could see and still the pedestrians, like robots, would not dare cross until the traffic light flashed the little green man. I mean it's a weird place. The vibe is like people feel they are being watched."

As if on cue, we all blurted out: "The stamp, the SHIT stamp." This passport stamp was infamous and one of immense traveler lore among fellow backpackers. The official stamp, which stands for Suspected Hippy In Transit," allowed the authorities if they suspected you were a hippy to stamp your passport, and make sure you were escorted out of the country within twenty-four hours; and not allowed to return for ten years. I went on to say, "I met this Italian guy in Turkey who had the SHIT stamp. He was so proud of it, as if he had earned the Medal of Honor.

It was so impressive, a full page of SHIT. We all broke out laughing, and quite honestly, we were envious of his achievement.

Being world travelers, each of us who sat at this table had been on the road at least two years. We took big time pride in having our passport stamped with exotic stamps of destinations where we had been, cherishing them as if they were battle wounds. We joked that it might be worth getting kicked out of Singapore, just to flaunt the SHIT stamp. Looking at Dieter, this tall, reed-thin German with blonde hair down to his shoulders, who struck me as a thoughtful, responsible, caring type, might be a candidate for exile.

With that long hair, it was like placing a target on his back. It might be only a matter of hours before the officials would be stamping his passport with "SHIT" and sending him packing.

"To Singapore," we all cheered, as yet another round of beers arrived at our table, as we toasted again.

Bllliinngg . . . bbblllliiinnnggg . . . bbbbblllllliiiinnnngggggg!!!

It was the unmistakable, ubiquitous ringing of a rickshaw's bell, as the driver of the rickshaw glided slowly by. As if on script, he let loose with his relentless sales pitch. "You want postcard, phone card, student card, city map, batteries, and cassettes?" All of us were so used to this annoying mantra; we just continued to eat and pay no attention, dismissing him with a shake of the head, as if shooing away a pesky fly.

Almost immediately, the rickshaw driver circled back and positioned himself right next to our table: "Hey, where you from?" We continued our chowing down, giving him no eye contact. The driver, not a young man, about fifty years old, short and slight with graying hair leaned in closer and said in a secretive, hushed voice:

"Hey, you want nice Singapore girl?"

You want nice 'sucky-fucky'?"

Brent, who was now probably on his sixth beer, got jacked up on hearing this:

"Yeah, Singapore pussy, let's do it!" The rickshaw driver responded to Brent with a concerned gesturing of his hand to tone it down.

Dieter and I just looked at each other. There was quiet. My own thoughts on first hearing this was, I really wasn't up for it. I had plenty of chances to partake of the prostitutes of Asia, but had never chosen to do so. I had my reasons. But the main reason now was being just too exhausted and weak and had no sexual desire. Because of my debilitating dysentery and extreme weight loss traveling in India, I was suffering from a lagging libido and sagging parts. Only in the past couple of weeks, traveling down the Malaysian coast I had begun to put on weight and started to feel stronger. Translation:

I was beginning to feel horny for the first time in almost eight months.

Brent, jumping in before we could even comment, said:

"Asian putang...come on!" I turned to Dieter for his honest opinion. I asked him in a genuinely concerned manner: "What do you think, Dieter?"

"I don't know. How much will it cost?" Dieter asked the driver.

"It cost $15 for a "go or $30 for entire night. And if you see girls you don't like, you don't take. Just come and look."

Brent shot back: "That's way too much." The driver pausing countered with: "Okay for you we make special price, $10 one shot, $20 for night."

Dieter muttered an almost inaudible, unconvincing: "Sure, why not?" With my brains between my legs and the booze talking, I nodded my head in agreement. Brent whooped a big: "YEAH, LET'S PARTY!"

The first obstacle, a practical one, was just boarding the rickshaw itself, as the rickshaw was only built to accommodate two. Krishna, the driver, informed us that it was against the law in Singapore to have three passengers on the rickshaw, and that we would be severely fined if the police discovered this. So Krishna instructed us, that if we spotted any police, one of us would have to hop off before being spotted. It was agreed that Bret would be the official "jump" person; and he would take turns sitting on our laps.

Okay, we were off. The ride to the "House of Nice Singapore Girls,"

I took for granted the ride would be short. Well, it was not short. The trip was more like a journey (into the unknown). The ride started with us being peddled down a heavily traveled main street that seemed to go on endlessly. It was over half an hour of riding, and it was not comfortable having Brent sitting on us. We began to question:

"Where is this place? How much longer?"

Krishna, sensing our concern, reassured us, "Not much longer, and it will be worth the ride for nice Singapore girl. Nice sucky-fucky!" His assurance of "not much longer" seemed to fire us up more and we began chanting:

"SINGAPORE SUCKY-FUCKY, SINGAPORE SUCKY-FUCKY!"

Krishna, the driver, turned his head, signaling us to quiet down: "You can't make noise like that in Singapore," he cautioned. Yet we continued to chant. Yes, we were flying high and in the mood for some Asian sexual adventure.

Soon our boisterous exuberance turned sober, as we turned off the main road to a dimly lit street, and quickly turned again. We were now down by the waterfront and despite us being high on booze, and in a party mood, we all noticed this was a rough looking area. It was dark, desolate and the buildings were stark looking, abandoned with broken windows and barbed wire.

We started to talk among ourselves that the area had a feeling of a place you'd see in gangster movies where you'd "dispose of a body."

Krishna, feeling our unease about the location, just replied with a laugh: "Area quiet but okay, safe." The rickshaw slowly rolled along another dark alley. It turned a tight corner and went down an alleyway so narrow, not much wider than the rickshaw itself.

The alley was so eerily quiet, it was unnerving. You could see and actually hear the rats running along the side of the boarded up buildings. About fifty yards ahead you could see a circle of light on the ground. As we got closer there appeared to be a man standing in the circle.

We had arrived. Slowly and cautiously we got out of the rickshaw. The man in the light stood frozen, as we approached. He looked Chinese, not tall, but he was imposing looking. His face bespoke of a no nonsense attitude. His jacket rippled with muscles. To me he looked like the type who might eat nails for breakfast.

He greeted us unceremoniously with all the warmth and charm of the lovely surroundings: "You want girl one shot or all night?" No one spoke.

To ease the tension I spoke politely with no disrespect, "Do you think we could see the girls first?" (To me it seemed the typical, proper way to conduct a business transaction). He grunted and led us up two dimly-lit flights of stairs.

The room we entered was of average size, stark and unwelcoming. The only lights were two florescent tubes which hung from the low ceiling, giving off a harsh purplish glow. There was nothing on the worn, crumbling walls. The only adornment in the room was a lone reddish couch pressed against the wall.

Our host grunted again, gesturing to sit on the couch. This couch was gross, a good portion of it torn showing the yellowish foam padding underneath. But worse it was badly soiled with stain marks all over it, whose origins you did not wish to contemplate.

He barked even louder in Chinese and nine Asian women walked out, or rather shuffled out, with significant disinterest, to the center of the room. They were all dressed in different types of sleazy lingerie.

I let my eyes run quickly across the nine women standing in front of us.

They came in all shapes and ages, from teens to the eldest probably pushing forty. In all sizes, from painfully emaciated to a couple that looked like they came off a Wisconsin milk farm, to one small girl about 4 feet six tall.

Now I took time to focus in closely, looking at each as an individual, I especially studied their faces. What looked back at me was so far from what I envisioned this experience would be. It was my first visit to an Asian house of prostitution. My vision was from the movie "The House of Suzy Wong," where there was an array of "lovelies" to choose from. But instead here before me, what I saw in these faces is best described in one word: "NASTY."

Did that girl second from the right have a couple of teeth missing? What about that woman directly in the center with the wild hair? Not just a tacky orange color, but cut almost in a severe Mohawk cut, or the one to her left, was she sporting a mustache? There were a couple that seemed to have skin so coarse and caked with makeup, you could light a match on it. Perhaps the oddest one of all, although her face was the most acceptable, had a huge bulge in her panties.

My gosh, did she get lost trying to find Bugis Street?

What they did all share in common was an attitude, an attitude of total diffidence: listless, yawning, scratching a crotch here, picking a nose there, no smiles, just frowns. Their negative body language, their "downer" attitude sent a message loud and clear.

"Let's just do it, but I have no interest in trying to entice you." (And who could blame them?) These girls looked used, exhausted, wasted. They were a total "turn off." I felt sorry for them. But scared of them too.

After the girls were on the floor for only a few seconds, our host, the brothel boss, barked: "Okay, which one you want?" There was a long uncomfortable pause. No one said anything, as I believe my two cohorts had the same feeling I did. It was not just that they were not attractive. It was more than this, they looked mean and dangerous and unclean. I had no desire to go behind a closed door with any of them.

I looked across at Dieter sitting next to me, and to Bret on the end of the couch. The silence hung. Dieter finally whispered to me that he did not want to partake. I could see that Brett just shook his head slightly with a "no."

Our host standing beside the last girl in line, moved forward toward us and demanded, in his intimidating barking tone: "Which one?" More silence.

Bret, nervously and lacking in his usual machismo ways he likes to display, said quietly: "It looks like we don't care for any of these girls."

Our genial host seemed to take this quite personally and moved forward threateningly to about five feet in front of us. In a deep voice with greater agitation he snarled: "Okay, I have more girls, but this better be no joke."

Off the girls shuffled and for the first time I noticed a hint of personality in one of the girls. The small one giggled under her breath as she skipped off, as if to say: "Finally now I can go back to sleep."

There was a brief pause, perhaps two minutes, but it seemed longer as the tension filled the room. The host was now pacing back and forth, curling his fists, and rearranging his black turtleneck under his tight fitting jacket. There seemed to be some commotion in the back, some yapping of the girls to one another. He walked back and pulled aside what looked to be a sheet which led to another room and shouted his orders.

Out they came. As bad as the first group was, this cast of seven was worse! At least three of the girls looked deformed. A couple of them were frightfully young, maybe twelve or thirteen. And a couple of others had bruise marks on their faces, as if used for human punching bags.

"OKAY WHICH ONE? WHICH GIRL YOU WANT?"

Silence.

I hoped against hope that Bret or Dieter might say: "You know that one third from the right, she is sort of cute. I'll take her." No response. Our host was not happy and became in-your-face confrontational:

"I bring you more girls, you get. Now you must make choice." He was now just a couple of feet away from us yelling: "Don't play game with me."

The sinister atmosphere hung heavy. I spoke as diplomatically as possible: "I think we are going to pass on the girls you have." I added, "However we appreciate you taking the time to show us your girls." (What a weird thing that was to say to him). This caused him to go to another level of intensity, as he crouched down with his face just inches from my face.

"Don't you play fucking game with me!" His head looked like it was going to explode. It was turning beet red. He was sweating profusely and the veins on his neck were bulging out.

Dieter, made the comment of the evening, which to this day still makes me smile when I think of it: "Look, the rickshaw driver said we come and just look and not buy if not satisfied."

Quickly his fist was thrown at Dieter, catching him squarely in the mouth. The boss was yelling something, screaming something like a mad man. I had no idea what. He was crazed like a bull. I sensed he wanted to kill us.

As he wound up swinging his big left-handed haymaker at Dieter, I jumped up. This does not sound very manly, and certainly not a move one would see 007 do, but I had a clear opening, and took advantage of it. I kicked him as hard as possible right in the balls. Doubled over, muttering and sputtering.

Dieter, despite being punched in the mouth, helped me trip and wrestle him to the floor. Brent jumped on top of him and went into his Black Belt attack mode, delivering a powerful blow to a vulnerable area in the neck. We were not sure if he was out cold, and certainly did not wait to see, as we headed toward the stairway exit down to the street, while assisting Dieter who was bleeding badly from the mouth.

It was interesting to note, and I thought about this later, that during the violent confrontation with the brothel boss, the girls of the "house" seemed not to overreact or express alarm. Instead theirs was a more of "ho-hum," been there, seen that before attitude.

It is said crisis situations demand "fight or flight" responses. This demanded both.

As we made our desperate escape to go down the stairs, a huge, as in hippopotamus, Chinese guy came charging up the stairs. His bulk was immense, completely filling the narrow passageway, preventing our exit. We knew we could not out muscle him, but if we could get past him, we could out run him.

He was obviously the brothel bouncer, and he had other plans. I sensed he had dealt with dissatisfied customers before. He was waving his massive arms ordering us to "stop." We instantly sized up the situation, that there was no way we could get by him. So the three of us just ran as hard as we could into him, using him as if a blocking dummy in football practice; and down the stairs all of us rolled. It was crazy!

We scrambled to run out, but he got hold of me just outside the doorway and started to pummel me. He continued to swing away, as Dieter and Brent struggled to get him off me. The real punishment was his weight. He was like a 350 pound hippo, and I felt I was going to be suffocated by his mass.

Finally, the repeated punches of Brent and Dieter started to slow him down, and somehow I got up from beneath him and he began to stagger.

We started to move away, but just when we thought we were free of him, he lunged at Brent with a knife, catching him in the arm. Brent was furious and wanted to meet his challenge, getting back at him with his Black Belt lethal tactics, impervious to the impending danger.

But Dieter and I yelled at Brent: "Come on, let's get the hell out of here!"

And so the raucous "good time Charlies" full of bravado, bad jokes, big laughs and cheap booze, were suddenly silenced and scared shitless, as bruised and bleeding, we bolted into the CLEAN, CONTROLLED, CONSERVATIVE Singapore night . . .

A sobering experience. Not my finest hour.

Chapter 19

SCOTLAND PASTRY SHOP: TWO ANGELS AND A WEE BIT O' HEAVEN

It was the driving rain and raw cold that drove me to the pastry shop. For three hours I stood along the road which led out of Glasgow, trying to hitch a ride north to the Highlands of Scotland.

In those three hours of wet, I sampled a variety of rain types: from soft bearable mist; to conventional downpour; to the brutal horizontal rain. This is a rain that is punishing like wet bullets.

Scotland! Oh Scotland! I have read your poet Robert Burns rhapsodize about your beauty. Your haunting scenery is legend in the Scottish Highlands with its wild heather which erupts in the Moors. But oh! Scotland, you have been trying . . . In my ten days backpacking I have had seven straight days of rain, rain, rain, rain, and more rain. I hope to see your bonnie face soon.

The pastry shop was simple. But upon entering, it could have been a Four Seasons Resort, so inviting was its warmth. It was dry, toasty warm and carried a delectable fragrance of baking bread. I was beyond wet. I was drenched, soaked. I was like a human sponge.

The pastry shop was empty. I stood at the counter and waited. I turned and looked around, went back to the counter again and waited. Was anyone here? "Hello?" A head popped out from behind the counter, an elderly white haired woman, with a generous open face with rosy cheeks.

"Good Heavens, lad, you look like you just had a swim in Loch Lomend," she said in a distinct Glasgow brogue bordering on the hard to understand.

As I sat my pack down in the corner and settled myself in the torn but comfortable chair, the white haired woman came scurrying around the corner with a big steaming pot of something, putting it on the table in front of me.

"I'm sorry, I didn't order this," I said.

"Sweetie, please it is hot tea with lemon, drink up," she insisted.

In a matter of seconds another woman, almost her twin in appearance, came racing around the other corner with a big thick towel. "You must dry off, love."

I thanked them and ordered some scones with cream. They were so good. But even better was the feeling of just being inside out of the wet. I took my time savoring the taste of the scones. Also I wanted to linger taking in the warmth and dreading going out into the downpour again.

But after about twenty minutes, I began to feel ill. Not so much a nauseous feeling, but the sweats, chills, and aches rushing all through my body. Although the rain seemed to have calmed down somewhat to a light drizzle, it still was raw, and I shivered at the thought of getting back on the punishing open road again. But I had to push on.

Going up to the counter to pay my bill, the kindly white haired woman #1 looked at me with grave concern and said: "Laddie, you look terrible. You are sweating and trembling."

"I do feel a little weak and feel some chills. But I'm sure it will pass," I tried to say with conviction. In truth I felt miserable and that I might pass out.

She continued to study me, shaking her head. "No, you should take some time to rest. What is your rush? You can rest at the shop here, and when you feel better you can be on your way." She called back: "Mary, fix up the cot, will you dear? Our friend is going to rest a bit."

Mary came out and smiled sympathetically, handing me a heavy wool sweater and said: "Put the warm jumper on, Love, and follow me."

The cot was small and sandwiched in the tiny back room among crates, cartons, cans and confusion. To be dry, cozy and stretch out on the cot, covered with a fluffy down blanket with tender, loving care, felt like heaven. Within minutes both ladies were at my bedside, one with another pot of hot tea; the other with shortbread cookies.

"Thank you so much for your kindness. My name is Scott by the way. What are your names?"

"I am Gladys and this is Mary."

I extended my arm from the cot to shake their hands; each had a strong grip.

"Now rest up, Love, sleep as long as you want."

"But what time do you close the shop?" I asked.

"Closing time is around six o'clock, but don't fret that, just rest up," they assured me.

So rest I did. I would sleep deep, only to be awakened in the evening with Gladys, Mary and a younger man holding a tray for me. "Sweetie, this is Robert. He owns a pub down the street and brought you some of his shepherd's pie."

Meeting Robert just represented the beginning of the caring people I would meet, as I lay in my little cot in the back room; it being a parade of kind Glaswegians, each bringing me their own personal warmth to make sure I was progressing well. I knew I was seriously ill as my burning up body alternated between shivers and sweating, which continued through the night.

The next day Gladys called for the local doctor to come. His diagnosis: walking pneumonia. He instructed me to take the medicine he prescribed and continue to rest.

I did so for four more days on this cot, a cot far too small for me, a cot that would sag in the middle and creak whenever I moved, and had a spring or two that would poke at me. This was my bed to recovery. And the doctor's prescription helped. But perhaps the best medicine that performed its magic was the big dose of healing TLC. (tender, loving, care).

As I slept or tried to sleep on my cot, I would constantly hear the women, especially Mary because of her louder voice, say things such as: "We've got a young American lad resting up in the back."

Everyone was curious and would ask things like: "What is wrong with him? Where is he from?" Some of them were allowed to come back and stick their head in and take a look. They were very quiet and considerate as they would gently open the door to the back room and take a look at the "young lad" resting, as if I were a rare extinct specimen.

But the ladies were always selective and discreet about those they felt would be advisable for me to meet, or that they felt I would enjoy meeting.

My "keepers" spent the first evening bedside, as I ate, learning things about me.

Then came a colorful collection of local folks who found their way to my cot to check up on me. This was not just kind, but an entertaining, enthralling experience in getting wonderful contact with the people of the country.

This included: an art professor from the University of Glasgow who introduced me to the Art Nouveau style of Charles Rennie Macintosh; an inspiring young playwright; a couple of fanatical soccer blokes, who gave me the low down on the bitter rivalry between the Celtics and Rangers; plus an elderly but fit, powerfully built gent who had climbed the summits of the five highest mountains in Scotland. And Sarah, well, she was just a lovely, young Scottish lass.

Each night around seven as the ladies were closing the shop; they would knock on my door and enter ceremoniously with my dinner. Every evening it was a different person from a different local restaurant that brought the dinner.

It was as if from my bed I was being served up a gastronomic representation of the best of Scottish specialties: from venison, in a delicious red wine sauce, to poached salmon which was known as "Tweed Kettle," to "Cullen Skink," which was a thick soup of smoked haddock and potatoes, and of course, Scotland's treasured national dish of haggis, an acquired taste, but I enjoyed it served with the classic "neeps and tattie" (turnip and potato).

After the rigors of the road, this was first class dining. But it was more, so much more . . . nourishing me in indefinable ways.

As I finished my meal, they would sit with me and have tea and chat for an hour or so and make sure I was feeling well and if I needed anything. Making sure I had enough covers. Making sure I was informed what was on the "telly." Making sure I had enough books and magazines to look at. Making sure I was comfortable. Just making sure.

It was so endearing their quality of caring. I "made sure" they knew how much I appreciated it. I called them my "two angels," who rescued me.

I always enjoyed our talks. Their presence was healing. They would ask me questions about my family, my thoughts on different matters, and where my future travels would take me. They were good listeners. And although they asked a good deal of questions, I could not encourage them to share much about their own lives.

The two of them appeared close in age (perhaps in their sixties) and had been close friends all their lives. They did tell me that neither of them ever married and now shared an apartment down the street.

By the time I woke up on the fourth morning, I felt much better. I was almost disappointed to feel so good, as my time on the cot in the pastry shop was such a rich, cozy, nurturing experience.

As I prepared to leave, the ladies gave me a bag of their favorite short bread cookies and a thermos of hot tea. They had taken off their aprons for a quick final farewell photo. And surprise! Appropriate for the occasion and their radiant spirits, the sun was finally out. An auspicious beginning and parting. A difficult moment.

I hugged them close and thanked them again for their immense kindness. "May your good deeds be rewarded? I shall never forget you." As I hoisted my too heavy pack on my back, I said: "I wish I could take you with me, my 'angels,' to keep watching over me."

"Not much room in there," Mary giggled.

"We will be," Gladys assured me.

A last embrace, and I was off.

As I made my way down the road and out of Glasgow, I could feel myself tearing up and looked back. Gladys and Mary were still waving in the distance. It was almost as though they were seeing their son off, wishing a fond farewell to that son they never had.

I waved a long final good-bye to my two "angels," who had watched over me, and shared so generously their wee bit o' heaven . . . until the city traffic swallowed me up.

Chapter 20

MUNICH TROLLEY STALKER

Sitting sandwiched between two portly men, she read intently. She looked up only slightly when jostled by someone bumping into her, caused by the twisting movement of the trolley.

I was pressed in the back holding on to a strap shared with three other hands. I was straining to catch glimpses of her between a man's armpit and a woman's grocery bag, which contained two large protruding sausages.

I could not take my eyes off her. No, this was not a simple romantic attraction, as she was probably twice my age. But this was stronger. Her presence drew me; it was out of my control. She was so glamorous.

Never had I seen such a woman. I had to be near her.

The trolley came to a sudden stop, and I lost my balance tumbling into others. By the time I recovered I noticed her seat was vacant. Where did she go? Without even thinking I pushed past those in front of me and forced my way to the exit door, just before the trolley pulled out.

I was more than two miles from the stop that I wanted. What was I doing? Why was I pursuing this woman? I was not sure. But I think it was because I was feeling dejected over the day's events and needed something to take my mind off my own self-pity.

I was feeling down because today I was officially notified that I was not allowed to work in Munich. I desperately needed the money. I had spent all day at the Official Work Office showing documents, presenting a letter from my potential employer and still got a "NO!" It was not as though I was competing for a highly sought after position with Munich's recent university graduates. I had exhausted almost all job possibilities.

The last resort was a job as a shoveler of shit at the Munich zoo. I tried many approaches to appeal to the stern administrator; even showing her my shoveling motion which worked so well during my interview for the leaf raking job in Sweden. She was not amused and shouted "NEIN!" even louder, fully enjoying exercising her petty officialdom.

As I bounded off the trolley into the chilly December evening air, I could clearly hear the six chimes of the Glockenspiel from the Marienplatz. I looked in all directions. Where was the woman from the trolley? Across the street I recognized her from the back, dressed in black with the unmistakable smart fedora. She was taller than I expected and carried a cane, adding to her allure.

I navigated quickly but carefully across the slick, icy roadway, not wanting her to get away. Now on the same block, I walked slowly behind her. She walked with a pronounced limp and the icy conditions made it difficult for her. The light changed to red and I stood with her on the same corner with several other people. I was right next to her, looking at her from the corner of my eye. Her bone structure was striking. I wanted to speak but couldn't. Her face had coolness about it. I felt intimidated. What was I going to say? It was not as if I were interested in asking her out for a date: I was just fascinated by her.

As the light changed and she walked on ahead, I continued to stay behind her. I tried to think what it was I was going to say. "Hello, my name is Scott. I was on the trolley with you and found you to have the most interesting face and wanted to meet you." HOW STUPID! I felt like a total buffoon chasing after this elegant woman. Forget it, let it be, go home! Leave this woman alone, I admonished myself.

And just as I was about to quicken my pace to move past her and abandon this ill-conceived escapade of meeting my mystery woman, she let out a cry and slipped on the ice. I half caught her as she fell, falling down with her.

"Are you okay?" I asked, as I slowly got up and helped her to her feet.

"Fine, thank you." Her voice was soft, almost shy, with a slight German accent, very pleasing.

During the fall some things fell from her shoulder bag, which I helped her retrieve. One item was the book, which I presumed was the one that so engrossed her on the trolley. Its title: *American Playwrights of the Twentieth Century.*

"Are you sure I can't help you?"

"No, please, I am fine." This time she said it stronger with more conviction, a la Garbo, as if she really wanted to be left alone. She thanked me and slowly began to walk forward, her limping more evident than before.

After a few steps she slipped again. Fortunately, I was directly behind her and made a clean catch.

"Please, I insist on walking with you to where you are going. It's too icy. You must be cautious. I'm in no hurry."

I then added (with an inspired, ingenious literary reference to the book on playwrights she had been reading), "Remember what Tennessee Williams wrote in *Streetcar Named Desire*: 'I've always depended on the kindness of strangers.'"

This got her attention and respect and produced a hearty laugh.

"Very good. Quick, clever," she said.

"Please allow me," I said in my most earnest tone.

"Yes, well thank you. That is very caring of you. I am going to a nearby café to meet a friend in about an hour."

As we walked we did not speak other than introducing ourselves by name. It was so slippery; I wanted to concentrate on getting her to her destination unscathed. Her name was Anna.

When we arrived at the café, I paused at the entrance to say "goodbye."

She said: "Scott, thank you so much for escorting me here. You are a 'kind stranger' indeed. If you like, let me treat you to a coffee or a glass of wine."

Without hesitation, though careful not to sound overly anxious, I smiled: "Yes, I would like that."

On entering the maitre d' spotting us, abruptly left those he was assisting to turn his attention to Anna. Despite the restaurant being packed to capacity with others waiting to be seated, he led us to a private table in the back.

As Anna made her way, those around us turned to stare. She commanded attention. So there I sat directly facing this woman of intrigue. On the trolley I caught only quick, partial views of her face, but now seated across the small round table, I could study her closely.

It was not just a pretty face; it was striking. The type of face that can take your breath away. The high cheek bones, the slight lift to her grayish blue eyes, and her porcelain skin appeared distinctly Slavic. She was not young, tiny wrinkles were visible.

Removing her fedora and shaking her shoulder length blonde hair, almost platinum in color, she resembled the old black and white photographs of movie stars I had seen in my father's book on the history of film. She had a definitely Garbo-esque quality about her. But there was someone else, who was it?

Then it hit me, Veronica Lake, that is who she very much resembled. (The Hollywood femme fatale of the 1940's).

She had an aura of savoir-faire about her, but in an unassertive way, gracious, as she exchanged a cheek kiss with the head of the establishment who had come over to welcome her. She introduced me and asked if I would like coffee and dessert. Nodding "yes" she turned to the gentleman, his name was Manfred, "Please get Scott the Black Forest Cake with Viennese Coffee."

The way she ordered, the way Manfred leaned in close, hanging on her every word, and noticing the other people in the café still looking at her, I had the feeling I was in the presence of someone who was "somebody."

And now Anna looked closely at me. Her gaze was direct and strong. What did she see? Anna launched immediately into lively conversation: "So, Scott, tell me what you have done since you have been in Munich."

"Well, I went to the Hofbrauhaus and watched the Glockenspiel move and chime, and went to the Englischer Garten."

Anna seemed to contort her naturally lovely face into a distasteful expression saying: "I don't care for the Hofbrauhaus at all to be quite honest, and the Glockenspiel and the Englischer Garten are so touristy, certainly loved by Americans."

It sounded like a putdown of sorts. "But, Scott, what about the Deutsches Museum or Schloss Nymphenburg?"

"No, I have not been to those yet," I stammered quite feebly. My hands felt damp, my throat dry. I felt I was drowning in front of her, when I wanted so much to impress her. Anna was such a presence. Sophisticated.

An unfair comparison perhaps, but she was such a dramatic departure from the college girls I encountered often shallow and vacuous.

There was quiet and Anna sensing I was uncomfortable asked me, "Scott, you seem to like theater. You certainly seem to know your Tennessee Williams." I told her I had studied some theater in college.

"So what are your thoughts about Munich's Rainer Werner Fassbinder and the works he has produced?" she asked.

"Who?" I stammered.

"Fas–binder, Fas–binder." Anna enunciating his name for me each time distinctly and slowly, so I would never forget.

"Scott, he is from Munich, he started a theater company called the Anti Theater. His works are avant-garde and daring. He is controversial and brilliant. He is something of an enfant terrible. He has also produced some films which I believe have been shown in the states, well at art houses perhaps, such as *The Bitter Tears of Petra von Kant*, and *Effi Briest*. His leading lady, Hanna Schygulla, has a most interesting look and strong stage presence."

I could not pretend to know. I could not fake it. Only the truth was worthy of this authentic, substantive woman. "No, I have never heard of him. Sorry."

An uncomfortable silence came over the table. Anna was such an amazing woman, exciting both in her beauty and intellectually. I felt so insignificant, so out of her league. She checked her watch. The quiet was interrupted by my knocking my fork off the table, it clanging loudly on the polished hardwood floor.

More quiet . . . I felt like I was going to cry.

I reached into my small daypack and brought out Thomas Mann's *Death in Venice* and placed it on the table. Anna sighed, "Oh, my, *Death in Venice.*" Her passion intensified, as she asked me what I thought of various characters, and if I had seen the movie with Dirk Bogarde.

Because I was only half finished with the book, she did not want to ruin the ending for me. Instead she focused on other Mann novels, which she recommended I read.

Thank you, Thomas Mann for saving me. (It is smart to travel with good books).

Anna continued to elaborate on the merits of Thomas Mann, enthusiastically talking about a novel called *The Magic Mountain*, then switching to Goethe and his book entitled *Sorrows Of a Young Werther*. She was enthralling to observe, this ice-cold beauty that could get so fired up over things of the mind.

We had been there about an hour, when I noticed she was looking at her watch again. I could sense she was anxious and somewhat agitated.

"Anna, are you okay? Is something bothering you?"

"Scott, I like your fine sensibilities. It is a privilege to be with you. And a pleasure." In one affirming utterance she had made my feelings of awkwardness and inadequacy vanish.

With almost no emotion she added: "What is bothering me is that my friend is late." For several minutes she looked away and checked her watch again. Abruptly she interrupted me and said, "Scott, my friend is forty-five minutes late, and I have tickets to a cabaret. It starts very soon, would you like to go?"

"Why, yes, but what do I owe you for the ticket?" (Who am I fooling? Me on a $2 day budget)

"Nonsense, you are my guest."

This was the beginning of being "her guest" at many extraordinary events.

We had to move quickly as the curtain was in twenty minutes. We seemed like old "pros" navigating the ice this time, as we were in step, she taking my arm, and not falling once. "A little better than our first try," I joked.

We arrived about five minutes before the curtain with Anna explaining that tonight we would hear the songs of Kurt Weil. I was not familiar with him.

"Weil was one of our country's greatest cabaret composers, before he passed away. The songs will all be in German, but I think you will still enjoy it."

Enjoy I did! After the cabaret, she insisted I join her for a nightcap at one of her favorite haunts. A place not even noticeable from the street, almost speakeasy-like, but inside dimly lit and invitingly warm. We each had a cognac, and it was here that Anna opened up and told me about her life.

She talked about her two daughters "both beautiful, accomplished and about your age. They are my life today, so important to me, as I lost my husband four years ago." Anna went on to say her husband's name was Franz and that he died in an avalanche skiing in Switzerland.

Anna expressed with both poignancy and joy that Franz had been a remarkable companion and father. He was a very successful business man, but he always had time for the family to travel and shared with her a strong interest in all the arts. "He was a man of intellectual curiosity, strong and masculine. Hard to find," Anna said nodding her head.

"And now being a single woman, this is very different." She went on to say that her friend whom she was to meet in the café earlier in the evening was a man that she had been dating quite seriously for eight months.

But she was getting fed up with him, as he had a roving eye.

"He is a cheater, a middle-aged playboy. I have no time for this type," she said with contempt and resignation: "No one compares to my husband. I am best alone." I felt inadequate to comfort her.

I told her my comparatively inconsequential woes and that meeting her was such a good thing, when I had had a miserable day. She asked why.

"I wanted to stay and work here, but was refused my work permit today, even though I had found a job at the zoo doing manual labor."

She inquired more about the position at the zoo and what "manual labor" meant; I explained "shoveling shit out of the cages."

Anna burst out laughing and we toasted each other with our cognac glasses.

She said, "Scott, I think I might be able to help you. I realize it is difficult getting a work permit in Germany even for a job such as that. My husband and I were donors to the zoo, and I know people on their board. Let me see what I can do."

And so it was the mysterious woman that I had first spotted on a trolley car who would turn out to be my savior in trying to get me work. More importantly, Anna became an inspired mentor to me in all aspects of the arts. Not only did we attend the opera, ballet and theater, but also talked hours on end about music, literature and our favorite artists.

I credit my mother for planting the seed to broaden myself with knowledge about all forms of the arts. The interest was there, no question. But Anna ignited that interest into a passion for the arts to what it is today.

I sensed that Anna's husband had left her well off financially, as cost seemed never a consideration for her. It was not just the very best of Munich we took part in, be it the performing arts, or dining at the finest restaurants, such as Boettners or Grunwalder Einkehr, but we would go on out-of town cultural binges.

She would have her driver wisk us up the autobahn for the three hour drive to Berlin, to see as Anna would express it: "Herbert von Karajan is like God conducting the Berlin Philharmonic Beethoven's 9th." To this day I have never been so moved by a classical music performance.

We would go to Vienna and not only see *La Traviata* at the world-famous Vienna Opera House, but go to the world-class museums like the Kunsthistorisches and the Albertina, and stroll the streets while Anna would point out important buildings designed by Otto Wagner and those built in the colorful Jugendstil architectural style.

It was amazing being with her. She was so deep and curious about everything. We grew very close and cared for each other in a very special way. Yes, she was twenty-seven years my senior, her age being forty-nine, but when we walked I liked feeling her next to me, as we would link arms. I liked how it felt holding her hand, lightly kissing her cheek and warmly embracing each other when we would meet, or when we parted. I liked her fragrant scent of expensive soap.

However, never did we become intimate. I can honestly say it never occurred to me. My feelings for her were on a lofty platonic plane. Being physical would have been like an impure act, and have complicated our relationship. It would have tarnished the shine of the cherished bond we shared.

No matter where I traveled in my trip around the world, I would feel her presence, and keep her posted with letters and postcards.

While I was in Istanbul, about ten months after seeing Anna last, I received an engraved invitation from her to attend a formal charity ball for the Munich Hellabrunn Zoo. I did not attend. But I did enjoy the sweet irony of life with its surprising, serendipitous twists and turns: from rejected zoo shit-shoveler to black-tie benefactor.

But demanding as life can be; we often get so involved and absorbed in our daily lives, that we regrettably lose touch with those we love dearly. Such unfortunately was the case with Anna. Our correspondence stopped.

The final letter came some twenty years later to my parent's old house, telling the news of her death. I regret I didn't receive the letter in time and had missed her funeral to honor the memory of this great lady.

Her impact on my life will always be part of me. Is this not what true immortality is all about? She had touched me deeply with her generosity and spirit and kindness, in everything from zoos to "strangers" like me, her "trolley stalker." She had graced the world with her extraordinary beauty, her intellect, her luminescence.

The stars would not shine as bright this night . . .

Chapter 21

BURMA: MY BUDDHIST SAVIOR - HERO

His name was Man Nai Win.

He found me in a cornfield, doubled over and vomiting.

He was a saint…his care restored my health; his pleading kept me out of a Burmese jail; his serenity sustained me.

Let me backtrack five days to Rangoon, Burma, and how I arrived in this position, and what would transpire.

"NO SELLING CIGARETTES OR LIQUOR" read the big bold black sign above the reception desk of the Rangoon YMCA, a hotel that was well known for "accommodating" backpackers. This referring to the illegal black market that was so prevalent in Rangoon.

The man at the desk, his head barely reaching the top, asked for my passport, and declaration form with a most official tone. Then following his approval, I turned to go to my room, when I heard a, "Pssst, hey do you have any Johnnie Walker or American cigarettes?" I pointed to the sign. He shrugged his shoulders, as if to say, "Forget about it," or "don't you understand you are in Burma? This is our way."

Burma today is called Myanmar. The horrific tragedy of the June, 2008 cyclone, taking 140,000 lives and the strict isolation for years from the outside world is well documented. In 1978 Burma presented a mysterious travel destination. Only very recently had it opened to tourism, and I had never actually met a person who had traveled there.

However, those whom I talked with who had heard from others, spoke of its lush landscape, dazzling pagodas, gentle Buddhist people and recommended heading north, to Mandalay or Pagan. But this rosy image was also tainted with tales of a country that was repressive, a police state that was run by a dictator and a strong armed military, plenty of red tape which allowed only seven days VISA for travel.

It was a country that you needed to be on your best behavior as a traveler and strictly obey all government "rules and regulation." Of which there were many.

It was this shroud of mystery and sense of being an intrepid explorer that captured my imagination. But, with only seven days, I would have to move quickly, and be in my best traveling shape. Unfortunately this was not the case, as I arrived in Rangoon via my two hour flight from Katmandu, Nepal feeling weak, exhausted and sick. My weight, as of yesterday had reached an all time low. It read 55.4 kilos or 122 pounds. Two years ago when I left the States, it had been 185 pounds.

I was especially disappointed that my health had taken a turn for the worst, as I had expected in Kathmandu, with a full week of just kicking back, eating good food, and recharging my batteries from the tough travel of India, to get better. But unfortunately this was not the case.

Katmandu, the capital and largest city of Nepal, was a place that is absolutely beloved by backpackers, including me. The heart of the city was made up of narrow, twisting streets with ornate wooden balconies and over 1,000 temples. Of special interest was the Living Goddess, a young girl, eight years old, who would every morning at nine o'clock open her window, and smile and wave to those below.

Restaurants with reassuring, inviting names such as Grandma's, California Café and Nirvana served up comfort food with familiar sounding dishes that travelers missed: macaroni and cheese, apple pie, meat loaf, lasagna and cheeseburgers. And that was the cause of the problem. Because the comfort food was so familiar, travelers would assume it was safe like that same food back home. They would not question it, as they would have in India, where you were always on guard and cautious about the food and water. In Nepal, you relaxed and the defenses came down and bang: food poisoning!

On my third day in Kathmandu I experienced this. My familiar sounding dish was shrimp scampi. Within fifteen minutes after finishing, I knew I was in trouble. It was not until I was ready to leave after I had eaten the shrimp scampi that I learned that Kathmandu, (with all its positive accolades) was known among travelers as "the dysentery capital of the world."

What also made Katmandu so appealing was its being a crossroads for international travelers. Istanbul had more travelers coming and going, but many of those were the short two month college summer vacation variety coming from Europe. Whereas Katmandu attracted the hard core, those who had been on the road a long time, the vast majority arriving overland were directly from India. And like me, they showed their travel time on their exhausted skeletal bodies.

Sitting at a café with my new traveling companion Jack, a British architect about thirty years old, whom I met on the bus from India to Kathmandu, we would sip tea and watch the sad parade of travelers walk by and play this game:

"Do I look better than he does?" As we would witness astonishing, rawboned wasted looking backpackers amble by, we would compare our emaciated bodies to theirs.

The results: I was about the norm; Jack looked a little better than most. But I joked with him that he had only been on the road for about eight months. And, also, his route was "softer," having spent most of his time in Bali and Thailand and only three weeks in India. India was commonly known among travelers as the most grueling of travel destinations. There was definitely a "look" to those that had traveled India. That look was weight loss.

I spent two days in Rangoon. Because of the lingering ill effects of the scampi, I spent the time just resting up for the train trip north to Mandalay. However, I did find the energy, thankfully, to visit the world famous Shwedagon Pagoda. Standing 376 feet, the bell shaped pagoda was mesmerizing in its golden glow, plated with over 21,000 solid gold bars. The very tip of the stupa was set with 5,448 diamonds, with 317 rubies, sapphires and other gems, 1065 golden bells and a single 76 carat diamond. Surrounding the pagoda were many smaller Buddhist shrines in silver and gold. It was dazzling, a mind blower. I had never seen anything like it. I felt like I was in the Emerald City of Oz.

The train to Mandalay was to be 445 miles, departing at seven a.m. and was scheduled to arrive thirteen hours later. As I boarded I felt fairly good, and in high spirits. The train itself was comfortable by south Asian standards, in spite of the seats being hard wooden benches. But it was clean, with good size windows, and most important not over crowded.

I was seated across from two young orange robed Buddhist monks. A middle aged man sat on my bench with a seat between us. He wore an old but classic Harris Tweed blazer with a red tie. With his silver hair and thick glasses, he presented a distinguished professorial look.

The Mandalay train chugged on in a slow unwavering line, passing simple huts made of straw on stilts, virtually in the shadow of the railway track. The children, their faces covered with the ubiquitous thanakha paste, (this the yellowish substance made from ground tree bark), would jump up and down as the train approached and run as fast as their little legs could go, hoping to catch up with it. Further out, you could see people in the rice paddies knee deep in mud. Pausing from work, they would wave, some giving the peace sign. All seemed to wear huge grins under their large bamboo triangular-shaped hats.

Yes, so far so good. The scenery was pleasant, my body functions seemed okay; and I enjoyed getting to know my train companions. The monks spoke no English and shared little conversation, even between them. But their faces were so peaceful; it felt good just to sit close to them, as if they had blessed our seats with good harmony. They shared with me their mixed assortment of nuts, and every so often they would look at me and just smile.

The man in the blazer, sitting to my left, I noticed had the book *Airport* by Alex Haley, resting on his lap. We began to talk. Our conversation was limited but enlightening. It was also a conversation that was cautious, spoken in a quiet voice, as if not wanting to be overheard.

His name was Kandin, and he was a high school teacher in Rangoon. As our talk took form, he moved to sit in the space next to me. "Burma is a repressed society. The government watches the actions of people closely." He went on to say that the book he was reading was one of only two western novels that were currently allowed to be purchased on the newsstand. Digging into my shoulder bag, I pulled out a beat-up copy of *The Sun Also Rises* by Ernest Hemingway. "If I gave this to you, could you keep it?" Kandin nodded his head as if disgusted. "No, I would have to hide it. The central government monitors what we are allowed to read."

I found meeting Kandin insightful, and looked forward to continuing our conversation on the remaining six or seven hours. However when the train stopped at the next town, a new passenger joined our bench, an army officer in his mid thirties. He was a large man and imposing in stature. Dressed in a tailored olive green uniform with gold buttons, there was a severity about his face, square jawed with a two inch scar under his right eye?

Hoping to maintain the ease and good feeling of where we sat, I greeted the officer with a "hello" in Burmese. He looked at me as if he smelled something bad, and spit a red stream beetle nut on the floor.

With the officer's forbidding presence in the car, the conversation between Kandin and me came to an abrupt end. He nodded ever so slightly "no" with his head, as the officer sat down. Even the monks' body posture and faces seemed to tighten.

It was also at this stop, that I jumped off the train and purchased some food to take back on. It was lunch time, and I was hungry. I was feeling good up until now. I should have played it safe and bought some oranges from the fruit seller. But instead I opted for curry with a questionable meat item.

Well, if my mouth had stopped speaking on the officer's arrival, my stomach started chattering very loud. I could feel the impact of the curry with its mystery meat almost immediately. Within the next hour I dashed five times to the toilet. My diarrhea had become so frequent, that I had to excuse myself from where I was sitting (explaining to Kandin, half smiling to the monks, rubbing my stomach). For the remaining four hours I would stand positioning myself by the toilet, and now adding to my discomfort, vomiting as well.

It was during my time of standing by the toilet that Kandin approached asking how I was. Looking over his shoulder, he handed me a piece of paper. Written on it was the following list:

Farewell to Arms – Ernest Hemingway
The Great Gatsby – F. Scott Fitzgerald
Sons and Lovers - D.H. Lawrence
Of Human Bondage – Somerset Maugham
Huck Finn – Mark Twain

I understood. He wanted books, reading material from the west. Kandin, looking over his shoulder spoke quietly, "If you could send me these, I would be so grateful." I nodded to him, "I will, I promise." He then added that there were two addresses. The first was his, but the second address was where to send the books. It was the address of his brother, who lived in a rural area. He added that the government would be less likely to open his mail there than in Rangoon.

"I wish we could have spoken more, it is just not possible with that officer. Perhaps he doesn't understand English, but the risk is too great," he said. I let him know that I understood, and asked if he would like my copy of *The Sun Also Rises*. A wide but controlled smile appeared on his face. And before getting off the train, I made the illegal exchange of the Hemingway novel.

As I exited the train station I felt totally spent. I was abruptly stopped by two stern looking men who greeted me with "Tourist Burma, follow this way."

I followed them back into the station and into a small side room, where I noticed there were two young, long haired travelers. I nodded. I heard a "salut," they were French. We were to show our declaration form, and fill in what we had acquired since we boarded the train.

I had trouble finding the form. I could sense they were watching me closely, as I dug through my backpack. Not a good way to start with the authorities. I could hear them snicker and felt their eyes closing in and studying my soiled, dirt caked backpack. I started to mutter, "I know it's here. I know it's here somewhere." Finally finding it, showing it to them, as if it were a gold medal, I sat in a chair and wrote in what I had purchased on the train journey.

As the inspector studied my passport, he paused, scrutinized me, looked at the passport again, and once more at me. It was as if he could not believe I was the person in the photo on the passport. I felt like exclaiming, "The photo was taken sixty-three pounds ago."

The three of us were then taken to the place we were to spend the night. We had no choice of hotels. The place we were assigned was fairly clean and acceptable but the cost was a full seventeen chat ($2.50). Wow, expensive! The French boys and I muttered to each other on this highway robbery cost. It was almost three times as much as the places I stayed in India. However, though irked by the cost, I had no energy to complain and crashed immediately.

Mandalay was Burma's second largest city, a place that Kipling wrote about in his famous poem. To me it sounded so exotic, so melodic: "Mandalay." Although my heart wanted to explore and drink in its color, I felt too lethargic and just went through the motions.

The Grand Palace, according to my guide book, was one of the two "must sees." When I was told it was about one mile away, I started to walk. It was so hot, and I felt so sluggish, I passed on that "must see." Instead I made my way out to Mandalay Hill, which according to the book, the walk to the top of the hill to see the magnificent view of the surrounding countryside was billed as a "not to be missed." This ranked higher even than "a must see." But when I looked up at the hill, and read that there were 1,700 steps, plus the scorching heat, and feeling just so out of it, I did miss it. I passed on something that was probably very special. I can't remember this ever happening before. A valid indicator how weak I had become.

I was feeling lightheaded and hungry. Hordes of local kids followed me and crowded around and stared as I sat at a food stall eating some stew. Hawkers started waving things in front of me to buy. I just did not feel good, and those around me demanding my attention were getting on my nerves. I just wanted some peace and headed back to my hotel. Feeling queasy, I stopped to vomit. A group of about ten kids watched, some laughing, others caringly running to assist me with water. This was, of course, the last thing I needed.

Not wanting to push my luck any further, I called it a day. I retired to my hotel. Writing in my journal, I thought of the school teacher I met on the train.

The next morning, still feeling nauseous, I thought it might be wise to explore a near-by small village, rather than deal with the noise and commotion of the city.

The train ride up from Rangoon had shown me glimpses of rural Burmese life. I was hoping now to discover some of this on my final day before heading back to Rangoon. I boarded a bus and headed out, not having any idea where I was going. I was seeking a village that just "felt right" to me. After riding the bus for about forty-five minutes, I caught a glimpse of a pagoda above a lake. I got off at this village named Taguntaing.

And this is where we pick up the story from the beginning... I had seen some pagodas straddling above the lake. But to get there I had to navigate through a dense cornfield. As the corn got higher, it became increasingly difficult to see where I was going. It was only 10:30 in the morning, but the heat was fierce. Surrounded by this corn, it was almost claustrophobic. My stomach was uneasy. I was feeling so incredibly weak that I could barely walk more than a few minutes at a time. Dizziness set in. I was doubled over vomiting, not once, but convulsively again and again.

As I was curled over, trying to get my bearings, I heard a rustling. I looked up and there was a short dark skinned man of about thirty years old carrying a machete. His machete looked menacing. But the look he gave me was not one of his being angry, but of surprise and concern. After explaining what I was doing here, he insisted that I come with him back to his house. Retracing some of my prior steps, veering off to the right, we continued through the corn field for another ten minutes before arriving in front of a simple straw hut, like the ones I had seen on the ride up on the train.

His name was Man Nai Win. Sitting on his wooden bench outside the straw hut, positioned between the cornfield and the rural dirt road which ran about thirty yards in front, he served me some milk tea and a biscuit.

"You look bad, you should rest." Feeling my forehead, he said, "you have a bad fever, come lay down over here."

He led me to the inside of the hut with a dirt floor. Kicking a couple of chickens away, and taking a hand broom and brushing the floor, he said, "I am going to go into the village to get something for your illness. You just take a nap."

By this time several young children of the village had gathered around the open window of his hut, jockeying for position as their eyes peered in at me with curiosity. Man Nai Win told the kids to scram, so I could get some needed sleep. Before leaving, he introduced me to an older gentleman named simply Billy who lived next door. He assured me Billy would check on me if I needed anything.

My sleep was deep and undisturbed. However, when I woke up I was sweating, but I was shivering as well. I called out, "Nai," but it was Billy who entered. Through hand gestures, he displayed three fingers, which I took to mean that Ko went somewhere and would be back at three o'clock. I gestured that I was freezing and needed a blanket. He gestured he understood and returned soon with a blanket.

I was in a daze, though recognized Nai standing over me. He sat on the edge of the cot and spoke quietly, almost hushed, but you could feel the strength in his voice. "I want you to take this." He held out several leaves on the palm of his hand. The leaves all green in color, about an inch in length, had the texture of sage, but no smell. I am sure he could read the hesitation on my face, and he said, reassuringly, "Please take. This will help calm stomach." I chewed the first couple cautiously, basically no taste. With no seeming after effects, I downed the remaining leaves with greater ease.

After a short time, surprisingly, my stomach actually did feel better. So I left my cot and joined Nai on the wooden bench. Together we shared a dinner, of boiled chicken with rice, followed by his home-grown plums, which were especially delicious. No curry.

As I sat with Nai and sensed the calm of the place, I felt at ease. The lonely dirt road, running in both directions as far as you could see with its thick green vegetation, was so tranquil and welcoming in comparison to the bombastic buzz of Mandalay. For two hours or so, we just sat looking out, talking occasionally, sipping our milk tea. A water buffalo would meander by; a woman supporting a long pole across her shoulders balancing two large containers loped past; a couple of bikers coasted by; each waving to Nai.

I felt so comfortable with him and protected. Even though knowing him only a matter of hours, I had trust in him to do what he thought was best for me. "Nai, thank you very much for your kindness in taking care of me," I said, as we had finished the chicken and now began to sip our milk tea. He nodded quietly, his face breaking into a slight smile. I looked over at Billy who was sitting behind us smoking a huge cheroot, a cornstalk about eight inches long and very popular in Burma. I noticed he was stirring something in the wok.

Man Nai Win was forty-one years old. However, with his smooth dark skin, open face and easy smile, looked easily ten years younger. He previously worked for government services for fourteen years. Living in Rangoon, he became tired of the noise and congestion and moved to this village of Tanguntaing five years ago.

He felt good also getting free from working under the controlling clutches of the government. He was now doing all he could to make it as a farmer growing plums.

"I love the peace that the village brings, and being on my own, doing my own business," he said. I asked him about his family.

"I have two young children, who live with their mother in Rangoon. I support them, but I prefer to be apart from them, to see them every so often. I like the solitary life."

Nai went on to talk about Burma, and not in a positive way.

"The country is not stable. The government is corrupt, led by a ruthless man named Ne Win, who has been in power for sixteen years. We are isolated from the outside world."

Nai went on to say that the Burmese are not allowed to travel out of the country; and if they do, they are never allowed back in.

"If I was to talk to you and a policeman saw me, he would likely stop and want to know what the conversation was about." He continued speaking of the oppressive measures.

"Mail is opened. Burma is a very poor country, and the government has power over private industry."

Many people Nai knew in Burma had crossed the border over the mountains to enter Thailand, and even India, as both presented more opportunities for the independent business person. Nai said he was strongly considering doing this.

It was now almost 8:00 p.m., the sky was turning soft violet and pinks, and a soft breeze gave nice relief from the humidity.

Billy called out to Nai. Nai got up and went over to where he was cooking. He looked in the wok, nodded, and picked it up and showed me. Inside the wok were what appeared to be grasshoppers frying. Nai nodded his head approvingly and said something to Billy.

Although my stomach felt better, I started to get the cold chills again. Nai gestured to go back to the cot and sleep. However, before I did Billy came forward with a glass of green liquid. It looked awful. "Is that drink part of that?" I gestured to the fried grasshoppers. Nai, nodded, "Trust me, this will be good for you, bring back strength." By this time, I had built up so much trust in Nai that I would probably eat or drink anything he suggested. It tasted like it looked, only worse; it was terrible! I only hope it does me good, I thought.

Just as I began to get comfortable in the cot and began to doze off, it just hit me. I remembered about having to return to my hotel in Mandalay, and needing to catch the 7a.m. train tomorrow to Rangoon, before my seven day VISA expired. How could I forget? How could I make such a serious mistake!

I called out to Nai. He joined me by my cot, and I explained to him the VISA restrictions and how I could be in big trouble with Tourist Burma. He was cool and collected: "We will deal with this tomorrow. But you are not going anywhere tonight. There are no busses that early. Just sleep well."

The next day I woke feeling better, but I was very anxious about my VISA situation and dealing with Tourist Burma. Would there be a big fine? Would I be put in jail? I once again expressed my concerns to Nai.

He just calmly said, "I am sure they have their strict rules. I will go with you and hopefully help the situation out."

As I began to pack, in order to catch the first bus into Mandalay, Nai said, "Scott, why do you need to rush off? You missed your train already. We will go in later. I want to show you something very special."

And with that, following a breakfast of plums and pineapple, I followed Nai through the stalks of the cornfield down to a lake. Kids were splashing about, jumping up and down screaming, some running to shore to say "Hello mister, hello." We walked for another ten minutes around the bank of the lake and waited for a small boat. It looked somewhat like a poor man's gondola, being pushed by a single oarsman, to pick us up and take us across the lake which seemed about a half mile wide.

The view was pristine and peaceful, with dense green forested hills rising from the lake. In every direction you looked you could see glimpses of white shimmering pagodas, resembling upside down vanilla ice cream cones.

Disembarking, I noticed Nai handed the old oarsman a small brown bag. We moved forward through thick vegetation. He told me that the temple we are headed for is named Kyack Taw Gyi and is one of the most famous in Burma. But because of its remote setting, it sees few visitors, he explained, except for the most ardent followers of Buddha, and probably no western tourists.

We occasionally would pass simple straw huts, kept in much worse condition than Nai's. And see undernourished kids sitting about, some crying. Nai would seek out the parents or elders and give them plums that he had in his brown bag. "These children are hungry. They need to eat better food."

We had now been walking over half an hour, and the vegetation was getting denser, almost jungle like. We pushed through a thicket and there was the temple. Nai mentioned that the temple was nearly 250 years old, that King Pagan erected the pagoda which was to be the reproduction of the famous Anand Temple in Pagan.

What especially made it memorable was the magnificent Buddha that rested inside. A sculpture of the sitting Buddha, probably 30 feet high, and this was carved out of a single block of marble. He pointed out two light green spots, one under the Buddha's chin, and the other on his chest. This is showing that it is mysteriously "turning" to jade.

We were the only ones in the temple. Flowers rested at the Buddha's base. A colorful flag of red and orange was draped behind his head. In the quiet, I could hear the sounds of song birds outside. Nai shared some of his thoughts about Buddhism and the importance of having "no desire."

Desire, he explained, was the source of evil. He only wanted to live a quiet simple life, being compassionate, living life in the moment, one breath at a time. And to raise his plums and pray to Buddha.

All this solitude, serenity and healing; and soothing surroundings had put me so at peace. But as we started back, I was snapped back to the harsh reality that I had to go face Tourist Burma and find out what hassle I was in for by overstaying my VISA time. I expressed to Nai that it really was not needed that he accompany me to Tourist Burma, that it would be too inconvenient for him.

It was my problem, and I would deal with it. But I thanked him for his kind concern and caring. Nai would have no part of this talk from me and said, "Scott, I will support you how I can. But believe me if you go alone, I think it will be very troubling for you."

Three hours later we were back in Mandalay. I ran into my hotel room and grabbed my backpack. The man at the reception desk, whom I had never seen before, informed me that an official from Tourist Burma was looking for me. He sounded quite distressed.

As Nai and I entered the Tourist Burma Office, it felt like a sweat box. There were two officious looking men standing arms crossed, looking pissed off, as they had been expecting me. One of the men I had not seen before. He was built like a bull. Nai stood with me but a few feet off to my right.

Before I could even speak, the chubby short officer, whom I had met yesterday, barked: "Where have you been? Why did you not check in last night?"

I began to explain my situation, letting them know that I was in the village of Taguntaing and became very ill.

"Why were you in this town? Why did you not notify us of this itinerary change?" snorted the bull. "This is bad, very, very bad," chimed in the other one.

The bull continued his rant, "You are on a seven day VISA, and now you overstay. This is a severe offense."

"I am sorry, I got ill. I did not mean it to be a problem. I am ready to return to Rangoon immediately on the train first thing tomorrow morning."

Nai quietly said, "Scott was with me last evening. He was a very sick young man." As he started to speak more, he was interrupted as a slight, older gentleman walked in. He was dressed in a dark blue business suit and a crisp white shirt. The other two officers seemed to come to attention with his entrance to the room. He was clearly the leader.

He walked over to me and challenged me: "You, Mr. Stone, made a serious mistake, not reporting to us. Now please I need to know the reason why you go to such a backwater little village when tourist sites are in Mandalay."

I responded in all truthfulness. "The reason is I wanted to get a better feeling of the quiet countryside of Burma and its people. And also when I took the bus I noticed the lake and the pagodas. It seemed like a nice village."

He fired back, "Have you been to the Golden Triangle?" This is the infamous corner where Burma, Thailand and Laos come together and is well known for its opium smuggling.

I responded, "no," that I had not.

There was quiet for a moment. The officer from yesterday said, "Please let's see your passport."

He took my passport and showed it to the leader, the little suited man; the bull looked on as well. The three heads bobbed up and down a couple of times, between gazing at my rawboned spare face, and what they saw on the contrasting passport photo.

The leader said what I knew the Burma Tourist office had been thinking all along: "This photo in your passport does not look like you."

I explained my situation, how that was really me and that two years of travel had taken a serious toll on my body, having lost over sixty pounds.

"You must do drugs to look this way," the bull responded.

"No, I do not."

The leader flipped through my passport. "Afghanistan, lots of opium to buy there. Did you buy drugs in Afghanistan?"

I responded firmly: "I don't do drugs, I don't buy drugs."

"What about Nepal? I see you have been there, all those hippies. That is a drug center."

"Sir, I do not do drugs, I don't buy drugs," I answered as calmly as possible.

This was followed by them insisting I empty out all the belongings in my backpack. I did this slowly. Out came my trusty blue jeans, three torn t-shirts, faded khaki shorts, a map of Southeast Asia, and a little gas stove. My movements were deliberate.

I was feeling nervous clearing out my backpack. For although I did not purchase drugs, I had firsthand knowledge of the horror stories of travelers who had drugs "planted" in their backpack by the authorities; if the officials wanted to "get back at them" for attitude or for doing a serious misstep. My friend by the way spent six years in an Indonesian prison. And to this day he denies that the drugs were his.

My backpack had been away from me over night. I knew that Tourist Burma was very unhappy with my actions. Would they seek their revenge by planting some drugs in my pack? I was sweltering in these thoughts of what I might find as I continued to take items out of my pack.

The bull was getting visibly annoyed with the time it was taking me to empty my backpack. So he grabbed it, unzipped the three side zippers, and held it upside down as if he were emptying garbage.

There was a clattering of items hitting the floor:

a couple of pens, loose coins, some Indian love beads, shaving cream, tooth paste, a flash light, pictures of family, postcards and some personal letters from friends. Also a couple of books; *Goodbye Columbus* and *Tropic of Cancer*.

The leader picked both up and exclaimed, "Filth," and tossed them to the floor in disgust.

The chubby small officer unzipped the bottom compartment of my backpack where my sleeping bag was. They proceeded to turn the bag inside out, shaking it. It was in this compartment that they came across six thick notebooks. These were my most prized possessions, my journals.

"What are these?" the leader demanded.

"Those are my journals. I do some writing when I travel."

"And what do you write about Burma, and who do you write to?"

"I only have written good things about Burma. Please you can read them if you want. And the writing is for me only. Travel journals are for travelers who never want to forget their journey." The three of them gave the notebooks a quick thumb through, and tossed them aside.

It was a surreal scene, sitting on the floor cross legged, surrounded by all my worldly possessions. It was airless, oppressive and tense in this room where we had now been for at least two hours. There was quiet deliberation. They talked to each other in Burmese.

I noticed amongst the disarray of tossed items, resting against the corner of my sleeping bag was something wrapped in white tissue paper. It was small, no larger than an inch with a slight bulge in the middle. It was taped. What was that thing? I did not recognize it. Was it dope? Had they planted this on me? I felt my head was going to explode.

"What is that?" the leader, now looking drained pointed toward my sleeping bag.

"What is what?"

"That white thing, what is it?"

I could feel my heart racing, extreme sweat coming over me. I answered him honestly, "I don't know."

The bull picked it up and the three of them gathered closely studying it. Then the chubby officer opened it. Inside there was…an orange, a small, withered orange.

I remembered. This was a gift given to me by a revered religious man in India. I explained to them. And that he blessed this orange and wanted me to always keep it for enlightenment and protection during my travels.

They each gave it a quizzical sniff and pinch, seemed satisfied, and tossed it to the floor. Never did I feel such relief. A simple orange, and a rotten one at that, had never looked so good.

There was an awkward prolonged silence. No one spoke. The heat was stifling, the tension palpable. After conferring a final time in hushed tones in Burmese with the two subordinate officers, the leader moved toward me, and with piercing eye contact, stated in precise English:

"Mr. Scott Stone, you should go to jail for what you have done. But instead, you will be fined 1,500 chat."

"What?" I looked at Nai in disbelief and said quietly, though the others tried to listen in, that is $200! I only have a total of $300 left, and this was to get me through my remaining four months of travel.

"There is no way I can afford this."

Nai up to now was quiet, and then began to speak. I do not know what he said. However, for a good ten minutes he spoke all in Burmese, focusing his attention on the leader. He would return Nai's words with a shrug, a nod, and an occasional "okay" or "yes," while the other two looked on as if mute.

And that was it the leader said, looking almost relieved,

"Okay, you are free to go. However, I will need to write you an official form to give to the authorities on your departure at the airport. I will have it ready for you this evening."

As we left, Nai who was my savior before, was now my hero.

"What did you say to him?" I asked. Nai just smiled and responded: "The leader, he is a believer of the Buddha…and he likes plums!"

When I embraced my savior hero for the last time, I was choked with emotion; not only with gratitude for what he had done for me, but in knowing Nai's kindness would forever restore my faith in humankind and the simple goodness and greatness of which man is capable.

At last when the plane finally made lift off from the binding borders of Burma into the free "blue skies yonder," with me on it, my spirit lifted off and soared with it "up, up, and away." Free again! Free again!

Exhausted, I could scarcely muster enough energy to fasten my seat belt and almost instantly surrendered to sleep. Not before reflecting, in reverence, for the "Man Nai Wins" of the world: the unsung heroes quietly making a difference each day, living simply, seeking justice, serving others, even a fallen American traveler in a cornfield. And asking nothing in return.

My Buddhist Savior in Burma

Chapter 22

KINDNESS AND KIMCHI IN KOREA

The touch on my shoulder was so light that I thought it was perhaps that of a butterfly. From the floor of the Seoul International Airport, I opened my eyes to see an Asian man standing over me.

He leaned down, and in a voice as quiet as if telling me the most hushed secret, said: "You can no sleep here." I muttered under my breath and rolling up my sleeping bag, made my way over to the nearest chair. The clock said 11:37 p.m.

"No, no sleep here, you go home with me," he persisted, as I tried to resume my sleep sitting upright in the chair. "No, please, I am fine, leave me alone." I getting a little testy because of a recent incident I had in Hong Kong that became uncomfortable. My male host became a little too on the "friendly" side, and I ended up having to physically wrestle him off me.

Soon a young Asian woman came into focus standing by his side. I was by now fully awake. She was attractive and spoke in good English. "This is my boss, Mr. Park. He is a very kind man and feels you need comfort of his home to sleep." She added that he had just gotten married a week ago, and his wife will make you a delicious meal. Hearing that food was in the offering I perked up, and learning that he was married made me feel more comfortable.

The woman said goodbye to us, and Mr. Park said, "Please, follow me." As we walked out of the airport, I with backpack, Mr. Park insisted on carrying my three plastic bags. These were filled with inexpensive tourist goodies for friends and family back home. After nearly two and a half years of rugged traveling, I played the tourist shopper in Honk Kong, as now I was on the home stretch.

Today was November 23.[rd.] I had flown to Seoul earlier today, arriving at 6:30 p.m. Tomorrow I was to leave on the Korean Airlines flight at 9:20 a.m. to Nagoya, Japan; and eventually catch the December 2 KAL flight out of Tokyo back to the States.

It was not until we were outside the airport, and he was hailing down a cab, that I introduced myself.

"My name is Scott. Thank you, this is very kind of you." It bothered me that I did not yet know how to say "thank you" in Korean, having just landed four hours ago.

"Pleasure me, I am Ronald," he said as we shook hands. He was short and slight, but his head seemed big for his body. He was animated and seemed to have energy about him even when quiet. I would guess his age to be early to mid-thirties.

As we waited for a taxi, I was amazed how freezing cold it was. I could see my breath and noticed the snow on the road sides. After over a year in tropical sun-drenched south Asia, I was now in a northern climate, and shivered wearing a thinly knit turtleneck.

"You have no coat?" asked Ronald with concern.

"No, this is it," I said.

The taxi ride was a brief, perhaps twenty minutes if that, leaving a main drag to a quiet street, another turn down a narrow lane. During this time I thought about the cold and my monetary situation. I had ten days left on my trip before flying out of Tokyo on December 2. I had only $82 left, which in India would last me six weeks, but Tokyo I had heard was ridiculously expensive.

With the weather cold and no warm coat, hitchhiking and even possibly sleeping outside could be a tough situation. But in my heart, I knew somehow I would work it out.

It was a little after midnight by the time we arrived at his home. It was an eight story apartment building. We took an elevator to the fifth floor. The apartment we entered was dark and still.

"Take shoes off, sit here," he pointed to a chair in the kitchen, which was dimly lit.

He came out about a minute later seeming to apologize for keeping me waiting.

"Sorry, please are you comfort?" I nodded yes. "My wife, she will prepare some food." He turned on the main overhead light, which displayed a small orderly room. It contained: a bright red sofa, two matching lounge chairs, books everywhere, and a record player with a healthy collection of records. Some very attractive Korean art works graced the taupe walls, and what appeared to be photos of family in sturdy frames.

I got up and walked over to the photo of a Korean couple with three boys, looking to range from five to eight years old.

"Is this mama and papa and your brothers?" He nodded. "Which are you?" He smiled and pointed to the boy in a bright green sweater with a huge grin, much more exuberant than his siblings.

"Nine years old in picture," he said.

"Very cute of you. Where is your family today?"

"All live in Seoul area. Mama though no more, passed last year."

"I am sorry to hear that." I could tell that Ronald was saddened. It was quiet for a moment. I moved to a photo with an elaborate gold frame which displayed Ronald and his wife, the recently married couple. Both wore controlled smiles and were dressed in traditional Korean costume: the bride's an elaborate top coat in luscious green with flowing sleeves in red. She had small pink circles on her face and wore a small crown. The groom was dressed in a maroon jacket with baggy pants tied at the bottom; he wore a dark cap.

"Now that is a beautiful picture. Your wife is very pretty."

He seemed to beam with happiness. And as if on cue, his wife came out. She was petite, probably not even five feet tall, but so pretty. She had a youthful innocent look about her, big dark eyes and porcelain colored skin. She looked younger than Ronald, perhaps in her mid-twenties. I had a feeling that she had been sleeping before.

"This is wife June." She smiled graciously. "She speaks no English," Ronald informed me, "but she is wonderful cook. She will cook for us now."

I nodded to her, without offering my hand, and said, "Nice to meet you.

Congratulations on your marriage," as I pointed to the photograph. Ronald translated and she broke out in a quiet giggle.

Ronald led me into another room. It was small and dominated by a gigantic television set.

"This is TV room," he seemed proud to announce.

"Yes, I guess so," I said jokingly.

He turned to me and said, "Before we eat, need to wash feet, change clothes, more comfort." Out from a small closet he brought a crisp neatly folded light blue jogging suit.

"Please put on, wash and come back."

A few minutes later via the visit to the bathroom, I returned with clean feet, and wearing the jogging outfit, which fit me snuggly.

"How do I look?" I striking a muscle-man pose, as his wife caught my image from the kitchen. She laughed, louder this time. Entering the TV room, Ronald smiled and gave me thumbs up.

He was seated on the yellow tiled floor and instructed me to sit down. To my surprise the tile seemed warm and comfortable.

"Dinner coming soon, please some tea," he requested. He informed me he had always wanted to visit the States, and hoped someday to live there.

"My company, I am in banking, we have office in LA and New York, hope to transfer someday." Before I could even comment, he said,

"Today is your Thanksgiving. We must have toast for this," and yelled to June something in Korean. It was surreal, sitting here on the floor of a stranger in Korea one o'clock in the morning on Thanksgiving. And to think in ten days I would be back in the States.

June returned with a tall green bottle with Korean writing. Ronald nodded to June and taking the bottle, he said exuberantly,

"This is Soju. It's Korea's most famous alcoholic drink, drunk by almost everyone."

I started to lift my ceramic white cup, he instructed me, "You need to learn correct way to receive and pour Soju. Please hold glass in left palm and hold with other hand." He poured slowly for me and I put the cup down.

"Now you pour for me. But you need to do as I do, hold bottle in right hand and with left hand you rest on elbow."

I listened carefully and performed my task. He smiled, "Yes, this is good. Pouring this way is tradition, promote spirit."

Lifting the glass, he called out "One shot to Thanksgiving, gun bae!" (Cheers in Korean) And down the hatch I drank, it tasting similar to vodka, though slightly sweeter.

Ronald was like a piston, so full of energy. He was upbeat and curious and fired question after question:

"What you study in college? Do you like soccer? What type of music enjoy? What state come from?"

With that last question, I answered, "Michigan."

He seemed to reach a greater excitement level as he said, "Scott, you should be here Saturday. It is Michigan – Ohio State football game."

I looked at Ronald stunned, "How do you know about that?"

"I love American football, that game big, big battle!"

I shook my head in agreement, but then added emphatically, "I have no interest in Michigan. I am a Michigan State Man!" (Referring to the university that I graduated from, and the rivalry between the schools).

"What about pro football, who's your team?" I asked.

"My team is Raiders. 'Just Win Baby,' this referring to the mantra of the Raider's controversial owner Al Davis.

"This year we not do so good, but last year, yes, Super Bowl victory over Vikings!!" Man this guy was incredible!

"Okay Ronald, do you have any Raiders' caps or jerseys ?"

"No, I don't, they don't sell here, American football not big in Korea."

"Who is your favorite Raider?" Without pausing to think he said,

"The Snake, Kenny Stabler, he is main guy."

"Ronald, when I get back home, I am going to find you a Stabler jersey and send it to you. I promise." He broke out in unbridled grinning.

I felt we could have chatted on about football nonstop. I had not seen any football during my travels. Hearing him so enthused, really wetted my appetite and got me fired up about the sport. But the gridiron talk phased out as June carried in a huge tray of over a dozen small dishes, placing them around us on the floor.

"Wow, what is this?" I stared in amazement at all the various small bowls and their contents and Ronald added, "These are all called banchan. The most famous banchan is kimchi, he pointing to a bowl containing an orange colored cabbage.

"Kimchi, like a religion in Korea, people crazy for, and so many variety over one hundred types."

I picked up the metal chop sticks and grasped a pretty healthy load as Ronald cautioned me, "Very spicy, be careful." I love spicy food, but took a cautious small bite. The taste was spicy, but not spicy like curry, more a hot biting and sour taste. I could taste a good deal of garlic and chili pepper.

"I like it," and I took another bite, this time more generous, and Ronald laughed, "I think you have Korean blood in you."

The other dishes spread out before me were delicate in their presentation. Some of the dishes looked strange; certain dishes I liked, others I did not care for. But I sampled them all. Ronald was excellent in explaining all that I ate.

Dishes named, Miyeok muchim, which was seaweed in vinegar and a white substance named Dubu-jorim. This was tofu simmered in soy sauce and did not agree with me at all. However, I did especially enjoy: Backkeum, stir fried shredded squid; Sigemuchi namul- spinach in sesame oil; Kongnamue-cold boiled bean sprouts; and Ganji namul-boiled egg plant.

The dining experience was remarkable. This unique, newly tried cuisine was washed down by ice cold Korean beer, called OB Lager.

"Ronald, this meal is so good, how do you say "thank you" and "delicious" in Korean?"

"Kamsahamnida is - thank you, and delicious is - a ju ma si seeyo" Ronald replied smiling broadly. I felt so comfortable as I leaned back and called out:

"June, kamsahamnida!" and heard her laugh from the kitchen.

And yet, believe it or not, there was more food to come, as June soon entered carrying a circular flat yellowish looking thing that resembled a pizza,

"This is Gamjeon, another famous dish, known in English as Korean Pancake," stated Ronald. I felt in awe of June's cooking, the couple's kindness.

I looked at them both and repeated "a ju ma si seeyo" This dish containing shrimp, squid and scallion was delicious! It was my favorite.

June standing above us, making sure all was in order, said, "Sleep, now." I got up from my seated position and this time shook her hand, not sure if that was correct, and thanked her again.

It was almost three o'clock by the time we had finished all our food.

During our eating, the conversation was mostly about sports: from American football to soccer, which he was crazy about, to golf which he recently had taken up. Golf was a sport that I had loved.

"I want to play that Pebble Beach," he sighed.

"To Pebble Beach" we toasted in the hopes that he would make it to the USA someday.

But now our talk left sports and became more varied, more culturally stimulating. Ronald, was not just some "jock," but a man of vast varied interests, a "Renaissance Man," if you will. He was like a thirsty sponge wanting to soak up everything about my travels, asking question after question:

"What was Paris like?"

"Did you go to the Greek Islands?"

"What about the Taj Mahal? Is it really magnificent?"

"Did you see Mount Everest?"

"Did you go to a bull fight in Spain?"

"Did you hear opera at La Scala?"

"Scott, you are so fortunate to see so much. These memories will be with you forever, you are rich inside."

He continued to ask me questions, now changing to more general topics, including favorite authors, music, art, film. He was so curious. I said to him:

"Ronald, you have such a hungry mind, you are the one that should travel."

He nodded slightly, "Yes, I hope so, I want to see much."

And when I inquired, he was pleased to share with me his "heroes," as he called them.

"Scott, I love some of your American movies, *Jaws, Cabaret* and *Star Wars*. But you must try to see some of our South Korean movies. Today in the Seventies films are being censored some. But in the Sixties we called it 'Korean Golden Age' for film, directors like Kim Kiyoung and Yu Hyun – mok, especially the film called the *Housemaid*, very strange, but sexy also." And from here we touched on writers, artists, musicians.

I shared with him that I was currently reading *Of Human Bondage* by Somerset Maugham. And though I still had forty pages to go, I was pleased to give him the book.

"Ronald, I have loved this book, you can keep it."

He seemed very touched and added, "My favorite Korean writer is Hwang Sun-won. He was great short story writer. Favorite of his novel is *Tree On a Slope*. He disappeared for a moment and came back with a dark bound book.

"This is it. I only have in Korean. You should look for translation."

"What is it about?" I asked.

"It is an emotional story of three lives of three soldiers in the Korean War. I wish had English translation to give you."

For a favorite singer, he jumped up and got out a record and played an artist named Kim Min-ki who had a unique sort of folk pop sound.

"He was very much revolutionary, helping the youth movement."

We even got into Korean politics, and the Korean War, and the friction between North and South Korea. And also Japan and how Korea was under their power for thirty-five years.

As I sipped on what was my fourth OB, I could not believe it was going on four-thirty. Just as things were winding down, he looked at me and cried out as if he forgot the most important thing of the evening.

"What about art? Did you go to the Louvre, Prado and that one in Florence?"

"The Ufizzi," I said.

"Yes, all of them and others. Art is one of my strongest passions. I regret, however, I know so little about Korean art."

With that Ronald sprang up off the floor again, disappearing into the other room, and in a few minutes reappeared carrying two thick hard covered books. One was written in Korean, the other said Gongsong Art Museum.

He sat closely as he slowly leafed through some of his favorite paintings and artists, "We have rich history of art, but favorite period was the late Joseon Dynasty, 1750 - 1850."

During this time there were three artists that were especially excellent. The artists' nicknames were: Hyewon, Owan and Danwon. They are known in Korea as "The Three Won."

It was extraordinary his passion to want to enlighten me. Here after all this time, so late at night, and now, so early in the morning, his desire in wanting me to understand the Korean culture. As I carefully turned the pages, he would comment.

I focused longer on a painter by the name of Shin Yuk-bok, and drawn to his painting called "Scenery on Dona Day." This portrayed several young very pretty Korean women in a pastoral setting. One of them in red was in a swing, while two men looked on behind rocks.

"This painter is Hyewon, and that is a lovely painting, one of my most favorites. 'Dona Day,' by the way, is a Holiday in Korea which comes every year of the fifth day of the fifth month."

Ronald suddenly said, "Scott, oh my, it is 5:15. You need to get up early, you must get sleep." And he bounded up and prepared my bedding, as he rolled out a padding mat of some type for me to sleep on. "I'm sorry, I kept you up so late," he said.

"Ronald it was terrific, thank you for an unforgettable evening."

As I lay my head down, I felt a little lightheaded from the OB Lagers and the Soju, but I was certainly clearheaded enough to realize what an incredible special evening it had been! Not just fun, but so enlightening. To think that just hours ago, I had arrived into Seoul's airport just to stay there for the night; and leave the next day without knowing anything about the country.

But instead, now because of Ronald's rare radiance with his big mind, big heart and this five hour gastronomic cultural cram session, I will be leaving so much richer in my feeling for Korea.

The morning came too quickly. Soon I was at the breakfast table taking my last tea with Ronald, which June would pour for us. It was 7:20a.m. The cab would be arriving soon. Ronald looked at me closely and with warmth in his eyes, as if we had known each other for a long time, said, "Scott, I have called a friend in Tokyo. His name is Tony Kawabata. He works for same company as me. He is very nice and he would be pleased for you to stay with him and his family for a couple of days when you are there. Here is his number. He is expecting to receive your call."

Just as I started to thank Ronald profusely, June scurried in carrying a huge winter coat and wearing a big smile. "Scott, you need warm coat also, you take this."

"No I can't, no, please," I protested. But they were insistent and together they put it on me. It was so big and warm and the hood covered in fur, I felt like a much beloved Eskimo, being rescued from the storm.

The sound of the taxi horn honked, it was time to say goodbye.

"Kamsahamnida, kamsahamnida," I said, and spreading my arms out I hugged Ronald and June in my fur lined coat, turned and headed to the taxi. I was off, but after about five seconds of driving, the cab stopped and Ronald came running up alongside the cab. "Scott, I forgot, these are for you," as he passed them through my rolled down window.

I did not look at his gift, until I checked my luggage and could sit quietly before boarding my plane.

Slowly I rolled down both scrolls, each an artist's print. And it was so like Ronald; he had attached a note with each.

The first was a print from Hyewon of a painting called "One Amusing Spring Day in a Field."

The other from the artist Jang Sueng – eo known as "Omon" and was of delicate flowers.

I was now in the air . . . I had left Korea, but Korea stayed deeply rooted in me, and has to this day, because of Ronald and his great kindness and passion.

Soon after I returned to the States, I sent my dear Korean friend my promised gift. It was not as elegant as his gift, but was sent with the same deep affection . . .

His RAIDERS jersey and cap to match!

TRAVELS WITH "PETE" (MOM)

Chapter 23

TRAVELS WITH "PETE" (MOM)
(GREECE, TURKEY, ITALY)

The rigors of the road can be tough and demanding. I was feeling exhausted, losing weight, and even a touch of homesickness was setting in after fifteen months of hard travel.

I had already done and seen so much, I told myself; perhaps it was time to return. I phoned home. I was choked up when I heard mom's voice from so far away. But I felt excited to tell her what I thought would make her ecstatically happy, that I'd be returning home soon. But my good news was met with an awkward silence.

After telling me how much they missed and loved me and how proud they were of me, she implored:

"NO, SCOTT, YOU CAN NOT!" IT IS TOO GREAT AN OPPORTUNITY. YOU MUST KEEP GOING AND CONTINUE ON AROUND THE WORLD. WE WILL COME SEE YOU INSTEAD."

She did. Unfortunately at the last minute my father could not get away because of pressing business commitments, but he insisted Mom go anyway. I have asked her to write of remembrances of our unforgettable travels together for five weeks in Greece, Turkey and Italy, which will be a bond between us forever.

MOM'S REMEMBRANCES

This chapter is entitled **TRAVELS WITH PETE.** "Pete" is the name of endearment Scott gave me at an early age. One Mother's Day he presented me with a special hand-crafted card with a personal message in his bold fifth-grade script that read:

"YOU'RE NOT LIKE NORMAL MOTHERS.
YOU'RE MUCH MORE.
YOU'RE MY PAL.
MAY I CALL YOU PETE?"

So "PETE" it was.

It is a privilege and pleasure to share my remembrances of that special travel experience with my son. It all began because I liked to give symbolic gifts. For Scott's graduation gift from college we gave him a transatlantic trip aboard the QE2. This gift symbolized presenting him with the world for him to discover. And discover he did.

His letters home dramatically documented this. They were both fascinating and thought-provoking. He would point out that a traveler is an attitude, a state of mind, a commitment to see and savor the world first hand. In a recent letter he wrote: "Many people travel. But few people are travelers. The traveler charts his own course, unrestricted by time or schedules or plastic pre-packaged planning. He travels light and lives lean. He gives up comforts and conveniences for experiential learning. He is open to learn, to grow, to enjoy. Mom and Dad, I know you've visited many different countries. BUT NOW I WANT YOU TO BECOME A TRAVELER."

And that's just what I intended to do when I finished talking to Scott on the phone. And he decided, with great enthusiasm and new energy in his voice, we should rendezvous in Athens, before he started his trek overland Asia to India.

My decision to not only become a traveler, but a "good traveler," was based firmly on three conditions:

1) Scott was a well-seasoned traveler. I would travel his style and on his terms, respecting his decisions and his itinerary.
2) He was as well an independent, self-reliant and mature individual now. I would not play "mother" (Very difficult with so many years of practice).
3) I would not complain at any cost.

The flight to Greece seemed more tolerable than most overseas flights, being in high spirits to see Scott again. It felt like I had scarcely been asleep, when it was announced we'd be landing in half an hour. I sensed my previous trips abroad would not properly prepare me for this trip that was to follow. But "different" does not have to mean "less," I reminded myself.

"THE SUBLIME TO THE REDICULOUS"

What I was properly prepared for (after hours of anticipation during flight) was the emotional impact of our long-awaited reunion. The flight had arrived in Athens right on schedule. Excitedly surveying the crowd on the other side of Customs, I suddenly spotted a beautiful head above the crowd. Was it, could it be?

Yes, it was! It was #1 son, Scott, that very special human being our family had missed so much: his basic goodness, his boundless fun-lovingness and his bottomless vitality. And now there he was looking tanned and fit and all smiles.

When we met there was nothing to do but wallow in our immense joy. We embraced each other midst tears, cheers and laughter, oblivious to the booming, buzzing confusion of the international airport that surrounded us. It was a poignant moment, sweetened and made more meaningful by our rich family bond.

The hotel room he had reserved to welcome me was a reliable indicator of what was to come.

"The sublime to the ridiculous."

A non English speaking hotel clerk silently directed us to the fourth-floor walk up. It was really not necessary for him to point out the communal bath down the hall. One just had to follow his instinctive sense of smell. A scurrying malnourished mouse greeted us as we opened the lockless door. The room was stark. The beds hard. The traffic-ridden view from grimy unwashed windows disquieting.

But on the bedside table was a single white rose in a Sprite-bottle vase with a card reading:

"MOM, I'M GLAD YOU'RE HERE! YOU'RE ABOUT TO BECOME A TRAVELER!"

I sized up the situation in a hurry. This trip was not to be the Hilton route. It was to be much more.

To Scott, by admission, it was the Plaza Suite compared to his usual modus operandi – roughing it in hostels; or just his sleeping bag on the floor of train stations; or just outside on the cold ground.

Out of respect for Scott as a hard traveler, I had followed his instructions to "travel light and live lean . . ." Although he allowed us both the indulgence of one, what he termed "DTK" (dressed to kill outfit)."

"FREE IS THE MAN WHO CAN TRAVEL WITH ALL HIS WORLDLY POSSESSIONS ON HIS BACK," he quoted me reassuringly. Complain I would not! I was shifting gears in a hurry.

And so the "pain and perils," the "pearls and pleasures" of travel started unfolding before me . . .

The "pearls and pleasures" were predictable. Our itinerary, embracing Greece, Turkey, and Italy was staggering in its riches: with all its man-made and natural wonders; its ancient historic landmarks, its lavish art treasures; and the enduring beauty of the Greek Islands and magical Venice.

To be able to share these riches with a world traveler, my son, only enriched it more.

The "pain and perils" were not predictable. The ubiquitous sublime: in the Greek Parthenon; The Michelangelo frescos on the Sistine Chapel ceiling, Istanbul's Hagia Sophia mosque contrasted sharply with the ridiculous. A for instance: the "excuses" for toilets. I could write a graduate thesis on "TOILETS I HAVE KNOWN AND LOATHED." With an enlightening Preface:

"There is no toilet paper on the road less traveled."

And my head being splat on by pigeons from the lofty Corinthian columns from on high.

Not once. Not twice. But thrice. Small bearable things like sea sickness during a storm and high seas while traveling in the Greek Islands, coming into port in Patmos.

Less than pleasurable, too, were the often unsavory accommodations that would elicit from the bowels of my being:

"WHAT IS A LITTLE OLD LADY IN TENNIS SHOES DOING IN A PLACE LIKE this?" Also unidentifiable foods and flavors.

"Should I risk eating this?" And stretching myself to keep up the pace on the trail, with a persistent inner voice pleading:

"When is naptime?"

"Where is my teddy bear?"

While reminding myself I did not want to be pampered. Only to survive. And scolding myself that I was not a tourist. I was a TRAVELER!

Mass "agony" was experienced on a torturous bus ride from Greece to Turkey. A price had been quoted for this trip. Then mid-way the bus stops at this posh hotel and we're told by the driver that we must stay here overnight at an additional fee. Everyone was grumbling and felt exploited.

These travelers were all on tight budgets. This was a set up. A case of collusion. We were being manipulated. We decided collectively to refuse to get off the bus. Always a champion of justice, Scott said I was at my best spear-heading the revolution. We negotiated with the hotel management, forcefully, for a compromise and were finally allowed to get reasonable re-duced rates and a good night's sleep.

During the bus trip we had befriended a sweet, shy Thai student named Pong whom we had come to know and care about. When Pong told us sadly he could not afford the hotel room, we welcomed him to stay with us. Pong, a devout Buddhist, was reluctant. Also, he didn't know how he would explain to his mother he had slept in a room with a strange woman.

Scott recounted this story to a reporter from our local newspaper who was doing a feature article on Scott's travels, after he returned home. Scott's version of the ending of this story, which I totally deny and abhor, is that we all slept together in one bed. Pong would never have agreed to this, nor I.

In truth, there were three single beds. Pong, painfully embarrassed, im-mediately chose the bed closest to the door, sleeping with his same clothes on and possibly his shoes for a quick escape if necessary. And I, sensitive to his embarrassment, selected the bed by the wall at the far end of the room. Scott's bed was in the middle. I can still visualize it.

I think Scott gets a kick out of confusing the issue and hearing my protestations. So which version is valid: three in a bed or three beds in the room? I have Pong as a witness.

We were concerned and upset when Pong was turned back at the border by Turkish custom officials for not having the proper credentials. It was a sad good-bye. We missed our pleasant traveling companion. But were glad we gave him a memory none of us would forget.

And then there was the "agony" I experienced in an acute physical sense. I often encouraged Scott to go out evenings to explore the night life. One evening as a safety precaution he locked me in my second floor room, and forgetting the bathroom was down the hall.

My kidneys have always been my finest feature, but I really put them to the test that night. To distract me from my escalating distress, I read, I wrote, I studied the ugly wall paper. I tried to sleep, to meditate. I listened for the key in the door. I finally reached that stage of urgency: "when nature calls". . . you go!

I went. Yes, in travel you must be inventive, flexible and earthy. The large potted plant in the corner seemed to be flourishing the next day, as a result of its nocturnal liquid fertilizer the night before. HELP!

Scott was such an exemplary "Ambassador of Good Will" abroad, that whining, complaining, "Ugly Americans" we had difficulty tolerating. We avoided tourists usually. But on a tour to the ancient Greek ruins of Delos, I overheard two American women complaining in disgust:

"WHY HAVEN'T THEY CLEANED UP THOSE RUINS BY NOW?" I turned around aghast and said: "THOSE ARE ANCIENT RUINS FROM 400 B.C!" To which they exclaimed: "I KNOW! I KNOW! YOU'D THINK THEY WOULD HAVE DONE SOMETHING BY NOW. NO YANKEE INGENUITY. BACK HOME THEY'D HAVE TAKEN CARE OF THAT BY NOW." (But at least they didn't say: "Who asked you; mind your own business!" which would have been justified). But quibbles all. Especially put in proper perspective.

But one discontent we both shared was our pursuit of "Zorba" in Greece.

As in "Zorba The Greek," the film starring Anthony Quinn as the highly-spirited Zorba. The Greeks seemed to be suffering from "tourist fatigue," instead of a Zorba "love of life." It became a running joke throughout our travels of Greece: "WHERE OH! WHERE IS ZORBA?" We had to go to Turkey to find him. Zorba was everywhere in Turkey! Being less traveled, Turkey had not yet been "turned off" by the invading tourists. They were joyous, laughed easily, took time to talk and joke and to welcome visitors with open arms.

We not only looked for Zorba, we looked and connected with all the people. Scott, with his natural animal magnetism, had a real facility for doing so.

But one facility neither of us had was with language. The rest of the "civilized" world was much better at being bi or multi-lingual. I had only university text book knowledge of French. But it was important to both of us to master all the basic courtesies in the language of each country we went to: hello, thank you, please, goodbye, delicious, beautiful, etc. Our pocket dictionaries were put to good use.

But despite the help of our dictionaries we felt an inadequacy, since foreign languages were being spoken fluently all around us, so we created our own foreign language called "STONE-IPSKI." This consisted of just jabbering guttural nonsensical rapidly, but with a heavy authoritative accent and expressive gesticulations.

For instance: "Hello" would be "kapok"
or "thank you" "latooka".

We were no longer highly identifiable Americans as soon as we opened our mouths, but of a mysterious origin that commanded attention. We felt we were getting some respect.

During our travels we did a commendable, comprehensive job of covering all the remarkable, recommended "MUST SEES" and "MUST DO'S. However, some of the most memorable and meaningful moments and highlights were not to be found in the guide book. It was the time spent at the end of an active day. We would seek out interesting places, kick back and leisurely watch the sun set.

Scott would rummage in his weathered knap sack to find some "aged" cheese and hardened black bread to nibble on to go with the local wine. Then we would talk and sip. And sip and talk.

A perfect setting for spirited discussions, ranging from: the meaning of life; and what is true success; to favorite books, music, art and movies. And how do you know when you're really in love.

INTERNATIONAL ROUND TABLE DISCUSSIONS

Other times we would share the sunset with other fellow packers, who would congregate in a special scenic spot to celebrate the sun setting together. There was a great shouting and cheering when it finally slipped below the horizon. We were all sensing, perhaps, the same deep satisfaction in knowing there are some things in life you can always depend on. Plus the comforting assurance that life goes on. Yes, "the sun will come up tomorrow." Yet another cause for celebration was witnessing the sheer outrageous beauty of it all.

Afterwards in the sunset's afterglow, we'd gather around an international table of young travelers and students for exchanging travel stories, lively discussion and good food and wine of the region.

Special privileges came with traveling with Scott. This was one of them: the unique exposure to these diverse groups of vibrant young people, sharing their energy, cultural heritage, their ideas, their dreams, and even their bad jokes.

I was grateful to him for opening up this opportunity to me. But the round table discussion grew tense one night when Nigel, an arrogant "know it all" from England, challenged me. We had been discussing ancient civilizations.

"YOUR COUNTRY, THE USA, HAS NOTHING TO OFFER. IT IS SO YOUNG. WHAT DO YOU SAY TO THAT?"

I have often maintained humor is the best way to diffuse difficult situations, especially with a combative Nigel type. No one won arguments with Nigel.

I agreed with Nigel, "YES, THE UNITED STATS WAS YOUNG. BUT IT DID HAVE SOMETHING TO OFFER." I told him not to consider the Grand Canyon, the Metropolitan Museum of Art, or the Smithsonian Institute. Not to consider we have the world's highest standard of living or our contribution in World War II. (I do believe we gave England a helping hand). "BUT NIGEL, YOU MUST CONSIDER WE DO HAVE ONE THING TO OFFER (pause)

. . . MODERN PLUMBING!"

The table exploded in laughter, because Nigel was tolerated as one of those irascible chronic malcontents. Or as an easy-going Aussie so aptly expressed it later:

"NIGEL ALWAYS HAS A PRICKLY THORN UP
HIS ARSS ABOUT SOMETHING!
YOU KNOW WHAT I MEAN, MATE?"

And so "the days dwindled down to a precious few" . . . All too soon my departure date was here.

The night before leaving we treated ourselves to a farewell dinner in our best "DTK" (dressed to kill) outfits. We were in high spirits, both looking back on what we knew had been a "once in a lifetime" happening; and looking forward to Scott's now challenging journey overland to India.

When we were finishing our wine after dinner, he presented me with a farewell gift, a small Florentine leather journal with instructions: "For Pete, a good traveler, fill this with good memories."

"Mom," he said, "when we meet again, I hope you'll share your journal with me. It will be as if we never parted."

When the next morning came, I was packed and ready to go. Scott had picked up my luggage, and went to wait for our cab to the airport. Now that I was leaving Scott, I felt vaguely melancholy and uncharacteristically apprehensive.

The "worst case scenario" negative thinking was getting to me. It occurred to me that I might never be in the presence of this "Life Force" again.

I felt an overwhelming motherly need to tell him a last time how much I loved him and to thank him. But with everything packed, and in the waiting cab for the airport, there was nothing to write on. Yes, travelers must be inventive. The only available paper was, of course, what else, toilet paper.

I could have used the whole roll to express what he and this trip had meant to me. But it took only three squares for a hurried "thank you" note:

"Dearest Son, thank you for the privilege and immense pleasure of being your traveling companion these last few weeks, and for being "Pete" to you for a lifetime. Special thanks for bestowing on me your highest accolade: "a good traveler." I had the best teacher. Always know how much I love and value you. Take good care of yourself. There's only one of you! May the great journey continue . . ."

Later I slipped it into his journal where I knew he would find it.

MELANCHOLY MOMENTS

Chapter 24

NORWAY: COMING IN FROM THE COLD

I had arrived at the farmhouse in the dark of the early evening. Only 5p.m., but in November this far north in Rindal, Norway, the sun had set for nearly two hours. It was bitter cold and the rain was biting. I needed shelter to come in from the cold.

Norway, especially the west coast, had enriched me with some of the most magnificent landscape I had ever seen. However, travel here is very expensive. I had to be creative as to how to save money, as I traveled about the country. This meant knocking on farm house doors and offering my work services in return for food and shelter.

After several knocks, a stoic looking man opened the door, just wide enough for me to slide him what I referred to as my "magic message." This was a piece of paper stating exactly what I wanted written in Norwegian. Through the crack in the door, I explained the best I could in my broken Norwegian, that I was an American student looking for work.

He nodded and walked back into the house. I stood outside the door, shivering, not knowing for sure what to do. When he returned, he waved with a slight motion, and I followed him. The house was dimly lit. In the next room around a long bare wood table sat the family eating: an adult woman, presumably the mother; an old man; a teen-aged boy; and two young children. The father pointed to the chair where I was to sit. He handed me a bowl containing two potatoes. Although I was starving, I took only one to be polite. At the end of the table was another bowl, containing what appeared to be a fish of some kind. But it was never offered to me. I felt it would be considered rude to ask them to pass it to me. So I just slowly ate my one boiled potato.

I looked around the table. No one spoke. No one smiled. No one looked up. No one seemed to notice or care that a stranger was at their table. I felt too uncomfortable to speak, but kept my head up hoping to catch the eye of one of the young children for a friendly wink or nod. But this did not happen. Usually, I could find humor in any situation. Not here. I did not even have a suppressed urge to call out cheerily: "HEY, WHAT'S FOR DESSERT?"

This bleak, lean meal lasted an interminable hour. Was this sullenness and silence because of me? Or was this their natural way?

I had always considered it a great privilege and pleasure to join families in their homes during my travels. I have found the family table a reliable indicator of their quality of life.

But as hungry and despondent as I felt here, I reminded myself to be grateful, that at least I would have a roof over my head tonight. I was conscious of the harsh, howling North winds outside, and that the rain had turned to a punishing sleet.

As the mother got up to clear the plates, the children disappeared like vapor.

The father came over to me and spoke for the first time: "You must go now." And so I did, out into the cold, cruel Norwegian night.

Chapter 25

INDIA:
WHEN THE GOING GETS TOUGH

L aying on the flea-infested mattress in my seven-rupee a night hovel in Warangal, India, I watched the blade of the ceiling fan rotate above. Around and around and around it went. I was fixated on the blade, as if in a catatonic state. My body drained and covered in sweat, I lay limp and lifeless. Two flies relentlessly buzzed about my face. A rodent ran across the room. My body was numb, my brain was numb . . . around and around and around.

I was starving, but I could not move. I did not want to move. I needed food, but I did not want to go outside and face India. Dark was setting in. I had been prostrate, just staring up at the blade, for I did not know how long, two hours, three hours, five hours. Yes, it had finally happened . . . India had gotten to me.

"India had gotten to me" is an expression I had heard as I traveled toward India, and meeting those travelers. Even those who were enthralled with it, seemed always to add, "But it will get to you. . . What did that mean? Well now I knew.

I did not move. I was fixated on the blade. At 116 degrees the blade seemed to just circulate the stifling heat more. As bad as the heat was inside, and as hungry as I was, I could not get up the energy to go outside. I could not face India.

Perhaps it was the eleventh straight day with over 110 degree heat; or because the oppressive crowds were so curious with their excessive in-your-face attention; or yet again another brazen rat would make its way up on my bed; or that my amoebic dysentery was now causing me to shit up to thirty times a day with no control. Yes, India was having its effect on me. It was getting to me. Around and around and around . . .

As I lay in my semi-conscious stupor, I tried to remember the fight slogan of driven, determined Lombardi-like football coaches: "WHEN THE GOING GETS TOUGH . . . "But what was the other part? Oh yeah, "THE TOUGH GET GOING!" Well, the "going" had gotten tough alright with the rigors of traveling the interior of India, pushing myself so hard in my weakened condition. But as far as the "tough get going" part, with my serious weight loss, I did not feel tough. I did not feel anything. Just let me sleep.

Morning finally came. As depressed as I was when I went to bed, when I awoke I knew I had to do something to shake myself from this despondent, lethargic stupor. I needed something to make me smile. I needed something out of the ordinary from my typical exhaustive India travel day. I needed something special to raise my spirits. Yes, I needed to be pampered somehow.

What could that be? Fantasies flooded my muddled mind. Was I delirious? Soothing thoughts of sitting poolside sipping frozen daiquiris, or splashing in the spray of Victoria Falls, or making angel designs in the snow, or dog sledding in Lapland. Or how about listening to classical music in an air conditioned concert hall? I yearned to be Gene Kelly dancing in a downpour in "Singin'In the Rain." Anything to get me out of my burned out on India funk. Anything!

But back to reality . . . the blade was still rotating around and around and around . . . And the reality was I was in Warangal, an ugly, filthy, dusty, boring city located on India's Great Plain in south central India. No, it did not hold the promise of London or Paris, or for that matter any large cosmopolitan Indian city. Warangal did not even have any redeeming geographic features: no water nearby or sumptous verdant hills to lend it some softness. It was a god-forsaken place that baked in its sizzling heat. My choices for special treatment in this place were basically limited to either a foot massage or an ear cleaning. Falling back on the bed, feeling deflated, I unfolded the map and pinpointed Warangal and checked the distance I had to go to reach Bombay, it was a good 500 miles away. The idea of the long grueling train ride made me feel nauseous.

Then it hit me: First Class Train Ticket . . . Yes! That was it. I would travel to Bombay First Class. Never did I expect to splurge on such a luxury on my meager money. However, these were drastic times that called for drastic measures. My weight had dropped fifty-eight pounds to 127 and being 6'2" I looked like a walking stick. But a greater concern than losing weight was losing my passion for travel in India, a country that until recently I was captivated by.

First Class . . . yes! I tried to visualize the experience . . . it was the same train, but a private car. A car instead of squalor meant peace and order; a car instead of oppressive heat meant air conditioning; a car instead of feces in overflowing toilets meant spotless pristine plumbing with plush hand towels. And best of all a car which meant an assigned seat, instead of "survival of the fittest," getting trampled in the fighting to get on. The idea of traveling First Class was cause for celebration. I bounded out of bed with a new found energy. I showered and shaved, washed my hair, and headed for the train station. I wanted to look my best for First Class.

I had a spring in my step, as I headed to the station, almost immune to the heat and constant harassment of the rickshaw drivers and demanding crowds. I was headed for a trip in a First Class train car. And I was feeling good!

Entering the rail station, the mass confusion for the ticket window line for Second Class passage was in full frantic swing with hundreds jockeying for position for a general boarding ticket. No thanks, been there done that. Not today! I glided peacefully up to the First Class window with only three people ahead of me. Just saying the words was empowering: "First Class ticket, please." I felt better already! I braced myself for the cost which was six times the Second Class ticket. Expensive, but justified.

It was one of those investments you can not put a price tag on. I paid the price, now I was determined to milk it for all it was worth. Part of that was gloating, watching the Second Class passengers board the train.

"Boarding" is not the correct word for getting on a Second Class train. It is more like "attacking." It is the ultimate Darwinian travel experience. The train arrives, the car's capacity is about 100 people, with 300 people demanding seats, well, go figure.

I watched as the aggressive, agitated, bustling mass of humanity forced itself into the one open door of the car. Everyone pushing and pulling at each other, some attempting to climb in windows, those inside not allowing those outside inside. A man dressed as a policeman whacked those with his club who got too hostile pushing and punching.

And me, I was still sitting comfortably, sipping my mango lassi and taking it all in. I hesitate to admit it, but it was with perverse pleasure I watched their discomfort. I had experienced this type of travel in India all too much. I played back in my mind the agonizing rides on India's Second Class trains. The rides where I would have to stand for eight or nine hours, chest to chest, or those where I was forced to sit in a hunched position in the overhead rack, or deliberately position myself next to the horrid smelling toilet out of necessity, because of my chronic dysentery.

No wonder I was enjoying this rare moment so much. I now observed the scene far down the track to the right, those boarding the First Class car. It was the polar opposite. There was a privileged sense of order and calm and civility, as professional men in crisp white lungies (the Indian version of a sarrong) and joyous families boarded the train. Many of the women were dressed in fine silk saris. Most of the passengers in First Class seemed to carry a little extra girth around the middle, a true sign of having achieved the good life in India.

I looked at my tired looking lungi; its once vivid aqua color was now faded and somewhat worn and torn. This ankle-length piece of cloth that wrapped around my waist had been my uniform de jour for the five months I had traveled in India. The lungi was not only a smart fashion statement, but it had practical advantages too. It was both cool and open. And importantly for me with my problematic bowels, it gave me easy access in emergencies.

This lungi, like me, had been through so much in its travels of India. I felt an affection for it and regretted not having time to wash it for the First Class train experience.

As I slowly boarded the three steps of the train of the First Class car, I paused to take a final look at the tortured masses squeezing into the Second Class train below. I was abruptly stopped and interrogated by the conductor. Dressed in a crisp handsome beige uniform, his angular hard-nosed face registered a look of disgust towards me.

"This is the First Class train car," he said sharply with the inflection to let me know I did not belong. Not someone like me, skinny, overgrown hair, and carrying a beat-up back pack. "There must be some mistake," and he repeated again with even more condescension, "First Class only," and pointed in the direction of Second Class.

Inside I was churning and wanted to scream at him: "How dare you act this way to me? I am paying the same as everyone else. This ticket cost me a lot. Be kind to me, please." But instead I was cool and well mannered. I was not going to have this pompous, petty government worker ruin my special first class travel experience. I politely gave him my ticket and even tipped him, as he led me to my compartment. He now was bowing with gratitude. I felt like saying, see us "suspected hippies" know how to behave.

As I entered my compartment the disdainful look of displeasure of the conductor was nothing compared to those that occupied the shared compartment. This was not just a family, but a poster perfect gorgeous Indian family. The family, impeccably dressed and well groomed, consisted of the young parents and their two children, the daughter perhaps twelve and the son perhaps eight years old.

I greeted them all politely with the classic Indian exchange of "Namaste" with folded hands. They just looked at me with no response, just a sneering stare, which made me feel uncomfortable, certainly not welcome. Not to respond to my "Namaste" was pointed enough, but to give me a look of such contempt, a look that said "What is this scum doing in our compartment," was discourteous to the extreme. I heard the man rudely whisper something to his wife in Hindi, and they both exploded in big laughter, and the wife commenting back, and more uproarious laughter.

I felt self-conscious and, yes, not wanted. Did they not realize this was a big day for me? Hey, I was traveling First Class, my first time ever. The price of this ticket was a big sacrifice for me. Please be understanding and let me enjoy this journey. I was determined not to let their derisive laughter and haughty attitude ruin my trip.

Yes, my hair was long. Yes, I looked sickly thin and my backpack was caked with mud, but I was clean. I had showered this morning, and shampooed my hair. And importantly I loved their country of India and traveling in it!

My bed was the top bunk. Before heading up, however, I slid my backpack under the lower bed, some of the dried dirt flying about, the two kids scattering over to the other side of the compartment, as if they had never seen dirt in their life.

So up I went to my top bunk. I thought they would appreciate me getting out of their way, no longer polluting their space. Despite their rejection and shabby treatment of me, I remained excited about the trip to Bombay. And the thought of stretching out in the bed, feeling the cool, clean cotton sheet and the soft fluffy pillow; this simple luxury filled me with happiness.

Then it happened. As I reached the top rung of the ladder and lifted my right leg up into my inviting First Class bed, I felt on exertion an intense squeeze in my stomach and *PPPFFFT*, an immediate emptying of my bowels. An explosion of diarrhea. I was not wearing underwear, so it came raining down, unimpeded, in full force. It gets worse. As I was climbing up, the lovely Indian woman looked directly up at me with disgust at the time of my full release. Bulls eye!

Welcome to First Class! What's the saying? "You can take the guy out of Second Class, but can't take Second Class out of the guy."

The husband was understandably extremely upset. He was screaming at me now in English and the children howling and crying. I pulled up my lungi and climbed down the ladder to the floor. I was deeply humiliated.

I struggled to apologize and tell them how sorry I was and how sick I had been with dysentery. But the father protecting his perfect family and perfect life would hear none of it. I could not blame him. I had violated his safe, sane, sanitized world in the most primitive, offensive way.

He was outraged, beating his fists on my chest and screaming for the authorities. His wife was horrified but unable to scream, as the excrement was still drizzling down her flawless face, and she was unable to do so. But she did gesticulate threateningly.

I was so upset that I grabbed my pack and stumbled down the passageway. And so distressed I hopped off the train just as it began to move.

So there I was . . . on the platform with my prized First Class ticket in hand, as the train pulled out without me. My hope for a special day to refresh myself, to regenerate my enthusiasm for India faded away . . . I felt totally empty, exhausted and alone, swallowed up again by the scorching heat and relentless teaming humanity.

My love-hate affair with India had always been "the agony and the ecstasy:" from the magnificence of the Taj Mahal to the grinding poverty of the masses. This travesty today was part of the agony. For the first time I knew what it felt like to be judged, shunned, scorned . . . like much of the oppressed world endures on a daily basis.

Chapter 26

AUSTRIAN SKI RESORT:
THE WORST OF THE *WURST*

Long before arriving at the Hotel Evergreen to find work, I had thought of how nice it would be to spend the Christmas season working at a ski resort, perhaps in Austria or Switzerland. I envisioned a bucolic alpine setting, a restful time to get off the demanding road of travel, and enjoy a welcome change of pace, along with the local holiday festivities. And importantly, of course, the opportunity to ski.

It was with these hopes that I arrived in Innsbruck and spent two days knocking on ski resort doors on the outskirts of the city between the villages of Mutters and Igls. I must have tried at least fifteen places. It seemed to be the same sad story everywhere: "We are fully staffed." I apparently was too late for being hired for the ski season. It was December 15 and most staff hiring was completed by late November.

So, initially, I was ecstatic when I found work at the Hotel Evergreen. It was located in Igls in a lovely setting, nestled in the Alps, about ten miles up the mountain road from Innsbruck.

The manager of the hotel, Herr Schmidt, was stern, an absolute neat freak, and with one way of doing things, his way or the highway.

Two of his stock phrases were: "We don't do it this way" and "When you aren't working, you should be thinking about working."

My unofficial title was "General Clean Up Man."

My daily jobs included: bussing dishes from the dining room, washing dishes, taking out garbage, painting rooms, shoveling snow, salting the driveway, occasional baby sitter duties, as well as carrying in luggage for the guests. For this duty I wore a cutesy green Alpine jacket and matching bellman's cap with a feather. The guests thought it was charming.

I worked hard, but my pay was a pittance: 2,000 Austrian shillings for the month, including room and board. That was $120 for a month or $4 a day. When I questioned the manager about the pay being incredibly low, he just said, "Then don't take job."

Needing to take a rest from the road for a while and looking forward to my day off each week to ski, I decided to stay, in spite of the unfair working conditions.

It was not a good situation. Every day I rose at six o'clock to the jarring sound of a clanging bell from a nearby church. It was no way to start the day. How quaint you might think. A church bell in a picturesque Austrian Alpine hamlet sounds lovely. But this bell would not ring, but CLANG and CLANG and CLANG. Okay, I'm up. I got it. I counted ninety-seven clangs each morning. Why ninety-seven? No one seemed to know. But it was irritating to say the least.

I would do my general cleanup from 7a.m. to 7p.m. working like a dog with a forty-five minute break for lunch. Herr Schmidt had much to learn about motivating his employees with his incessant, complaints:

"You are the worst dish washer in the world."

"You are a lazy American."

"I must teach you strong work ethic."

"Don't just stand around, look for work to do."

Even when it came to eating, there was controversy. Breakfast consisted of bread and jam. Whoopee! I don't wish to sound like the whining ugly American, but the continental breakfast was dull and not enough to satisfy my laborer's appetite. Where were the eggs, hash browns, bacon and toast?

The quality of the food for lunch and dinner was okay but tiresome with only the Austrian-German basics: sauerbraten, bratwurst, wiener schnitzel and goulash. And the portions were small. There just was never enough. I worked non-stop. I was expending a lot of energy and required more food.

One night during dinner in the kitchen with the chambermaid, the part-time electrician, and Herr Schmidt and his wife, I summoned my courage and asked Herr Schmidt politely about my urgent need for more food. I offered to actually cook an extra bratwurst for myself. He glared at me incredulously, as if I were demented and barked: "You eat too much, enough for two people. You eat only what you have. No extra bratwurst for you!"

I continued to feel constantly hungry. In desperation I decided it was worth approaching him one more time. But this time I would approach it from how beneficial an extra wurst could be from a work production point of view. So the next time I was alone with him in the kitchen, I broached the sensitive topic again.

"Herr Schmidt, I want to be the best worker possible, but to do this I must be stronger, and that means I need to be properly fed."

His reaction was not good. I imagined steam coming out of his ears. He had reached his boiling point.

"If I can have one extra wurst a day, I can be more productive," I persisted. With this he grabbed my arm, shoved me to the refrigerator, reached in and waved the wurst at me.

"Don't you understand? We can't afford to feed you. Your stomach will be *das* ruin of the hotel." His face was fuming red like a big tomato head. I did everything in my power to restrain myself from laughing.

His obsession in keeping me from the wurst was pathologically "nuts." However, one good thing did come out of his tantrum: I saw where the wurst was stored in the refrigerator. YES!

The wurst situation got worse. I was driven to do something I had never done in my life: STEAL.

Around ten o'clock when things were quiet, the kitchen was closed and Herr Schmidt had retired upstairs with his wife for the night (they lived in the hotel), I would sneak a wurst out of the refrigerator. Then take my little gas sterno burner, sit outside in the freezing night air, out of sight about 300 yards down the road. Shielded by tall trees, I would cook and savor my wurst. Not that I was a glutton for wurst, but I was just so painfully hungry. Desperate circumstances call for desperate measures.

These thefts continued for three nights, until Herr Schmidt noticed. Knowing his anal ways, I was shocked it took him so long to discover the heist.

Not surprisingly, I was called "on the carpet" as suspect Number One.

"We have a wurst missing," he declared. His seriousness had the grave tone that a major crime had been committed.

"Last night there were seventy-three wursts, today only seventy-two. You took the wurst. I know you did! I know you did!" he shouted.

The next day there was a padlock on the refrigerator door.

That weekend I was pressed into service to help put up the hotel's festive Christmas decorations and lights. The cheerful, colorful glow of the Christmas lights made me sadder than usual.

My first Christmas away from home.

Warm memories of home and family started flooding in as my tears started flooding into my cabbage soup. I was sitting alone in the kitchen with only the kindly, portly pastry chef, having another meager meal. I could not hide my sadness from her. She observed me with caring concern. And although she could not speak English, she understood, nodded her head, patted my hand and stammered the words: "mama . . . home."

Conditions continued getting increasingly worse, since the wurst incident. But it was not just the lack of food that made me start to seriously contemplate getting out of this place; or as I liked to call it "making the jail break."

The discontents were mounting. On taking the job Herr Schmidt clearly stated I would have one day off a week, "probably Tuesday."

When the first Tuesday came, I was looking forward to skiing, but Herr Schmidt informed me:

"No day off. Too much to do."

"But what about my day off, as you promised?" I asked.

"Promise canceled because of work situation," he stated emphatically.

Then it happened again the next Tuesday . . . and then again.

Let's review the cold, cruel facts:

* long thankless hours at hard labor
* no days off
* slave wages
* starvation diet
* demeaning, inhumane treatment

Not a good situation. Plus boring nightlife, no relaxation, variety or fun; nor time on the slopes. No change or release, just work, work, work, then banishment to my cubby hole of a room every night.

Time to take action – "JAIL BREAK".

That evening after I got my weekly paycheck, I was feeling in an especially despondent mood. Herr Schmidt, the warden, had handed me my weekly paycheck, grumbling and growling in his restless, demeaning way: "Your work not good. I doubt you should get check at all."

These were the last words I would ever hear him snarl, as that night I had decided the "jail break" would take place. I reflected how, along with the gift of life, comes the power and privilege of a thing called "choice," and the need to choose wisely. I had.

Since the Schmidt's lived in the hotel, I had to be very careful making my escape. Around eleven o'clock when all was still about the hotel I took my backpack and quietly crept past their room toward the stairs. The stairs down were dark, and I had to feel my way along the wall as I went down.

The hotel was over 150 years old and its handsome staircase with its highly polished wood and ornate design was extremely creaky. I stopped every other step. The combination of the creakiness and the darkness made the escape difficult. I had to keep cool and not rush it.

I was about half way down. I could now see the main entrance door. My heart raced with exhilaration and excitement, as I could sense that in a matter of moments I would be FREE and done with the terrible tyrant of the Hotel Evergreen.

Suddenly my foot slipped, on what seemed to be a ball of some sort, and I fell crashing down the stairs. I was in pain, but I did not have the time to examine my wounds. Immediately I saw the lights go on in Herr Schmidt's room and his booming voice bark out in his guttural German. Not hesitating, I bolted for the door, not worrying now about the noise I would make. I had to get out!

Throwing open the door and running into the cold dark night, down the lonely ice-covered road, slipping and sliding, I felt empowered, as I made my great escape.

I was gone! Gone! I didn't know where I was going. But it had to be better than where I had been!

It was going to be a Happy New Year. VERY HAPPY!

ROMANCE OF THE ROAD

Chapter 27

FLORENCE: UFFIZI GALLERY
TITIAN ART TREASURE LEADS TO BOTTICELLI BEAUTY

A s I stood in the foyer of the revered Uffizi Gallery in Florence, I could instantly distinguish the Italians from the tourists. And I did not even have to look at their faces. One needs just to see the shoes, sweaters, blazers and scarves they wore with such flair. Looking down at my faded blue jeans and well-worn blue oxford shirt, I looked, well, certainly not like an Italian.

I had been at the Uffizi about two hours, browsing its glorious Renaissance art galleries, including the rooms of Filippo Lippi and Giotto. It was when I entered the Botticelli Gallery, that I saw her. Tall and slender, she was dressed in a black leather skirt and black angora sweater. Her face was classic with its high cheek bones. It was also a face that was open and sensual with fine flawless skin. But most striking was her long, reddish gold titian hair. She looked as if she were the captivating central figure in Botticelli's famous painting "Birth of Venus," which I had just viewed.

I was beginning to feel like a museum prowler, as I stealthily trailed her through yet another gallery. My "Botticelli woman" was exquisite. Her beauty stirred me. I must meet her. I was also intrigued by her being a genuine student of art. We would have much to share.

She was now focused on the Flemish painter Hans Memling's "Master Delarosa." I wanted to wait for the right moment, the right painting before approaching her. A Memling was not it. Although I was familiar with this 15th Century painter, a fantastic talent, he was not my strength in terms of making enlightened or clever comments worthy of her attention. In fact this entire gallery was all Flemish and German masters, and the latter was not among my favorite painters.

I observed I was not her only pursuer. Three other guys in the gallery were hovering about her, studying her much closer than what hung on the walls. I felt anxious knowing I could not wait too long to strike, as one of these slick, sharply dressed Italians would take off with her.

She moved slowly studying each painting closely, seeming totally oblivious to the preying eyes following her. After looking at a Hans Hoblein, The Younger, she turned abruptly and went to the next gallery. I quickly checked my gallery guide diagram, as to what artists were coming up, hopefully the right gallery for me to make my "move." I was in luck.

Following the one we were now entering would be the Titian Gallery.

Yes, Tiziano Vecellio, known as Titian, was one of the masters I was most passionate about. And relevant to this current situation of wanting to impress this stunning art lover with whom I was so infatuated. Titian was an artist whose paintings I could speak about with some degree of authority.

The three young men still hanging around were all smartly dressed and good looking, especially one with dark, wavy hair and olive skin. He looked like an Italian cinema idol. Conscious of my grubby jeans, I felt my chances might be on the long side. But just then the handsome one was standing right next to her. Without looking at him, or acknowledging his presence in any way, she coolly walked to the next painting. He immediately followed. He waited an awkward moment, seemed to say something to her, then abruptly turned, and walked out of the gallery. Hmm, perhaps he didn't know his art.

So one down, but two others were still lurking. "Please come on!" I almost seemed to say it out loud, as I was mentally urging her to move to the next gallery. My time and luck were running out.

Finally reaching the Titian Gallery, it was now my turn to enter the picture. I was hoping she would quicken her pace and just to glance at the lesser paintings leading up to the main event.

"Please move on to my painting," I thought. The painting everyone in this room is here to see . . . "Flora." But instead, she seemed to take an excessive amount of time studying these lesser paintings.

Three more paintings to go when one of the guys hastily positioned himself very close to her. He didn't speak to her, but looked ready to pounce. He was now almost pressing against her, he was so close. My heart sank. Perhaps he had the same mindset I did being well versed on Titian and saddling up to impress the hell out of her with his own art speak. He was about to steal my Flora shtick! The competition was getting more challenging.

With determination I started to make my move, jostling several other craning necks. I had her in my sights; it was time to strike, when I heard a woman's voice call out:

"MARIA! MARIA!" My Botticelli woman, Maria, returned a cheery greeting.

"Shit!" I thought, as she was introduced to an older woman and a little girl of about three years old.

So now what? Would they view the art together as a group? I hoped not. I decided to move down to the further end of the gallery and watch the progress of the group from a safe distance. For about ten minutes they were extremely demonstrative with gesticulating hands and repeated hugs and suppressed laughter. Yes, it was frustrating to wait. However, it turned out to be a good thing; as the Italian guy, who was my competition, got visibly impatient and stomped out of the gallery, scarcely giving a nod to "Flora."

Maria, was now saying what looked to be her final, "ciao" and made her way back to the painting she had been viewing. Good, get ready, Scott. "Flora" is up next! I crossed the museum gallery, which now had become quite crowded.

There were probably a dozen people gathered about the painting. Maria, was up front, but squished, in the middle between an elderly white-haired woman on her left and a man in a wheel chair and his attendant on her right. I could only position myself in the back, behind her with a couple of gangling teenage boys between us.

It was hard to even see her. Obviously this position was not conducive to making conversation.

Damn! I could not get to her. My hope was that she would take plenty of time to study the Titian masterpiece, as the other viewers moved on to the next painting. Well, the Art Gods seemed to be with me, as the man in the wheelchair was being backed away, leaving a free space by Maria. I did a quick end run around the group, positioning myself right next to her.

I did not want to verbally barge in right away, as it would look like a contrived pick-up line. I wanted to examine the painting for awhile, and even make a few studious facial expressions, just in case she was looking. But I also, had to be aware of her movement in case she started to leave. I noticed out of the corner of my eye that she looked at her watch, and it looked as if she were ready to move on.

"Do you have the time?" I asked.

"Oh, yes, it is 2:15." She turned her wrist to show me the watch face. She had a soft inviting voice.

"Grazie," I thanked her. Adding with feeling: "This is one of my favorite Titian paintings."

She cooed: "Beautiful, yes."

Without wasting any time, I unleashed my "Flora" trivia . . . "So, can you find Titian in this painting?" I asked.

"What? I don't understand," she responded.

"Titian scholars have revealed that he painted his profile in the painting. Can you find it?

She studied the canvas quietly and laughed:

"No, I don't see it. Show me."

Now we had drawn the attention of a few others, especially an oversized American middle-age couple, each carrying a Tauk Tours travel bag over their shoulder.

Maria's curiosity was genuine. Encouraged, I continued. "Check the hair, the left side of the hair. Look carefully, do you see his profile?"

Maria got very close to the painting. The American tourists were now examining it, too.

"I am sorry. I still do not see it," she confessed.

I moved in close to her, pointing my finger over the canvas, tracing Titian's profile. An overly zealous museum guard was nervously watching me and gruffly admonished me to "MOVE BACK!"

"Si, Si, yes I see it!" Maria exclaimed excitedly. The American man's strident, nasal voice rang out: "Wow! That's neat!"

"Thank you for showing me that," Maria said warmly. "I love that painting and am surprised. I never knew that." I played it cool, but felt that I had succeeded in making in-roads with my art chit-chat.

The gallery that was so busy and crowded before seemed to empty out, as we comfortably walked from one painting to another. We allowed ample time to pour over Titian's masterpieces: "Venus of Urbino" and "Venus and Cupid."

Her name was Maria and she had lived in Florence all her life, the youngest of three daughters. Strolling, we were now talking a little more than looking at the art. She went on to say that she recently took a job in the financial world as an analyst and found it dry and unsatisfying. So today she was treating herself to an overdue, much needed break from the routine of work.

I noticed that she checked her watch and I asked:

"Do you have to go now?"

"Not right away, in about half an hour," she answered. She said she liked how much I not only valued and appreciated art, but how I genuinely enjoyed it. I assured her that was true.

"Yes, especially the art here with its embarrassment of riches. There is so much to see, and I only have four days in Florence."

"That is too little time," she scolded, shaking her head. Maria was not only lovely and fascinated with art, but appeared to be a person of quality and substance. I wanted to know her better.

"I have a request," I said. "I know your time is limited, but could you show me a painting that is very special to you, that I probably don't know about?"

"Oh! I have so many paintings I cherish!"

"But one that is unusual, somewhat undiscovered," I persisted. Quiet prevailed. I enjoyed watching her flawless face, as she gave my request a good deal of thought.

"I like the question . . . follow me," she said, as we briskly walked through several galleries to her special painting. It was a portrait of a woman with a scarf wrapped around her head. It was entitled "Gypsy Girl" by Boccaccio Boccaccino. An artist I was not familiar with.

The painting dated 1504, was simple, but the expressive face was eloquent and spoke volumes. Looking at Maria, I asked, "Why this painting?" She thoughtfully replied: "I feel her face says 'hope.' She has had a hard life, but she keeps believing." I nodded in agreement and I let her know I liked her choice, and that it resonated with me as well. I thanked her for sharing it with me.

"Now, Scott, how about you sharing a favorite painting of yours with me?"

"That's easy," I said. I will show it to you on our way out." This time I took her hand and led her directly to the Botticelli Gallery.

As we silently gazed in awe at "The Birth of Venus" . . . she sighed: "Ah! Botticelli's masterpiece!"

"It has become a favorite of mine," I said, "because it reminds me of you. Didn't he capture her hair beautifully? Like yours."

"I am touched," she smiled.

There were only three others in the gallery now. We spoke in hushed voices:

"I enjoyed meeting you, Maria. I wish we could have spent more time together."

"I feel the same, Scott."

I asked: "Would the Botticelli Beauty like to join me for dinner this evening?" She looked both pleased and disappointed.

"I would like to, but it is not possible. I have a family commitment. I am sorry. But perhaps if you are free tomorrow, I would be happy to show you around Florence."

I enthusiastically accepted her kind invitation, and we agreed to meet at eleven o'clock the next morning.

We said "goodbye." But before exiting the gallery, she gave me a spontaneous two-cheek kiss and a final wave before she left. I could not wait for tomorrow.

We met the next day as scheduled in front of the Uffizi, Maria pulling up on a red Vespa. She looked so chic in tight, bright yellow jeans and a jaunty green jacket with fur-like trim.

"Ciao, Scott. Hop on! You're not afraid to ride a scooter, are you?" I laughed, shook my head "no," and then exclaimed: "You Italians!"

"What about us? She shot back.

"How you dress, always looking so smart, as if you just stepped out of a fashion magazine."

She laughed, as I pointed at myself dressed in the same tired jeans and bland tan parka.

"But, Scott, you look so comfortable. And remember the important thing is not the clothes, but the man in the clothes."

"Grazie, Maria. How kind you are," I said, and asked: "Any special directions before taking off?"

"Yes, as the driver, I am very safety conscious, so please keep your arms tightly about my waist at all times, Scott."

"Those are directions I shall love to follow," I promised. So off we went, and it would not have been possible to choreograph a more perfect day of seeing the real Florence guided by a native.

Sitting on the back of the Vespa, I marveled as Maria artfully zigzagged through the traffic; and puttered down quiet, cobbled side streets; and over the over the timeless Arno. From everywhere the great cathedral Il Duomo, the crowning achievement of Renaissance architecture, was visible dominating the cityscape. I was intoxicated with this enchanting, culturally rich, high-fashion city and my gracious guide with her titian hair blowing freely in the wind.

And so began . . . four amorous days and nights of "La Dolce Vita" with my Botticelli beauty . . .

From sunny vineyard picnics, colorful trattorias, museum art treasures, and sunset views atop Florence's romantic hilltop square, Piazzale Michelangelo, with its iconic sculpture of "David;" the days were filled with Renaissance magnificence and magic. And the memories . . .

Ah! The Sweet Life!"

Chapter 28

AFGHANISTAN: ROMANCE AND RAPTURE IN THE HINDU KUSH

I t was in the back of a pickup truck in the Hindu Kush Mountains of
central Afghanistan that our eyes locked.

Her name, I had no idea. But for the past three hours, I could not
stop taking quick glances at her: jet black hair, olive complexion, catlike
green eyes, and sensual full lips. I was totally captivated.

Following my immediate infatuation, my first thought was, "What's a
girl like you doing in a place like this?" On the Asia overland journey, I had
seen few female travelers. Those I had seen were rather "rugged looking."
One that resembled a young Liz Taylor seemed out of place.

She, like the other eleven of us, were packed into the limited confines of a battered pickup truck, as we made our way on a grueling nine
hour journey to Bamiyan; along a precariously bone jarring, thread narrow
mountain-clinging dirt road.

The town of Bamiyan, located about one hundred miles northwest of
Kabul, was home to the two monumental statues of the standing Twin
Buddhas. They were the largest of their kind in the world. And ever since I
saw a postcard from a German traveler I met nearly a year ago, showing the
majestic Buddhas carved into a side of a cliff, the image stayed with me. It
was a "must" that I see this.

The pickup truck. This was NOT supposed to be the vehicle of transport. No, the journey was advertised to be aboard a "luxury minibus." This
was just another cruel example of the traveler's trials and tribulations in
dealing with transportation in Asia. An entire chapter could be dedicated
to this.

So in classic Asian overland transport fashion, this current fiasco played
out. Arriving at 7a.m., the black minibus, looking surprisingly in half

decent condition, picked me up in front of my hotel. There were already several passengers aboard.

However, the driver did not drive on, but turned off the engine, got out and began talking to an elderly Afghan man. This gentleman with a flowing white beard, ancient dark face, and turban, was completely robed head to toe in gold. He carried a cane and looked over 200 years old. They seemed to be arguing about something, as the "Father Time" figure did most of the aggressive gesturing.

With our driver back on board, he a young Afghani with intense black eyes and moustache, in remarkably clear English said, "I don't have enough passengers. We need two more, or we no go to Bamiyan."

The pickup truck slowly drove up and down Chicken Street, the main drag for backpackers, and its side streets, as he yelled out, "Bamiyan, Bamiyan." Until, finally, after a full ninety minutes we attracted the two we needed, as two scruffy looking Italian guys waved the minibus down.

Finally, we were ready to go, two hours late, not too bad. However, after traveling not half a mile we stopped. Our driver got out. He seemed to disappear below the bus. About three minutes later he got back on and announced: "Sorry, bus is broken; wheel is bad, get out."

The eleven of us emptied out, and stood on the corner looking at our minibus with the questionable bad wheel. There was obvious frustration. But with such a seasoned looking group of travelers, it was tempered with an attitude of "been through this before." We waited only about five minutes, when a dirty mud splattered red pickup truck arrived. Our driver gestured toward the truck, "Ride to Bamiyan." What's going on? Are we trading in our advertised "luxury minivan" for this old beat-up pickup truck?

Now there was frustration, as several agitated voices rose up objecting: "What the hell, what the shit, this is not fair, no way"! How could we possibly fit in this thing? We demanded a discount of some kind. The driver just snorted, "No discount, take the ride or go away."

I believe all the travelers were thinking the same thing I was. They had heard the news about a big storm coming in tomorrow. If this were so, we might be stuck in Kabul for a week and not be able to leave and cross the mountain roads. This was our best choice. We were off!

From the back of the pickup truck where I sat, my lovely mystery woman being positioned on the opposite side in the front, I would continue my gazing. I was trying my best to be subtle, not obvious, especially because she was seated by some guy she seemed to know. The type of relationship they had, be it friend or boyfriend, I certainly had no way of knowing. However, picking up their words, it was German with a slight upward inflection, probably Swiss.

Finally, after some three hours of being in the truck, she caught my eyes looking at her. I held her gaze: she did as well. She then broke out laughing. Her lilting laugh faded away, and she resumed speaking with her male traveling companion, touching his arm as she spoke.

What was behind that laugh? Was it a laugh that said, "I am glad you are looking at me, I want to know you." Or did it say, "Why do you keep staring at me, give me a break, I'm not interested?"

I would continue to look her way on and off throughout the pickup truck journey, hoping she would shoot me a subtle smile, a playful wink; give me some kind of opening where we could start a conversation. Or just some sign or expression that she was interested. But it was not to be, not once did she again look my way.

When the pickup truck stopped for a short break, I made a last effort at friendliness with a harmless, "Hi, where are you from?" Her diffident monosyllabic response was simply: "Switzerland." Within seconds her male companion (as if a chaperon) crowded in at her side. That was it. The laugh two hours ago was my most engaged moment with her. She seemed obviously to have zero interest in me. I got the message.

Though my heart felt a pang and my ego deflated from the no go connection with the Swiss Miss, I felt enthralled by the journey, as the pickup truck shook, rattled and rolled its way toward Bamiyan.

Being seated in the back where the wind would whip through the canvas flap, it was cold, but not unbearably so. Nothing like the thirty-three hour icebox of a bus journey I made two days ago from Herat in western Afghanistan to Kabul. The cold on the pickup truck was bracing, invigorating, I liked it, and this position also was clearly the best seat for viewing the astonishing landscape. I would throw open the canvas flap and take it all in. The vistas looking back were staggering, a sea of barren rugged mountains, with hues of red blending into gold. Some even had a tint of green. All of them set off by a distant backdrop of jagged snow-capped peaks.

But with this awe inspiring landscape I was witnessing, the ride also was one that produced a high degree of anxiety. This was a journey that was terrifying at times. I have been on many bus rides in my travels, many longer, others more uncomfortable, but this was to me the most dangerous ride I had ever been on.

The danger was not to be blamed on some mad crazed driver who enjoys racing on blind mountain curves, as is often the case. No, we had a good driver, in fact an excellent one. This journey was terrifying because of the road itself. It was dirt based with gaping pot holes, extremely narrow with hair pin turns, and with no guard rails around cliffs that fell some 6,000 feet below. This was all compounded by bad weather conditions of a driving snow that created poor traction and limited visibility.

Because the road was two-way, our pickup truck when coming face to face with another vehicle, especially a bus or truck, would need to move over as far as possible on the side of the road. A couple times as I stuck my head out the back, I could clearly see that the back wheel extended over the cliff.

As we climbed higher, the pickup truck moved ever so slowly as it approached the Selang Pass at nearly 12,000 feet. It began to snow stronger and visibility was poor. And as the pickup crossed the pass the snow broke out with a crazy driving force creating a whiteout with virtually no visibility.

The driver thought it too dangerous to continue and stopped the vehicle; where we sat waiting for the snow to ease up. The snow continued to pound down. It became very cold. All the travelers aboard became quiet, an anxiousness filled the air during this waiting period, sensing that perhaps we were in a seriously dangerous situation.

When the snow finally eased, a good hour wait, the pickup truck started to move again, it proceeded with much caution. Because of the heavy snow, the pickup could not get the traction needed on the slippery mountain road, and several times most of us would jump out and give it a push.

The most dramatic heart-pounding moment occurred when the truck trying to go up on a steep grade could not make it and began to slide back, the brakes of no use, and it continued to slowly slide down the frozen road and gaining speed as it headed for the cliff's edge. Everyone was screaming as the pickup continued to slide back. The edge coming closer and closer, it looked for sure that we would be going over the cliff. But somehow, someway the truck stopped, coming to rest just six inches from going over.

A spontaneous cheering broke out and the Dutch guy pointed to the heavens and said "Hindu Kush Gods are looking out for us, we are blessed." I opened the back flap and looked straight down the cliff to the valley floor below at what could have been fatal, and thought, yes, perhaps today we were blessed and said a little prayer silently.

Our pickup truck was a little UN of travelers. Representation of the following countries included: two from each England and Italy; plus one from France and Holland; the two Swiss; an additional American; plus the two Afghanis. All passengers were men, except the Swiss Miss, all seemed to be in their twenties, except for an American named Philip, who was probably in his mid-thirties. There were five travelers seated on one side of the truck and four on the other. The Swiss gal sat closest to the front, the two Afghanis sat on the floor.

I have observed that with travelers there seems to be that initial aloofness, each traveler feeling in his or her heart that they are the superior and the most experienced.

But this attitude usually disappears quickly. Such was the case in our group. The two British guys sitting directly across from me, one very tall and one short, but each with hair down to his shoulders, speaking quietly about something called Pondicherry. When I heard the word, I thought it was a cocktail. But a guy sitting two spaces down from me in a heavy French accent said, "You've been to India?"

And within seconds the two Italians were chirping in. Between the five of them they volleyed words and phrases back and forth: a Goddess called Kali; a pilgrimage to Rishikesh; houseboats on Dal Lake; ghats of Varanasi;

some food item called dosai. These words were foreign to me, but I was caught up in their enthusiasm and moved in closer to take in as much as possible. It was as if in their travels to India they were part of a private club with its own unique language. They were not snobby about this, but there was a definite rapport between travelers who had been to India.

One other thing about travelers who had been to India was that they all seemed to share a common physical characteristic. They were sadly so frail looking, boney and desolate. Despite wearing cold weather gear which padded the bodies, the five travelers all looked scrawny and undernourished. The French guy especially, named Claude, with a shaggy moustache, looked scarily so and very tired. I felt I looked healthier than these travelers, my weight 162pounds, down some twenty pounds since leaving the States. It would be interesting to see what toll India would have on my body.

Although there was not a great deal of conversation on our pickup truck journey, much I think having to do with the anxiety of the ride itself, there seemed to be a good bond; such as sharing of fruit, spreading out sleeping bags across legs when it got especially cold, and getting out of the truck to push the truck in bad traction.

My fellow travelers on this journey for the most part I liked, although I found the American who sat next to me, named Philip, obnoxious. He was stocky with a red beet face and a crew cut. He came from Phoenix and spoke loudly and crudely of his sexual adventures in Thailand. My Swiss dream girl and her male companion seemed to be the only ones that stayed to themselves and did not enter into any conversation.

Around 4p.m., having now traveled for about eight hours, the pickup truck started its descent on the town of Bamiyan. The birch trees with golden leaves and the clay roofs could now be seen. I got chills, not from the weather, but the exquisite feeling of being so "alive," and loving where I was. I felt wistful as I reflected on last night's farewell dinner in Kabul with my four prior traveling companions, and how much they would cherish this journey to Bamiyan.

The five of us: Joe from Los Angles and the three Brits; Alex, Nigel, and Allen from the Midlands of England had been together since Istanbul, where we began the overland Asia journey on November 17th. In those seventeen days we had traveled nearly 3,200 miles. With the amazing travel experiences we had shared, we had grown very close as friends as well. (See Chapter 31).

Last night was Thanksgiving. It was our final evening together. As we crowded around a worn deeply gouged wooden table at the Mustafa Hotel's restaurant, we were in a celebratory mood. We gorged ourselves on classic American comfort food: macaroni and cheese, spaghetti, burgers, fries and pizza. Biting into my juicy cheeseburger, the taste was so delicious and longed for I thought I was going to pass out.

We were high on the travel, the distance we had come, and we had plenty to be thankful for on this day of giving thanks. But with this euphoria, there was as well a palpable poignancy that hung over the gathering; knowing tomorrow we would all be going our own different ways. And that the special joyousness that we shared from travel would be ending.

Yes, they were terrific travelers and great fun to be with. I could almost feel them with me now. As the truck passed sandy reddish barren dunes, the late afternoon sun seemed to make them glow in a surreal light. When the pickup reached ground level, it turned right on what seemed to be the main road leading into town.

Suddenly there was an excited commotion: "Look over there."

"Yes, that's it!" Heads began ducking down, twisting and turning to see what looked to be a massive carved out area in the mountain, where, yes, there was the huge standing Buddha. I was in awe. And just seconds later appeared to be another Buddha, this was even bigger.

Piling out of the pickup truck, my back was stiff and aching, but I was thrilled to be here. My first thought was to grab my backpack and walk the mile or so back along the road to see the Twin Buddhas. However, dark was setting in, and I felt it best to get my first visit early in the morning; plus negotiations were going on with respective inn owners for a night's sleep.

Sleeping accommodations in Afghanistan are very casual. In most cases sleeping meant crashing on the floor in your sleeping bag in a tea shop or café that you would share with other travelers. Some of the cafes had a bed or two positioned off to the side for an additional cost.

All floors, believe me, were not created equal. They could be comfortable, if they were well carpeted and had warmth; or a nightmare, such as my experience in one of the places I stayed in Heart in western Afghanistan. Seventeen packers, that's right seventeen of us were jammed in a room not much more than 12'x12'. The floor consisted of splintered wood and dirt that was shared by a healthy amount of active little worms as well.

About a dozen Afghan men and younger kids greeted us, each wooing us to their respective café for sleep accommodations. "Best sleep over here, mister." "My place most comfort." "Best price, only 8 Afhs."

With the nine of us we had greater negotiating power in numbers, but the American, Philip, thankfully, drifted off on his own; as did the two British guys. It seemed that there were four main proprietors pleading with us to stay at their place. About twenty minutes later after visiting each of the cafes, all within a fifty yard radius, it was an easy decision that we would go with a man named Abdul. His place was called simply Abdul's Café.

Though it was slightly more expensive, costing 12 Afs ($0.25), it was clearly the most inviting. On entering there was a big fireplace with a roaring fire to greet us. The floor was covered with three colorful thick rugs in good condition and generous-sized pillows tossed about. It had a warm welcoming feel about it, and would provide a comfortable place to sleep.

The walls were adorned with a large detailed map of Afghanistan and four posters of close cropped iconic faces of Afghan men with the word "AFGHANISTAN" in bold print underneath. There was also an impressive collection of black and white photographs of Bamiyan, both current and from many years ago. Also, in their attempts to make travelers feel at home, signs were printed: "We have Western Food;" "We serve breakfast 'omelet;'" "We have Afghan and Pop music."

They even had a Monopoly game board.

And like any of these little places, it is the spirit of the person that runs it that makes the difference and makes it come alive. Abdul was so open and gregarious, "Please make yourself comfort. Here I have hot tea, all day all night tea, no cost."

There were seven of us. As we positioned our bags on the floor, I took a casual look at the Swiss Miss, as she and her male companion placed their bags down in the most removed corner. I had basically given up on her, knowing she had no interest in me. But I still found myself looking her way now and then. I positioned my bag near the fireplace. The Dutch and French guys were closest to me.

That night as I slept, feeling very comfortable in my bag, I felt a tapping on my foot. I awoke startled, expecting to see a rodent of some kind. But instead it was the lovely Swiss Miss herself! Was I dreaming? She crouched down, looking back toward her corner, and whispered to me, "Do you want to visit the Buddhas with me tomorrow?"

I felt confused. This girl, the Swiss Miss whom, I was so keen on speaking with, but who on the pickup truck showed no interest at all in me, now was requesting my presence. Feeling thrilled inside, but still baffled, I responded, "okay." As she got up to leave, I whispered, "What's your name?

"Marianne," she said.

"I am Scott." She carefully tiptoed back around and across the array of sleeping bags back to her corner, but stopped and looking back at me held up two hands saying lightly "ten o'clock."

Next morning, like the Swiss trains and clocks, Marianne was on time. At 9:55am I spotted her, dressed in her familiar puffed out dark blue parka. She resembled the Michelin Tire Man, as she walked toward me on the birch tree-lined road.

I greeted her with a "Hello," an awkward delayed handshake. I felt uneasy. On seeing her in the morning sun, the first thought was how healthy she looked. Her green eyes so clear and her cheeks took on a rosy color from the cold air.

We looked across at the two majestic Buddhas about a half a mile away, and slowly began to walk along the quiet road toward them. The weather was crisp and chilly, the sky a luminous blue and the sun gently warming. Invigorating weather just the way I love it. The Buddhas seemed to be positioned about three hundred yards from each other.

I had a lot of unanswered questions that I wanted to ask her: "Who was this guy? What is your relationship to him? Why do you want to be with me?" But I felt it best not to ask these questions. Instead, just continue to walk quietly toward the statues. However, after just a couple minutes of walking, she stopped and said to me, "I want you to know that guy is just a friend, nothing more."

"So he doesn't mind if I spend this time with you?" I asked.

"Well, it's a little complicated," she replied. "He wants more, if you know what I mean."

I nodded and continued to walk in silence. She added, "He is going back to Kabul tomorrow, and I am not." I expressed to Marianne that I felt uncomfortable about this and did not want to cause any problems. "No, it's not about you. I just need to be away from him. It is not good for me to travel with him."

The Twin Buddhas were absolutely overpowering. We stood back a distance, so we could view them together. They were enthralling. I felt frozen with awe, unable to express myself. The guide book stated the small one was 121 feet and the larger one 182 feet. They were built in the 6th Century. You could also see countless cavities in the mountain next to the Buddhas that had been carved out probably to create living dwellings. However, as we got closer and examined them, they appeared to be empty now.

From here we headed into the barren reddish hills that ran above the Buddha, creating our own path as we hiked up.

After about forty-five minutes of brisk walking we sat down and rested, as we snacked on some grapes and apples that I brought. The view overlooking the town of Bamiyan coated in late Autumn colors was lovely.

As we sat she asked about my background, and she spoke about herself. Her full name was Marianne Schmidt. She was twenty-three years old, and was a high school gymnastics and dance instructor in a suburb outside of Basel. Her parents were overly religious and extremely strict, especially her father. She had had enough of their "narrow views" and just had to get away. "They were very displeased with my travel plans."

We moved on and climbed further up and across, for over an hour. She navigated the steep hills like a mountain goat; I had to press myself to keep pace with her. When we reached what was an amazing vista, we sat again, and looked out. The view was achingly beautiful. The sea of gold and crimson hills seemed to go on and on, and the mountains snowcapped, jagged, powerful. And with this awe-inspiring panorama, the stillness was astounding. The quiet was so extreme, it hurt my ears.

It was here, that I brushed her face softly and moved closely to kiss her. She paused and responded with a kiss as well. Her kiss was nice but it was reserved. When I tried to kiss her once more with feeling, Marianne held back. "Scott, I don't want to move so fast." I smiled and shook my head, "I understand," I assured her.

However, I had to ask her why she seemed so indifferent to me before on the pickup truck. "Scott, that guy was so miserably possessive, I could not breathe." And she added, "I liked you when I saw you. You look like a very good friend of mine. And you said some funny things in the truck."

"Funny?" I asked.

"Yes, I loved that story you told about the wurst at the Austrian ski resort. Scott, I was attracted to you at once but was not free to express it."

It was now late afternoon. We decided we had better head back, as in about three hours it would be dark. Also, Marianne said, "I want time to talk with Stephan, make sure he is okay. Even though I don't care to travel with him, he is not a bad guy."

As we walked back, I asked her, "So what are your travel plans after Bamiyan?" The wind was kicking up and she stopped and smoothed the hair away from her face and said, "I was planning to go to Band-e Amir, return to Kabul, and then go on to India."

I took it all in. It was quiet for a few seconds. Then she asked, "What about you?"

"Pretty similar, though after Bamiyan, I was hoping to travel to the northeast part of the country, up to Mazar-i-Sharif, Kabul, bus through Pakistan, and of course India."

Her eyes seemed to widen and she added, "Wow, almost the same route."

"Yes, Marianne, you are not following me are you?" I joked.

Marianne laughed, and I held her tight and kissed her softly and pressed my forehead against hers. Looking directly into those liquid green eyes I asked, "Marianne, would you like to travel with me? We could head out to

Band-e Amir tomorrow morning, and travel to India together." I said this with such deep felt earnestness that it was as if I were proposing.

Marianne broke into a big grin, nodded, "yes," but added, "It sounds so good and exciting. I do want to be with you, but I can be difficult at times, a little moody."

"I'll take my chances, what do you say?"

"Yes! Yes! Let's do it!" She shouted with exhilaration, her voice ringing through the pristine pastoral setting. We hugged again. Taking her hand, we began the approximate three hour walk back to town, enveloped in the glorious late afternoon light, which would evolve into an explosive vivid sunset of flaming reds and oranges.

Back at Abdul's Café we agreed in advance, that we would be very low key and undemonstrative toward each other this evening. Being sensitive to Stephan, we kept our distance from each other.

That night my sleep was especially comfortable, with the roaring fire in full view, the melodic strains of "Nights In White Satin" on the 8-track, and the anticipation of travel with Marianne tomorrow. A new adventure . . .

The next morning Stephan had left early on the 8:30 bus back to Kabul. I had gotten up even earlier. I did not want to see him depart. Also, I felt the need to be alone and walked along the main road which provided a direct view of the Twin Buddhas. I relished this quiet, alone time to take in their grandeur one more time. However, in the back of my mind, I was questioning if I were doing the right thing by traveling with Marianne.

It had happened so fast. I was completely bowled over by her. It had been so long since I had been close to a woman I cared for. But by nature I always preferred to travel solo. Now with India coming up, which I knew would be fascinating, but also knew how tough the travel challenge would be; did I really want to have another person to worry about as well?

This disturbing feeling of doubt just seemed to inexplicably be bothering me. Just yesterday I felt so thrilled and certain. As I headed back to Abdul's to get ready for the 9:30 ride to Band-e Amir, walking slowly in a confused state, I saw Marianne running towards me with open arms. "Scott, Scott, we are free now to travel together!" She was jumping up and down and hugging me. Let's go, let's go, the truck leaves in one hour!" Her enthusiasm was so joyous, so genuine, that I could not help but get caught up in it. I thought to myself, "How could I pass up this opportunity to share my travels with this vibrant woman. It will be fantastic. Don't balk now."

So following our good-bye hugs to Abdul, we boarded the same pickup truck as yesterday, joined by the Italians and the Dutch guy. As we pulled out Marianne letting loose with a spirited "wwwooopppeee."

The drive to Band-e Amir was about sixty miles directly west of Bamiyan. This drive did not have the same rugged terrain, as it was mostly on a straight, though rough road. The view was striking, as the colorful mountains rose up and spread out in every direction, and the fresh snow from last night gave a vivid contrast to the reddish rock.

Our driver was the same as yesterday, named Mohammed. He informed us that the ride to Band-e Amir would take about two hours; and where we were being dropped off was not really a town, but just a café in the middle of nowhere, where we could spend the night. In the back of the pickup we just sat quietly, as it bumped along the potholed road. We said very little to each other. But our silence was one wrapped in comfort, as we held hands and snuggled close. Embracing this special moment, we continued to marvel at the astonishing landscape surrounding us.

I then turned to Marianne and said, "Why don't we get out now? Why wait until tomorrow? Let's get out now and walk.

She looked at me surprised, but smiling. "How do you know where to go? "How far is it?" she asked.

I told her, "I am not sure, but it can't be that far away, let me check with Mohammed."

I knocked on the back window of the truck and made a gesture that I wanted to speak with him. He stopped and informed me that we were probably about ten miles away. When I told him my idea, he said, "It is not a difficult walk, pretty straight. Just be aware that you will be all alone. This is a desolate area and you will be likely to see no one."

It sounded fantastic. I explained the situation to Marianne. It took her about five seconds to digest the information, and let loose with a "Let's do it." I loved her spirit!

Out of the truck we tumbled, waving hearty "goodbyes" to the others. We stood as if frozen, just absorbing it all. The landscape was huge. An endless vista of pure white snow set off by reddish rugged rock formations; and backed up by towering mountains, as far as the eye could see. "Wow!" Marianne exclaimed. But her voice was hushed with reverence, in respect for this still frozen cathedral we worshipped in.

We walked on savoring our journey. At times moving slowly and thoughtfully, and silently, appreciating the solitude. And other times, being silly, making bizarre noises, rolling around in the snow, making angels, hugging, kissing. We both were crazy happy. After walking for about two hours, we took a break and rested. It felt delicious as we both stretched out on the snow, feeling the sun's rays and looking up at the blue cloudless sky. We just stayed still for some time. It was too sacred a moment to speak. It was glorious.

When we got up to resume our walk, we were shocked. Sitting no more than twenty feet above us, were two Afghan men. Where did they come from? They both possessed incredible faces. The older one, perhaps eighty, had a dark deeply lined face with chiseled bone structure, a white beard, flowing blue robe and matching turban.

What is it with the older Afghan men, they all look so fantastic! The younger man, he as well dressed in flowing robe and turban, his age was hard to discern, perhaps forty years old. But where the old man's face bespoke wisdom and that of a prophet, the younger man's face looked fierce, that of a warrior. I noticed that he had a long barreled rifle setting beside him. This certainly did not make me feel comfortable.

As we stood up, they remained seated and just looked at us with no expression. I walked slowly towards them, trying to think of the phrase for greeting in Afghani.

I said "Salam alekum." This confused them. They looked at each other as totally baffled, as if to infer, "What the hell did he say?"

Marianne, sounding like an Afghan native, immediately followed up with just the right words, to which they responded warmly. Welcoming smiles and handshakes were exchanged.

We still had some bread and goat meat left over which we offered to them. They appreciated our good will overture and devoured it ravenously. The older man in kindness produced a bong and gestured for us to smoke. We looked at each other, and I shrugged my shoulders to Marianne, still not knowing her long enough to know if she even smoked grass. I said "Well…when in Rome." She laughed and was definitely up for toking away with our two new found Afghan friends.

The smoke certainly had its effect on us, as we not so much continued our trek, but instead ambled along; seemed to giggle a good deal; and kept breaking to chew on our loaves of bread. However, the final two hours of the walk, now back in our normal clear-headed condition, was the most spectacular of all, as we had come upon the Band-e Amir Lakes.

The lakes, five of them located all next to each other, as if joined were filled with amazingly clear water. Each seemed to reflect a different startling color: one being a deep blue; another sky blue; one almost a purple shade; and the other a clear, crystal aqua. These lakes were framed by steep, vertical 300 foot limestone cliffs that soared straight up. The terrain seemed almost otherworldly.

We had now been walking for about three hours. The wind had started to pick up, clouds began to form and it became colder.

I pulled Marianne close and kissed her passionately for the first time. It was a deep embrace. We were breathless, as she said so sweetly, so sincerely, "Scott, I can't remember a time I have been so happy."

"I feel the same," I told her. And I did. In some ways, this day, this walk with Marianne, was one of the happiest days ever, up to this point of my life. The staggering beauty and hypnotic presence of those powerful peaks that enveloped us, had worked their magic.

Darkness was setting in as the café came into view. It was situated alone in the shadow of a towering red rock formation. On entering, the Brits were in their sleeping bags on the floor. We waved. The manager of the café greeted us with a toothless smile, "You can have sleep on floor for 10 Afs, or bed for 25." We took the bed.

When we fell asleep in each other's arms that night, we knew we had experienced something extraordinary… an intoxicating, euphoric moment of rapture in the mystical Hindu Kush of Afghanistan.

It is said: There are no perfect lives.
               Only perfect moments.

This was such a moment.

*Note – *In 2001 the Twin Buddhas were dynamited and destroyed by the Taliban. UNESCO is currently involved in restoring the Buddhas.*

Chapter 29

YUGOSLAVIA: RAUCOUS FAMILY AND RAKIA DO NOT A ROMANTIC RENDEZVOUS MAKE

It was to be a quiet, "get to know the mother" lunch. I had met the stunning, young Tatjana two days earlier at Sarajevo's art museum. She had kindly invited me to her home for lunch.

I was greatly anticipating the romantic rendezvous in the intimate setting of her home. Not only the pleasure of meeting her mother, and finding out more about Tatjana and feeling closer to her, but the opportunity for uninterrupted moments alone together, after a delightful lunch, when mother would thoughtfully excuse herself, hopefully.

I have always loved and valued mothers, and gotten along well with them. Tatjana seemed to have a close bond and much affection and respect for her mother, which I found touching. Therefore, I was deeply honored and moved that she wanted me to meet her.

I had already envisioned us, once we were alone, cuddling close on the sofa, a soft sonata playing in the background, slowly sipping wine, and looking soulfully in each other's eyes. And now the day was here and the "romantic rendezvous" about to unfold.

Tatjana's home located in the gritty outer ring of the city was actually an apartment on the tenth floor of a tired, crumbling apartment complex. It was a "walk-up" on this day, as the electricity was out. No elevator. No lights.

The mother, equally attractive and probably no more than seventeen years older than her daughter, greeted me at the door with a demonstrative welcoming smile and hug. She led me to the dining table, covered with an inviting white lace tablecloth, a wild pink roses centerpiece, and a selection of tastefully displayed salads and assorted dishes.

Assuming that the mother, who insisted I call her Mila, was as culturally literate as her daughter, I began discussing the work of Marko Celebonovic, one of my favorite Yugoslavian painters. However, this cultivated, quiet talk over lunch was strangely and abruptly interrupted by five jarring phone calls within the next fifteen minutes.

Each time Tatjana, being seated closer to the phone, would answer it, in a somewhat embarrassed and agitated tone. Twice Tatjana's mother went to talk on the phone. The two of them, highly irritated, heatedly discussed together in Bosnian what seemed to be upsetting them both. To resolve the nuisance, Mila, emphatically, disconnected the phone.

We had scarcely had time to resume the "get to know mother" luncheon, when there was a loud, demanding knock at the door. Two huge men bolted through the door, welcoming themselves in, each waiving a bottle of what looked to be vodka. Before Tatjana or the mother could introduce me, they greeted me with open arms and in boisterous voices bellowed: "HELLO MY AMERICAN FRIEND. WE DRINK TO YOU!"

Their names were Srecko and Miroslav, the brothers of Tatjana's mother. With their bold "presence" there was no question what the phone calls were about. The word was out that a young man was seeing Tatjana, a young foreign man, a young man from America, and the extended family was curious. Tatjana saw it merely as a caring gesture in her best interest.

The brothers were exuberant as they slapped me on the back, rubbed my head and filling my glass as raising theirs. I swallowed the liquor down expecting to taste Vodka, but it was not vodka, it was stronger, and pretty nasty.

"Whew," I let out in disgust shaking my head, the brothers laughing at my reaction, "that is called Rakia, our country's national drink, drink more, you get use to it."

Not wanting to be a party pooper I joined them doing my best to take part in Rakia, the firewater tasting fruit brandy. I would raise my glass and shout "Ziveli, Ziveli" for "cheers" after them.

Three rounds of toasts later, there was a loud and constant honking noise coming from the street below.

Looking down from the window, I could see two cars and what appeared to be about twelve people piling out. Another car then pulled up with five more people.

Tatjana was visibly embarrassed and blushing and tried to explain to me: "I am so sorry. I wanted just a quiet time for you to know my mother, but the family is just too close. They love and care for me too much."

The two brothers opened the apartment windows. Those down below started shouting up and waving wildly to come down. Mila came over to the window and began yelling down something else to dissuade them. Tatjana looked confused and anxious, but still so lovely.

Those on the ground below were more persuasive in insisting we join them. So down the ten floors we scrambled, juggling picnic baskets of food. The "moveable feast" continued with the five of us jammed in the brother's tiny car, following the other three cars. In about an hour, we arrived at a picture book, pastoral setting, complete with a narrow river meandering through green woods.

When the four cars stopped, it was as if on cue. Doors swung open, large loud bodies bounded out; car trunks popped open displaying a staggering amount of food and drink. A volley ball net went up. And a cassette player blasted a lively Yugoslavian polka tune. This pristine, bucolic setting was being swallowed up by unbridled, spontaneous spirited festivity.

With already three rounds of Rakia, and it not even one o'clock, I had a "buzz" on, as I was warmly introduced to the extended family. It was a big family with big exuberance, big voices, big laughter and big people with big appetites for food, drink and showing their affection.

For the next six hours we would be here eating and eating and eating. And with the eating came toasting and toasting, and drinking and drinking.

Between gorging myself on juicy grilled lamb kabobs and an appetizing selection of savory local dishes, I would listen and partake in toast after toast which always concluded with a joyous "Ziveli", or "Hvala" from seemingly every member of the family, most of it in Bosnian in my honor, including from the eldest family member, Tatjana's great grandmother.

She, I was told, was 93 years old and was amazingly spry. The family included all ages: from the very old to the very young, even tipsy toddlers and an adorable set of ten year old twin girls.

I was beginning to get a little "tipsy" myself after so many toasts. These bon vivants really knew how to party.

Well, I was way out of their league and feeling seriously "seized." When I began to stagger, the family members, especially Srecko and Miroslav, caringly suggested perhaps I should not completely fill my glass anymore. When it came to rakia, they could see I was no stalwart Slav. But they seemed to respect my spirit for joining in to show my appreciation.

I now had blurry vision... And blurry thinking . . . But in spite of this, one thing was crystal clear: "A RAUCOUS FAMILY AND RAKIA DO NOT A ROMANTIC RENDEZVOUS MAKE!"

No, it had not been the quiet, intimate day I had expected. The only quiet thing was the ever-smiling Tatjana, who sat serenely by my side, holding my hand the entire day. She would sweetly kiss my forehead from time to time to make sure I was still alive, still surviving her out-of-control, over-the-top family, and still apologizing for them. I, in turn, apologized to her for the "zombie" I had become.

In my stupor, I loved her tenderness and caring and her whole family's bigger-than-life generosity of spirit and GUSTO for celebrating the great festival of life.

Yes, the day had been many things: confusing, surprising, disappointing in some ways, but delightful and joyful in other ways. But decidedly "NO!" it had not been the day I planned. It had been much more . . . I'll drink to that!

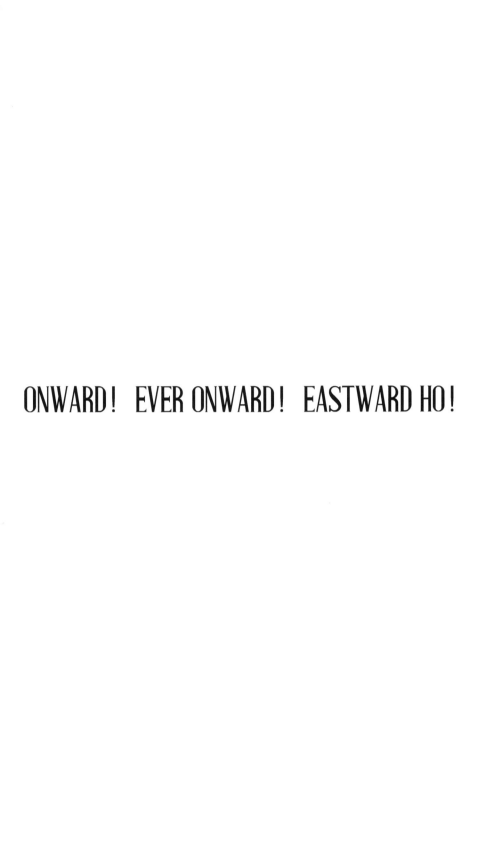

ONWARD! EVER ONWARD! EASTWARD HO!

Chapter 30

ISTANBUL: "CROSSROADS OF THE BACKPACKER'S UNIVERSE"

The "crossroads of the universe." To backpackers in the 70s that is what Istanbul was. It no longer is (due, of course, to current world events), but back in the late 70s, to backpackers, Istanbul was it . . . the "Crossroads of the Universe." Like a modern day Silk Road, Istanbul situated half in Europe, half in Asia was a frenetic, colorful intersection for backpackers leaving Europe for Asia; and those from Asia heading to Europe.

There were other backpacking "meccas" such as Bali, Kathmandu, and Goa which were magnets for packers and were beloved. But for me, and I think most travelers would agree, none compared to Istanbul in terms of the constant flow and diversity of the backpackers from all over the world. Coming and going, sharing stories, seeking information.

And if the city of Istanbul represented the universal crossroads for backpackers, the undisputed epicenter was The Pudding Shop. The Pudding Shop was a modest, somewhat grimy restaurant; serving up average food, sitting in the shadow of the Blue Mosque in the old section of Istanbul. This was the spot, beyond all tourist destinations where packers headed first.

The Pudding Shop unfortunately is no more . . . However, to catch a view of it, see the heart- pounding 1979 film *Midnight Express*.

I was captivated by Istanbul, and agree it is a fascinating city, especially coming from Europe. The city has extraordinary museums, mosques and bazaars; but in some ways I feel what I experienced by just sitting in the Pudding Shop, and watching and listening, was in its way equally fascinating.

I relished watching as wave after wave of backpackers came through... British, French, German, Dutch, Swiss, Spanish, Italian, Swedish, Israeli, Australian, Canadian and New Zealanders. Sure, on my travels through Europe I had met travelers from all these countries. But never concentrated together, centered in one place. A powerful dynamic.

The merging of nationalities for the most part coexisted well, but at times there seemed to be a definite one-upsmanship and national pride kicking in. The Canadians seemed frequently to display their nation's flag front and center on their pack, and were quick to remind you that they "were not American."

The Australians were loud, the Israeli's were very cliquish, the French always looked scraggy and haggard, and the Brits seemed to carry an attitude of having all the answers. There were lots of Germans and few Americans.

Because backpackers shared a common goal, traveling, exploring, there was a natural language which was easy upon meeting someone. Not the basic, stilted: "What is your profession?" so one can instantly categorize someone's monetary worth or social standing. But instead very "in the moment," focused on the now, of what you are experiencing or have experienced in your travels. "Where are you coming from? How was it? Where are you headed?"

One thing I found interesting as I observed the travelers entering the Pudding Shop, was I could usually tell those travelers that were going to Asia and those that had been. Those that had been, not only looked more gaunt, but also carried an air about them that seemed more sure, and had experienced something very special, as if they "had seen the light" and knew things that we could not comprehend.

To overhear conversations of those that "have been" just seemed more colorful. Even the names of these places; Esfahan, Poona, Mazar-i-Sharif, Yogyakarta, Hunza Valley, Chang Rai, had such a magical ring to them.

Where were they, what did they offer? Listening to these places I became envious and excited of what lay ahead.

Having traveled for nearly eighteen months in Europe, I carried a senior status among fellow travelers, or so I thought. I say this for in my travels on the Continent rarely would I meet someone that had traveled as long, or been to as many places. Most travelers I would come in contact with in Europe seemed to do the 2-3 month Euro Rail trip.

So fellow packers I would meet would often say in admiration: "Wow, you have been on the road for a long time."

Or: "You have seen so much." And, yes, I was proud of my travels, my time on the road, and did feel I had a superior status to be respected.

This somewhat cocky attitude of mine was quickly brought down to earth on meeting other "seasoned" travelers, or hearing the incredible travel stories that came through the Pudding Shop. There were packers here that were on the road for three, four, seven years. I was still a baby compared to these road-weary warriors.

Another concern I observed about the travelers coming into the Pudding Shop, was that some of them looked extremely seedy and sick. As if the traveling had just exhausted them: from the physical demands of traveling so long; or from drug use, a major and with some people the only, reason they travel. Asia had gotten the better of them.

From hanging out at the Pudding Shop, I also encountered for the first time travelers with no money at all. The begging for loose change by packers, going from table to table, was common and often done with an aggressive tone.

The Pudding Shop was not known for its high quality food. The Turkish cuisine served was nothing special, but was cheap. They also served up food that was "familiar" home country type dishes: meat loaf and mashed pota- toes to bratwurst, to fried eggs with hash brown potatoes.

This made the fatigued packer feel good. But what was best about the Pudding Shop was the contact and information you got from fellow travelers. Food was secondary. Many travelers, including myself, would sit for hours on end nursing a cup of tea, taking in this virtual United Nations of backpackers. At times I would be pro-active, introducing myself to a table and join in on the talk; but other times just sit back and listen from afar. I really loved this place, and I know most packers have a special feel about it as well.

The Pudding Shop had a helpful message board, huge about 7feet by 3 feet, with the entire space covered with diverse messages including the following:

"Need a cheap ride to Athens?"

"Where can I score some good, cheap pot?"

"Job wanted, drive Mercedes to Munich?"

"Have World Series tickets?"

"Looking for clean shaven guy to act as courier BIG $$?" (This was hidden speak for someone to transport drugs).

Because I had a rather clean-cut image, I was hit up twice while in Asia to do some "courier" work. No thanks!

For those headed east, and I of course was one of them, the question was: do I fly from Istanbul to India; or do I travel via overland to India? These were the two schools of thought.

The first being: by flying, yes, the initial cost would be more but it would be quick, taking only six hours; instead of going overland via local bus or train transport across Turkey, Iran, Afghanistan and Pakistan. Those who favored going by air could not understand why you would subject yourself to those thousands of miles of punishing travel, when you can arrive in India faster and fresher.

However, for me, there was never a question which camp I was in. OVERLAND!

I had heard the stories of how tough the traveling was, and that it could be dangerous. But, I could not imagine just flying over four countries, four ancient civilizations: Turkey, Iran, Afghanistan, Pakistan; and being deprived of a wealth of great cultures and experiences. Also coming directly from Europe to India was just too jarring. I had heard how India was a true culture shock. I felt the overland land experience would help me adapt and prepare me for India, to better value it and take advantage of its rich cultural diversity.

Travelers I met were dogmatic in which way to travel. Rarely did I meet anyone who waffled, not being sure if to fly or go overland. I was emphatic where I stood, and thrilled about what the unknown overland route to India experience held.

Chapter 31

OVERLAND ASIA TO INDIA
(TURKEY, IRAN AFGHANISTAN, PAKISTAN)

Sitting on the edge of a soiled torn red velvet sofa, in the drab, dimly- lit common room of Istanbul's Yecelt Hostel, I looked closely at the five faces around me. Faces that until two days ago I had never seen were now going to be joining me as constant traveling companions. Tomorrow we would be embarking on our first leg of traveling overland to India.

Our group consisted of: three Brits, Nigel, Alex and John, each with a strong Midlands accent, and each with scruffier hair than the next. Joe a lanky laid-back American resembled a young blonde Abe Lincoln, and Jocelyn a rather dazzling redhead from New Zealand. I could already imagine the amount of "attention" she would be subjected to during this trip.

The six of us were all in our twenties. I was probably the youngest at twenty-three, and Joe the eldest at twenty-eight. We met earlier over a shared table, in where else, the Pudding Shop. We were all coming from other destinations, but were now drawn together by traveling overland to India.

Joe took out a map. Not just a general map of Asia, which I had. But one that read "Rand McNally Near and Mid East." This map was more detailed, concentrating on the areas we would be traveling. With the help of Nigel, they unfolded it and laid it on the floor. There was something so pure and almost spiritual about this moment. The six of us focused on the map leaning closer taking it in. No one spoke, just quiet, transfixed. Looking at the map, with our own private thoughts, as in giving respect or awe to the countries and travel challenges that lay ahead of us.

The first thing I noticed on the map, were the deep shades of brown. This made me happy. The deep brown represented high mountains (above 15,000 feet). It was dark brown in color, darker than I recalled seeing on my European map. Having grown up in the flat Midwest, I now had a burning desire to travel where I would see these dark brown patches. And on this map the dark brown color clearly was seen between each border we would cross.

The light began to flicker and the electricity went out. The Yecelt, my home in Istanbul for the past four days, was a dump, no question about it. However, the people who ran it, Mohamed and Mohamed, were so kind. They quickly brought in a couple of flash lights. So now down on our knees, the flashlight slowly moving across the area to travel, the names of the biggest cities we were sure to go through, calling out to us: Erzurum, Tehran, Mashhad, Herat, Qandahar, Kabul, Peshawar, Lahore . . . and India.

"It's a little over 3,500 miles," said Jocelyn.

"About eleven inches on the map, not even a foot," John jested. It being early November and now about 9 p.m., the room was becoming cold. We could see our breath. But we were too excited to be bothered by frigid air.

We were together in our decision that overland was the only way to go. No plane travel for this group. However, we now had to decide train or bus or a third option by boat to eastern Turkey, which Joe found out about earlier today. All of us individually had been checking on the array of transport operators during the previous days. We had done our research. So these were our choices:

Express Train to Tehran was the cheapest, costing just $14, but taking a staggering seventy-seven hours. Ug!

Or: Express Bus to Tehran costing more at $26, and taking just 64 hours. Seemed like a sprint in comparison.

The third option, which Joe shared with us, I liked best. He said, "There is a boat sailing the Black Sea that leaves tomorrow at 10a.m. and arrives two days later at 1p.m. in the port city of Trabzon. From here we can catch a bus that goes to the town of Ezurum in eastern Turkey; then connect for the express bus to Tehran."

Joe went on to say that the price was amazing! With a student card it cost only 50TL ($3.50). Joe added that it was the lowest class and the room would probably be a "shit hole." And ironically as he said this, a rat ran across the Yecelt floor. No problem with that, we were ready for the accommodations that lay ahead.

Except for Alex, who had initial misgivings about getting seasick, we were in agreement that the boat would be a nice respite from the endless grueling, bus rides that faced us. And leaving out of Istanbul by boat had a romantic feel about it.

Erzurum, Turkey Overland Asia Day 3

Among a gathering of Turkish men, I awoke in my sleeping bag from the floor of the Dogubeyazit, Turkey bus station.

Some were standing over me, others squatting. As my eyes came into focus all seemed to be wearing little knit caps and sporting moustaches. On a quick glance they all looked so similar, as if they could be from one big related family.

Initially, I was somewhat taken back with the group of about fifteen Turks staring so intensely at me. But raising myself up on one elbow, I slowly and carefully studied the faces: weathered dark skin, but calm, not threatening. I yawned and said "gew nahy dohn"(good morning in Turkish.)

This created a few smiles, some nodding, others pulled away, two hands outstretched with a cigarette offering which I politely refused with a "no." A young boy, about ten, pushes through the crowd with soulful dark eyes and gestures to clean my boots. He asks about tea. "Yes," I opt for tea.

Checking my watch, it is 5:12 a.m. I pull out my Journal. This brings everyone even closer and holds their interest, but not for long. Soon the group focuses their attention on Alex who is sleeping. I must admit he was quite a sight to behold. Alex is a big lumbering bloke, easily 6'3" and weighing about 250 pounds, with a huge head and sporting a wild unruly mane of black hair. He lays flat on the floor sleeping, his gaping mouth wide open, arms stretched wide out and making booming beastly snoring sounds. The young boy arrives back with my tea, smiles and sits next to me. His name is Derin.

This diversion of attention to Alex sleeping is welcomed. It gives me time to reflect and do some writing on the first days of the Overland Asia trip. I did not expect to be writing from the town of Dogyubazit, but a bus breakdown (the second of the evening) caused the driver to pull into the station around 3 a.m. The bus journey has taken ten hours, and we have traveled only about one hundred and seventy miles. The town is located just twenty miles from the Iranian border, and is in the shadow of Mount Ararat, Turkey's highest mountain.

A smile came to my face, as I wrote about our two day boat trip across the Black Sea to the town of Trabzon. What a terrific way to reach Eastern Turkey to begin the overland route!

The sensation of pulling out of Istanbul, and cruising slowly up the Bosphorus Straight, I found spellbinding.

I positioned myself near the bow of the ship, and with no one around me I took it all in: this complex fascinating city of theByzantine and Ottoman Empires, this city that straddles two continents. Behind me the Galata Bridge with all its crazed color and frantic energy was saying good-bye. And now the magnificence of the minaret-studded Old Town sky-line, with the unmistakable architectural jewels of Hagia Sophia, the Blue Mosque, and further up the hill was the Suleymaniye Mosque, and soon the jaw dropping grandeur of Topkapi Palace.

As Istanbul faded in the distance, I found the sight not only breathtaking, but poignant. I felt a lump swelling in my throat. I thought back on the near one and one-half years traveling Europe. I found myself smiling, but yet wistful saying goodbye to Europe and welcome to Asia, and the wonder of what lay ahead. The sight of leaving Istanbul and the feelings I had at that time is a moment that has always stayed with me.

Our cabin for sleeping accommodations was seedy and cramped. Our group of six was now up to nine, as we met two Swedish girls and a guy from Canada. We had to fit in five beds, which were in a space no larger than 15x10 feet. The beds were not really beds, but just thin mattresses resting only a foot off the floor. The mattresses were yellowed, stained and ripped, and as we later found out contained a healthy supply of bed bugs.

Normally none of us would have had a problem sleeping on the floor. However, this floor contained what looked like two pools of an oil slick that would slush back and forth to the ship's movements. There also was a large beefy rat.

This was without question the largest rat I had ever seen. It looked almost as large as a loaf of Wonder Bread. And it was a rat with "attitude." No quick scurrying around for this rat. No, it would come out saunter around, check us out carefully, and then disappear into a hole which had a good six inch opening.

Alex, Joe and I approached the front desk to complain about the rat situation. The totally disinterested middle-aged Turk looked up and said with no sense of concern, "Hey, for what you paid, what do you expect?" And that was the end of the conversation. And any further complaints.

So with no one wanting to bed down on the floor, the sleeping arrangements were very cozy. We all doubled up, except allowing Jocelyn, the sole single woman, her own bed. Yes, we were gentlemen. With the bed no wider than thirty inches I shared my bed with Nigel. He was the smallest of the three Brits, a wonderful guy with a fantastic high pitched laugh. But still, sharing the mattress was way too intimate; especially as he had a rather robust gaseous quality. In other words, he farted a hell of a lot. We made the best of it.

But despite our filthy quarters, there was a strong camaraderie between us, and spirits were high. We were at the onset of the Overland Asia trip, and none of us wanted to be burdened with over-complainers. I think all of us were conscious that it being the start of Asian travel, accommodations would be sub standard. Traveling would be rough. No one wanted to appear to be a spoiled traveler. We were headed for Asia, and we must be prepared for change. So suck it up!

The days at sea were consumed by: sitting out on the open deck; taking in the brisk winds and bright November sun; playing cards, reading; and meeting other fellow travelers. There were a total of seventeen backpackers on the ship. Those that I spoke to seemed to have accommodations on par with us.

Two Germans I spoke with did not have any oil slicks in their cabin. When I started to feel cheated, they added that the lights in their cabin kept flicking on and off all night. Hmm! I think we got the better deal.

The dining experience aboard the ship was unusual and different from what we expected. To our amazement breakfast and lunch meals were not included. We had to fend for ourselves. Not being aware of this before and not prepared, I virtually starved waiting for dinner to come; making due only on tangerines and Turkish potato chips that I got from the vending machine.

When dinner did come we were desperately anxious and hungry. Two bells would ring for First Class (not us). One bell for Second Class (still not us). When do we go to the dining room? When do we eat? We waited and waited and then approached the dining room apprehensively.

The sadistic steward, a man looking in his thirties, with jet black greasy hair and oily pimpled skin, seemed to get pleasure, as he snapped: "No Bells for Tourist Class." He directed us, not to the main dining room, but another dining room.

Well, in no way could it be called a dining room. It was just a nondescript dank room with dirty brownish walls with a few tables and a buffet table.

I did not care that the surroundings were unappetizing, I was starving and ready to chow down.

In unison we all let out with exclamations of disbelief: "What?" or "Shit" in our native tongues, as on the buffet table was a sign: 70 TL. How could this be? The total two day voyage cost 50TL, but for a simple dinner it is 70TL? They had our stomachs hostage.

But we would not allow this! So much for being a non-complainer. We staged a protest. Joe, the Californian, whom I had early-on pegged as a laid- back Californian, repositioned his tall frame in a sitting position. "It's a sit-in against food. I haven't done this since my days at Berkeley."

After about fifteen minutes of haggling on the overpriced buffet with a man that spoke no English, the same lovely man to whom we spoke earlier about our rat- infested, oil-slicked accommodations, grudgingly agreed that we could purchase food a la carte. I settled on a 20TL lamb kebab that was passable.

So the two day ship voyage across the Black Sea, which included a brief two hour stop at the port city of Samsun, and later disembarking in the port city of Trabzon, plus a five hour bus ride to Erzurum, put us in position for the scheduled 11a.m. Express bus to Tehran, which was to take an "estimated" 27 hours. I was impressed that the boat journey was so punctual on its leaving and arriving time. The same could not be said about our Express bus to Tehran.

The scheduled 11a.m. departure had several false starts, alterations and changes prior to our finally leaving. We did not push off until 7 p.m. (Only eight hours late). This the first scheduled bus ride of the overland journey was to be a challenging lesson in dealing with the frustrations of bus travel in this part of the world.

A good motto is: "expect the unexpected." Be patient; be cool, for this is not bus travel in America, and certainly not Switzerland. Having been somewhat inpatient in the past, I knew that Asia's transport would be a tough test for me.

I was surprised to see such a large number of backpackers at the bus station, milling around the busses. I would say about forty from a quick glance. Some of the packers I recognized from the ship's voyage, some from the Pudding Shop. But most I had not seen before.

No one seemed to know what was going on. What bus to get on, or when it was to leave. It was like the blind leading the blind. And in addition to the backpackers were the local Turkish people also trying to navigate what bus to take. Some of the men were hauling huge cumbersome bags, which required them to climb a ladder, attached to the back of the bus, to get them on top. Others juggled crates containing squawking chickens and snorting pigs on top, and being yelled at for doing so. This brought on heated, fervid arguments with flailing hands, and the animals were forced to be brought down. They would travel inside the bus with the passengers.

Confusion, disorganized . . . YES! But at the same time this mass bus chaos had an immediate energy about it, which I found colorful and exciting. Pigs on a bus! Why not!

There were several busses in the lot, but no one knew for sure which one went to Tehran, or if one went to Tehran at all. As my *Lonely Planet* guide book said, "Busses for Tehran most likely left at 11a.m. three days a week, but that the days of departure seemed to change."

Where was the information desk you ask? Where is the person in charge? Yes, this is how the western mind works. Information desk... timetable, should be able to get the facts. Well there seemed to be a different system here, a different rhythm of when and why the bus left, or did not leave.

There actually was an information desk, run by a mean looking bear of a man. He was Turkish, dark and grizzly about forty, that could not speak English that well, except for saying choice words like: "No," "go away;" all peppered with foul four letter swear words. We called him "Mr. Nasty."

When he was pressed to answer questions like "why is the bus late," or confronted by some backpackers, he would explode with a barrage of vile obscenities. "Suck my dick" seemed to be his favorite. Even to women his language was equally outrageous: "No, don't know bus come. Get cunt out of office."

One had to approach this man carefully. You want to get the information, but if you anger him, he would withhold a ticket from you. I warned Nigel of this, as Nigel's temperament by nature is confrontational. Just as I cautioned him, moments later we witnessed a long-haired backpacker, I believe German, raising his voice and challenging Mr. Nasty. A mistake.

The Nasty man lashed back: "No ticket for you. You not allowed on bus." So it was.

When we saw this, we all agreed we had to handle this testy guy with "smarts." Since there was no need for each of us to approach Mr. Nasty, we decided to send Joe, the tall, soft spoken angelic-looking Californian to represent us. He had an easy manner. We felt that he was our best hope in dealing with Mr. Nasty to obtain information and get answers.

Joe's question: "When does the bus for Tehran leave?" asked in the most gracious way, was met with: "Maybe 11, maybe 2, maybe not at all."

When Joe probed a little deeper, asking: "What does it depend on?"

Mr. Nasty responded: "Out, get fuck out of office. You will know when bus goes."

But despite this confusion, this time delay and wondering will we ever get on the bus to Tehran, there was something crazy and exhilarating about the experience. I know it sounds weird to say this, as it was a frustrating experience, just waiting to go and not knowing. The air was charged with such pent-up anticipation of finally moving on, getting on the Tehran Express and heading East.

Rumors abounded between the travelers about the state of the busses, ranging from: "I heard that all busses today have been canceled."

Or: "No there is a 1p.m."

Or: "A special midnight bus is to leave."

To: "There aren't enough tickets, they are going to raise prices."

A little man dressed in a big fur cap ran out waving his hands: "Tehran, Tehran, Tehran!" and pointing at the bus parked alone in the far corner of the lot.

On hearing these words, our group of nine sprinted among the other colorful backpackers to the bus that would take us to Tehran.

To get a seat on the bus, that grubby, exhausted looking bus was all that mattered. As I dashed across the dirt lot, the bus being about one hundred yards from the information area where most of the packers were gathered, it appeared there were many more people than seats available.

We were not just competing with other backpackers for the seats, but local Turkish and Iranian travelers as well. The locals seemed to know the tricks of the trade, as they would not even run to the bus door. Instead they would throw their luggage in an open bus window then climb in to secure their seat.

Thankfully Alex was out roaming about the lot, away from the main area; and when he heard the call to action, he had a natural head start and did his best to save some seats for us. With lots of pushing and shoving we had made it on and had our seats, as we breathed in a deep sigh of relief.

But just as we began to give each other high fives, the little man with the overlarge fur cap came on the bus: "Tickets…Tickets"

What? Damn. All of a sudden there was a rush back off the bus to get the ticket from Mr. Nasty. We decided to pool our money and send John to get our tickets.

About fifteen minutes later we could see John coming back. He was skipping with elation, as he held up five tickets in his hand triumphantly. Ah, yes, now we have our tickets.

But just as we were beginning to get comfortable, I could see some people in the front of the bus, getting off the bus. They were all locals and someone was giving a direction I could not understand. A couple of the backpackers in the back moved forward to get off. What was going on? I stuck my head out the window and called to anyone who would listen, trying to figure out what was happening.

A couple packers yelled back, "you are on the wrong bus."

The provider of this updated information was none other than the gracious Mr. Nasty himself. He appeared in front of the bus now pointing with a long extended arm and barking "Tehran over there."

Ug! So off we came, as we hurriedly grabbed our backpacks from the storage below and raced across to another bus.

This bus, about the same size as the previous one, was even more dilapidated looking. By the time we fought our way onto it, three of us didn't get a seat. Those with seats, Alex and John vowed that they would take turns sharing their seats with us.

The thought of standing a good deal of the way on a twenty-seven hour bus trip was not fun, but at this point I just wanted the bus to move. But the bus did not move. Half an hour went by, then an hour. We did not even see our driver.

The travelers were getting restless and a couple of Australians yelled out the window in the direction of Mr. Nasty: "When the hell is the bus leaving?"

This was followed by: "This bus company sucks." Everyone was laughing, as you could see Mr. Nasty getting pissed off, but he could not see who was yelling.

About fifteen minutes later, Mr. Nasty got on the bus and looking grim and pissed. He announced with what seemed like suppressed glee:

"Bus cancelled! Next bus 3p.m."

With this there was an eruption of groans and moans and catcalls.

"BITE MY ASS!" retorted Mr. Nasty.

So off we came. It was now 1p.m. For another couple of hours we went to a local restaurant. When we came back, no Mr. Nasty could not be found, just a sign on the closed door that said: "3p.m. BUS CANCELLED. BUS TEHRAN 7p.m."

Shit! The sign was graced with a couple of nice graffiti comments such as "eat shit;" "stick this bus up your ass."

Damn! What a fiasco. All of us were so sick of this bus company. No explanation, just saying "cancelled." Would it really go at seven o'clock, or would it be delayed again? I was mentally spent; we all were. We felt helpless. It was like we had no control at all over the bus situation. Why was it cancelled? Was there a real reason, or was Mr. Nasty just being his normal loveable self? We had four hours to kill and no place to stay.

A very dark skinned, short middle-aged man with a bad limp approached us. He introduced himself by the name of Gorkem. He had a kind, soft-spoken way and said that we could pass the time at his hostel/café; and if we wanted to rest, he would not charge us. Isn't it an amazing contradiction how different people can be: from a soul-destroying, wretched "Mr. Nasty;" to a life-affirming generous gentleman, as kind as Gorkem. The challenges of travel expose you to both, and everything in between.

I followed the man with our group, but I had no plans to hang out there with the others for six hours. I wanted to explore Erzurum; and equally important I had a strong and needed yearning to be alone.

The five I had traveled with for the past few days were good people, interesting and fun to be with. But by nature I prefer to travel alone. And now I ached for this, even if it was just for four hours.

As I walked down the main street of Erzurum, it felt different than Istanbul. Though it was the largest city in Eastern Turkey with a population of 170,000, and had a colorful market, the pace was slower. I stayed on the main street for about fifteen minutes, and then cut to the side streets to explore.

I walked on, leaving one small side street for another and finally continued on this one for a good ninety minutes. The street, more of a mud track than pavement, led me out of town and heading directly into the steep rugged mountains that dominated in the near distance.

My casual walk out of the main city area seemed to transport me to another land. Erzurum and Istanbul are both cities in Turkey. But the outskirts of Erzurum seemed like a different country. It had a much more orthodox Islamic feel; as the men seemed mostly dressed in dark draped clothing, and the women veiled. Some were completely covered from head to foot with only tiny mesh slits for their eyes. Pigs and chickens squealed and pecked about the pathways, as men would chase after them with a cleaver.

The place was more primitive, raw. I felt somewhat uneasy as I pressed on exploring the rural dirt pathways and narrow alleyways. But at the same time I felt empowered and confident; it was exciting exploring this new area on my own.

I had now come to a clearing where the little mud houses seemed to end. In front of me was an expanse of burnt landscape leading up to the higher mountains. Over to the side I could see a group of kids kicking a soccer ball. Before I even started to head over to them, they seemed to notice me.

They stopped their game and began waving to me; all of them began running over to me. "Hello mister, hello, name, what's name?"

I responded with a new phrase I had learned earlier today, while waiting for the bus to Tehran: "My name is Scott."

I was in the middle of this group of about a dozen kids, most around ten to twelve years old. I moved around the circle slowly, shaking each of their hands in a ceremonious, over-exaggerated fashion up and down. This handshake always seems to get a laugh out of young kids, and this was no exception now. Moving out of the enclosed circle, I jogged toward the field and yelled: "Let's play!"

My travels in Europe and the countless pick-up games with European children made me a better soccer player. Growing up in the Midwest, I can claim never having even kicked a soccer ball, focusing instead on baseball, football, and basketball. I didn't even know of anyone in my town who played soccer. But in Europe, as in the rest of the world, (outside the USA) soccer is king. My travels gave me an opportunity to improve my game and respect for soccer.

The kids were not that skilled, but they played with much enthusiasm. The playing field was a mixture of torn up grass and dirt and was uneven with a couple areas with gaping holes in the ground. The goal posts at one end rested on two oil cans; and the other looked like two large milk crates.

Our team was losing, but we were having fun. The game was not overly serious. Many shots that went off target were met with laughter, rather than disgust. When I made a goal, coming on a close-in deflected shot, it was celebrated with high fives and calls of "Pele!" These shouts referring to Brazil's famed soccer star.

As I played, I noticed a man dressed in a severe dark black robe standing at the side of the field. He just stood with his arms crossed. He did not make any motion to any of the players, or seem as if he were watching a son or a friend. And he did not react when a goal was scored. He just stood still and watched. He watched me. Not the game. But wherever I went, his head seemed to follow with my movements.

When the soccer ball went off the field in his direction, and I retrieved it, he would say to me: "Tea Me. Tea Me." I did not know what he meant, but just quickly picked up the ball and returned to playing.

The wind started to kick up, and sand from the field was being blown about. It made the visibility difficult and stung the eyes. After about an hour the game had ended. Our team lost 5-3. There were exchanged congratulations all-around between the players; seconds later, as if in a fire drill, the kids scattered running in the direction of their homes as fast as possible. Some turned as they ran to yell and wave "good-bye" to me.

As I walked off the field, still accompanied by two of the kids, the man watching me so intently while I played, followed slowly behind us. After a good ten minutes of walking back in the direction of the café, where my traveling mates were, the man came up beside me and said: "Tea, Tea."

I shook my head and kept walking. The two kids did not make any indication that they knew who he was. Soon they each dashed off, each shaking my hand and saying, "Good game mister." Another said: "game tomorrow, you play?" With the unpredictable bus fiasco, who knew, maybe I would be playing.

With the children gone, just the man walked along by me now. I kept up a brisk pace, and he kept up with me. I did not feel uneasy, just a little annoyed, as the man kept repeating: "Tea, Tea."

I assumed he was trying to sell me something. Instead of just shaking my head saying, "No thank you", I stopped, and looked at him closely and asked: "What do you want? I don't need tea."

He was an attractive man, about forty -five, fairly dark, with greenish eyes and a small moustache. His face was welcoming; he did not seem aggressive.

With direct eye contact, he uttered a new word to tea: "Tea Home." He pointed to an alley we had just passed.

Now I seemed to understand what he wanted: for me to join him for tea at his house. My initial reaction was to keep on walking, as I wanted to get back to the hostel to eat, and get ready, hopefully, for the 7p.m. bus departure to Tehran.

So many times during my travels the ordinary person reaching out with a simple gesture, as was happening now, had rewarded me with a rich experience of close contact, and a more intimate, meaningful understanding of their lives and culture. Some travelers in this situation might turn away thinking that it was a set-up to get ripped-off, or too dangerous to enter a home in a remote area in a foreign land. If travel has done one thing for me, it is to trust that man is basically good.

He repeated it again, this time with pleading warmth, "tea, home," adding the gesture of pointing at me and himself, and the direction we would go.

Reaching inside his black robe, he took out a photo of a young man and a small post office-sized envelope that was addressed to the U.S.A.

"Son, Ohio. College."

He said these words with pride and a touch of sadness. With those familiar words and the photo, any previous doubts about the man's intent vanished.

I followed the man.

His name was Berkay. The walk to his place changed from a muddy narrow road, through an even narrower alleyway, flanked by high mud walls on each side. The alley was a tight fit, at times pressing me against the wall, to allow a cart pulled by a mule to pass. We walked on, leaving one alley after another. I started to feel anxious, as wherever he was taking me seemed removed. When I asked, "how much further?" He just shook his head and waved his hand forward.

As I walked I tried to remember the winding route. (Unfortunately unlike Hansel and Gretel I had no bread crumbs to drop). He trudged ahead at a quick pace, not speaking. I did my best to keep up, as I dodged packs of screaming children, yelling to me as they ran by.

It was now snowing. The sky was losing light. In another hour it would be dark. I had now been following him for about thirty minutes, leaving one confusing narrow alley after another. It was a true maze. I felt nervous. My mind conflicted: Who really was this man? Was that photo really his son? Was I going to his home for tea? Or did he have something else in mind?

I stopped. Just as I began to tell Berkay that I wanted to go back, a man with three children (ranging in ages from five to infant) ran into us and gave Berkay a warm embrace.

Berkay beamed and turned with outstretched arms: "Scott, U.S.A!"

The man, about twenty-five, shook my hand eagerly, and spoke English to me: "Nice to meet you. I grew up with Berkay's son. He was my close childhood friend."

With this endorsement I was feeling more at ease. Onward with tea!

Five minutes later, we turned into a courtyard, and through a low doorway, we arrived at his house. It was a small room, lit by a dim overhanging light. He quickly moved to operate three kerosene lamps, supplying more illumination. The floor was stone, with a torn, faded green area rug over it. The walls were adorned with what appeared to be portraits of old distant family members. There were also some Islamic posters on the wall; one a photo of the religious pilgrimage in Mecca, known as the Haj. The other picture was the stern- looking face of a high holy Muslim Cleric perhaps.

Over in the corner of the room a fire burned, supplying the small room with some suitable warmth. Berkay gestured for me to join him at the dining table. The table was made of heavy dark wood. It looked old, as it was weathered and worn in many places.

Berkay sat next to me but looked away and said something in a loud commanding voice. He spoke in Turkish, and apparently not to me. Seconds later he said something again, even louder with a more demanding tone.

Who was Berkay talking to?

Suddenly two hands appeared through a beaded curtain, covering a small window in the wall at the end of the table. In one hand was a tea pot, the other were two cups.

Seeing this startled me. The hands covered almost completely by black cloth, looked tiny, bony and worked. I wanted to say, "What was that?" But, I was well aware that women in Turkey, those of the strong Islamic orthodox faith, especially in these rural areas, were required to be submissive.

Berkay took the tea pot and cups and led me over to a dark brown sofa with a white lace covering. He gestured for me to sit, turned and snarled toward the window again. He did not seem happy. There was a short silence, as he stared toward the little window. I could sense the tension. It seemed like an eternity.

A small dish then appeared which Berkay grabbed, grunting something at the window, as he did. They were tea cookies. He poured the tea, pointing toward the cookies.

"Eat," he said. I took a bite of the cookie that was covered with a white sugary powder. It was too sweet for my liking; I still did the polite, expected universal response: "mmm, mmm!"

Berkay disappeared into another room. I felt a little anxious and on edge.

Berkay reappeared holding a record album. He announced a name as he put it on. I did not catch the name when he first said it. The music was a man's rich baritone voice, sung in Arabic. The voice was glorious in its power and resonance, and haunting.

I sipped the tea and bit the cookie; I sank down deeper into the sofa, taking in the enthralling music. The voice was trance-like. Just a few minutes ago I was tense, but now feeling utterly relaxed.

Berkay and I just sat on the sofa in silence. Listening. Just listening.

I felt contented and now at peace as the exquisite voice washed over me.

Time went by...

The bus!! I snapped to attention and jumped up. What time was it? I searched for a clock in my backpack and franticly unzipped the side compartment where I kept my cheap Timex watch. Oh, SHIT! It was 6:25!! The Tehran bus was to leave in thirty-five minutes. I could not miss this bus!

"Bus, Berkay, Bus!!"

He understood this time. I quickly drew a BIG "7:00" on my journal paper.

Berkay immediately got up and led me out. He took me by the hand, navigated the narrow dirt loose stoned alley ways. But it was too dark and dangerous to go faster. After just a couple minutes of this precarious walking in the dark, Berkay stopped and gestured for me to stay put. I stood in the blackness of the alley, questioning where did he go? Nearly five minutes went by, I was getting nervous. Berkay, where are you?

Suddenly a beam of light flashed. It was Berkay carrying a flash light.

With the powerful beam leading us, Berkay moved out at a quick pace with me right on his tail. Turning, twisting, the maze was even more dizzying at night, but soon we approached a main street.

My Timex said 6:50 p.m.

It went through my mind that this is Turkey, and if the past inconsistent false starts of the day were indicators, the bus might not leave on time.

We were on a main road, jammed with all types of traffic, I still had no idea how far away we were. Berkay stopped his fast- paced walking and stood in the road, as a bicyclist approached. He signaled the bicyclist to stop; and talked to him rapidly. The young man on the bike nodded; Berkay pointed me to get on the bike.

It was quite the balancing act to get on the small seat on the bike. Berkay held my pack as I sat side-saddle on the bike, while placing my pack over my shoulders. A quick farewell embrace with Berkay. We were off.

The cyclist was not the fastest, as he navigated the dimly-lit road for huge potholes. I wanted to scream: "faster, faster," but decided against this. The man was certainly doing his best, and doing me a great kindness.

My watch now said 6:58. Oh, please be typical, tardy Turkish Time Schedule (meaning "late"), I prayed to myself. The bike took a sudden turn to the right, I coming close to falling off the bike. A sharp turn left. It was the gate to the entrance of the bus station.

My watch was now 7:05. We were late. Please still be there. As we entered, a bus was just pulling out. I could not tell if this was the bus to Tehran, but we had to stop it to make sure. My cyclist was up on his legs now, peddling as fast as he could. He cut in front of the bus and read the "Tehran" sign. He jumped off and waived his arms to stop. I ran to the bus door, banging on it, as it moved forward.

The bus continued to move. I moved with it, still banging on the door. It finally came to a halt. I JUMPED ON.

I looked out the window, saw the cyclist standing there watching with big smile. I waved my arms fiercely shouting: "THANK YOU THANK YOU." I hoped he heard me.

I pushed my way through those standing, straining to see any of the Brits. From the back of the bus, I heard my name: "Scott."

Working my way back, Alex was in the midst of a heated argument with an older bearded Muslim man. The man spoke English and apparently the discussion was about Alex "saving the seat" for me.

I felt badly about the situation and asked the man: "Would you like to sit, perhaps we can share?"

His red fuming agitated face calmed down, and responded appreciatively: "You are kind."

So the three of us right there decided, it only fair that we each take turns standing in two-hour shifts. The way I felt now, so elated just to be on the bus, I certainly had no problem standing.

The "Tehran Express" is a 756 mile journey with an expected travel time of 13 hours and 44 minutes. I questioned the time, being fully aware of the travel problems in Turkey I experienced so far.

Pulling out at 7:05 p.m., and this being November 17, it was dark, and it was cold. There seemed to be NO heat at all, but regretfully enough power to generate the pounding, blaring Arabic music.

I was disappointed that the bus ride was at night, as I value seeing the land I travel on. Some travelers prefer a night journey, so they can sleep, but this is not the case for me. Alex had the map of Iran out, which included eastern Turkey, showing me the route.

Our Muslim "seat sharing" companion mentioned the Iranian border was about 200 miles away and it should take about four hours. He estimated we should be arriving around midnight. His name was Vahid. He was from Tehran, now living in Istanbul and going home to visit his grown daughter and her family of three children. He pointed on Alex's map to the village of Orumiyedh, where we would cross-over.

The road was straight and seemed in surprisingly good condition. There was little traffic, and we were traveling at a good clip, estimating about 60 mph.

Perhaps the "Tehran Express" was really living up to its name.

About two hours into the ride, right after I changed my standing position for Alex's seat by the window, and feeling assured that this was indeed a smooth ride, I felt a sharp swerve to the left, a jolt back, followed by a big thud and a jarring sudden stop. We were tossed forward, as everything in the overhead rack came tumbling down. Although it was certainly upsetting, no one on the bus appeared injured. The bus stopped and the lights came on.

What was happening? There was lots of talk among the passengers. Many of them were now standing up; moving forward on the bus to try to learn what was going on. The driver, a tall wirery, dark bearded young man, spoke something in Arabic; and disappeared off the bus. After about fifteen minutes of waiting and wondering what was happening, our Muslim friend Vahid went forward and left the bus to check with the driver.

Vahid soon returned: "bad news, the bus hit a boulder and damaged the rim of the wheel." He went on to say that the bus had a spare tire, but the rim needed to be replaced. The driver felt it would be sometime before this could happen, as it would have to come from Erzurum.

Even the driver was not sure when he could get the help he needed, but said (this being translated through Vahid) "to just sleep now, nothing can do." And with that the bus became dark, and the abrasive Arabic music was turned off. Thank God for small favors. Silence.

Well for awhile at least, as a couple hours later the axle fixed, on our way again, before another unknown mechanical problem, the bus limping into the town of Dogyubazit very late.

One reason why I called the bus the "Tehran Express" was because Alex, Nigel, John, Joe and I all wanted to get across Iran as fast as possible. Our goal was to get to Kabul, Afghanistan before the winter conditions became too severe, and the inland mountain roads to Bamiyan and further north to Mazar-i-Sharif became too dangerous for local transport to navigate; or even attempt to travel on.

These Afghani roads had reputations of being among the most dangerous in the world to drive on. In fact if we had our way, we would not even stop in Tehran, but have chosen to go straight across the country to Afghanistan.

This was not possible. We had to stop in Tehran to pick up the required visa for travel in Afghanistan. (Jocelyn, by the way, the young lady from New Zealand who was part of our original gang of six when we left Istanbul was no longer traveling with us, as she met up with a friend in Trabzon and was now traveling with him).

It's funny how things work out. The breakdowns, the crashing on the floor of the bus station, at first annoying, turned out to be a "blessing in disguise." I say that because when we finally boarded a "working" bus in Dogyubazit, the morning sky was a glorious pastel of colors as the sun began to rise.

After about thirty minutes of travel the bus stopped, and the Islamic faithful got out with their small prayer mats, and bowed on hands and knees in the direction of Mecca. The five of us got off as well.

It felt fantastic to feel the piercing icy wind in this wide open space. Behind me was Mount Ararat. This mountain, (17,000 feet), perfect in its classic volcano shape, with its snow-covered peak was a sight of extraordinary beauty.

On taking in its magnificence, I thought of my college friend Arthur, he of Armenian descent. Arthur had told me much of Mount Ararat and its cultural significance to the Armenian people, as up until the atrocities at the hands of Turkey in 1915, this mountain was part of Armenia. I took one last look at Ararat before boarding the bus. Between its beauty and knowing of its history, I was filled with awe.

Our bus soon crossed the Iranian border. In the early morning sunlight, the soil an amazing burnt red color, contrasted dramatically with the mountains on each side. But what really moved me, was out in this very remote desolate area, periodically, the bus would whiz by a hut or two with little children sitting dangerously close to the road. These huts made only out of mud, the children and parents seemed to have insufficient clothing and protection against the frigid weather conditions. This gravely impoverished scene played out, sadly, for too long a distance, as we drove across the harsh landscape.

The bus rumbled on non-stop, except for a brief lunch restaurant break. But nine hours later from the time of the bus being repaired, we now made our way into Tehran. The city, Iran's capital, looked huge with its urban sprawl and bustling crowds. It seemed a world away from the simple, stark conditions of the countryside. The city was situated in a valley, surrounded by looming mountains beyond. A layer of grayness hung over it. This grayness was smog, the worst I had ever seen. Joe, my American cohort from Southern California, joked that the smog made him homesick for Los Angeles.

Arriving in Tehran, our goal was simple: to get our Afghanistan visas as fast as possible and leave the city. So urgent was our time that we immediately headed for the Afghanistan Consulate, before finding a place to stay for the night. It was nearing 3p.m. We were starving and tired, but business first. We made it to the consulate just before its closing at 4 p.m. They informed us that our visas would be ready on Wednesday morning. Today was Monday. Not ideal, as we were hoping to leave the next day. But not too bad, as I have heard stories from other packers of a visa "for some unknown reason" taking up to a week to get.

The two days in Tehran were filled with the five of us taking in the top "must sees" in the city: The National Museum of Iran, and the Saadabad Palace, were extremely impressive; and the mind-boggling Bazaar, very colorful and entertaining! But the true highlight, (that is not the right word), the "most memorable experience," was an explosive incident involving me and an ultra-orthodox Islamic woman.

I was with Nigel walking on one of the busiest streets of Tehran, packed with all types of people. I was just commenting on how very pretty some of the Persian women were. Some of the women were dressed in the fashion of western clothes; others in concealing shawls with veils covering half the face. Others were completely covered in what is called a burqa.

The entire body and face are covered, except for fine mesh, similar to mosquito netting, to breathe. Despite the physical attractiveness of the women, we were well schooled and culturally sensitive to proper conduct to be reserved and respectful; and not act like a couple of sailors in town for a "good time."

As we walked down the bustling promenade, we approached a building which had a decorative mirror about three feet wide running vertically up the first floor of the building. A woman dressed in the black burqa, had stopped in front of me to look in the mirror to adjust her covering. I briefly glanced in the mirror to check my loss of weight. (I had not seen a full-length mirror in over a year). As I passed, our eyes made contact. It was fleeting. It was a mistake. The woman turned and slapped my face, and started screaming at me in Farsi (the Iranian national language), and shaking her fists violently.

I was aghast, totally shocked. Speaking English, I exclaimed, "Why did you hit me? What did I do?" My words meant nothing to her, and she only increased her wild ranting at me. I was terrified by her.

Soon our confrontation was being watched by the locals, as they gathered around the two of us. The woman just continued to yell. Her voice was a shriek, as she continued to wave her hands uncontrollably. I just stood there shaking my head in disbelief and repeating "WHAT DID I DO?"

In a matter of minutes the crowd had grown, forming a circle with me and the burqa-covered hysterical woman inside. There were some angry rumblings in the crowd. Tension was building.

Then a man, a very pious looking, middle-aged man, with a flowing robe and dark long beard made his way through the circle over next to her. She spoke emotionally to him, he speaking back. I did not know what they were saying, but I had an uneasy suspicion. There was no question that he was supporting her side, as he stared back at me accusingly. He moved toward me, only about six inches apart. I felt nervous but was determined to hold my ground, but not to over-react.

Nigel at this time, was standing on the side, but remained silent. This actually was a good thing, as he has a trigger temper. And at this tense time it was essential; we keep our "cool" and not do anything foolish.

This heated "conversation," now mostly coming from the bearded man, with an occasional outburst from the woman was directed at me. The crowd now was not only increasing in size, but the circle was growing tighter, as it pressed in on the three of us. I was feeling anxious and helpless as my continued pleas of "What did I do?" fell on deaf ears. Just stay in control I told myself, hopefully this will pass.

It was then that a young man in his early twenties, tall, clean shaven and ruggedly handsome stepped into the circle. He spoke in clear English, with a slightly clipped British accent, "What is the problem? Can I help? My name is Ahmed."

The bearded man and veiled woman started to over-emote, to loudly jabber at him. He gestured for them to be silent, and encouraged me to explain. I told him about the woman slapping me, as I passed her, and did not know why.

He was confident and composed. He had a slight smile, amused, as if he'd seen this sort of situation play out before. Ahmed explained to me that the woman felt that I was making strong "suggestive" eye contact with her in the mirror.

I responded with firm conviction, but keeping cool: "That is not the case. I did look in the mirror briefly, but the reason was to check my own body; which I was concerned about, because I had lost so much weight during my travels."

Ahmed returned to consult the other two nearby. He addressed the woman first, his voice calm in tone. She moved her head back and forth, as to acknowledge not believing any of it. After patiently speaking with her for about a minute, she just turned in disgust and briskly walked away, pushing through the circle of the crowd.

The bearded man now was confronting Ahmed. His tone was aggressive, almost growling. He abruptly disappeared into the gathering crowd of people who were watching us, and silently judging me. He gave me a threatening look, as he left, and raised his fist.

"Thank you so much, Ahmed for intervening. I was very upset and at a loss as what to do. I know crowd mentality can be explosive, and dangerous, especially for foreigners." He nodded his head reassuringly. He understood.

I asked him, if he would like to join me and my friend Nigel for tea. However, Ahmed said, "Sorry. I am in a hurry to take an exam at the University." I was impressed. I thought this guy sounds like "Superman." Saving an innocent stranger, a tourist, and now bounding off to take an important exam.

Before he left, he turned to us and said with upmost seriousness and concern: "Be careful. Tehran is going through a change. There is a strong extreme Islamic presence here that is over-zealous policing of what they consider bad behavior." With this warning, Nigel and I headed down the street with blinders on, being cautious not to look at a woman, or in a mirror.

That night in the snug confines of our frigid Tehran guestroom, we sat on the edge of two large over-used mattresses, bundled up in our heaviest warm clothes, eating ravenously of beef and chicken kebabs.

We were in a celebratory mood, as we looked at the map of Near and Mid East spread out before us; and realized that we had just surpassed the midway point of the overland journey to India.

The heavy penned line on the map, starting in Istanbul showed our route. Since beginning six days ago we had traveled 1,729 miles. We had 1,751 miles left to reach the India boarder. Or as John liked to say: "We have just five inches to go!" He referred to it as the eleven inch overland journey.

The travel from Istanbul had been exhausting, and each of us sporting shaggy first time beards (had not shaved since Istanbul) looked extremely undernourished. And yet each of us felt spirited and charged up for what we had seen and what lay ahead. Our final destination on the Overland trip was of course India. However, our most pressing goal, because of the threat of severe weather conditions shutting down roads, was to get across Afghanistan to Kabul as fast as possible.

The next morning we were up achingly early. The room was so cold that ice patches had formed on part of the floor. The "road" ahead of us (to Kabul) presented a pair of bone-jarring, endurance testing, icebox bus journeys; starting with the Tehran – Herat, 644 mile, twenty-one hour ride. A ride which was both enthralling in its majestic mountain land-scape; and heart-pounding, as in snowy conditions the dilapidated bus inched and creaked its way up, down and around over extremely steep icy passes.

This was followed early the next day with the Herat- Kabul journey, 712 miles. This journey simply put was brutal. It was a harsh, freezing cold punishing ride, with three breakdowns and taking an agonizing thirty-three hours. We were all in agreement that this was the most demanding bus journey yet.

But despite this misery, the terrain which the bus rattled across was awe-inspiring, and like none I had ever seen; endless golden sand dunes which ran on and on and on. I felt mesmerized as I watched an envoy of probably seventy camels slowly make their way across this vast and so remote land in the early morning light.

Each of our bodies ached, feet frozen, stomachs so hungry. We were burned out, fried, and completely spent. But as we reached the city limits of Kabul we were sky high and jubilant. Kabul, finally, we had made it!

It was here in Kabul that the five of us began to go our separate ways. Joe, needed to be in Delhi as soon as possible, so he left the next day. The Brits: Nigel, Alex and John spent three more days in Kabul.

For me, Afghanistan was an exotic place I had long dreamed of. It contained landscape that was rugged, remote, otherworldly. And the chiseled faces of the people, so powerful, especially the older men, so weathered, proud and strong. I wanted to explore more of the country.

I spent another two weeks in Afghanistan before heading into Pakistan: The infamous Khyber Pass with its bandits (our bus being shot at); the frontier "wild west" atmosphere of Peshawar; and the cultural riches of Lahore.

On December 5th I crossed into India.

Chapter 32

SRI LANKA : "PARADISE FOUND"

It was early on in my travels at a youth hostel in Belgium, that I first heard "Hikkaduwa" mentioned. I caught the name in passing as two backpackers were heading out the door. "Man, Hikkaduwa, what a place!" One of the fellows bellowed.

Then three months later on a crowded subway in Rome, I heard a woman's high pitched (sounding very nasal American) voice coming from the rear of the car: "Oh, you've got to go to Hikkaduwa and Kandy!"

As a traveler it was frustrating. I still did not know where these places were located; and knew less what made them special. This being 1977 the dinosaur pre-internet days, I had no immediate source to reference. But wrote a reminder in my journal: "Inquire about Hikkaduwa and Kandy."

Then almost a year later, it was a tea-house in Pakistan that I heard that name again. Three young male packers seated two tables over, one of them with a pronounced French accent say, "Such beautiful beaches in Hikkaduwa, and what about that tooth in Kandy."

Okay, that was it! Beautiful beaches, a tooth, what was going on? I needed in on these places. I approached them and apologized for seeming to eaves drop on their conversation. I admitted my ignorance and asked where was Hikkaduwa located. "We are talking about Sri Lanka, mate. A glorious place!

It's paradise," the Aussie exclaimed with authority in his strong Australian brogue.

Three days later I crossed the border into India at Amritsar, the Sikh pilgrimage city famed for its "Golden Temple." I would travel north to south making my way down the western part of the country, focusing on the states of: Rajasthan, Karnataka, Kerala and Tamil Nadu.

As I traveled, those who had been to Sri Lanka sang its praises of the vast white sand beaches, lushness, ancient Buddhist ruins; and how mellow and relaxed it was. "It is PARADISE!" That's the phrase that I heard over and over. Yes, it sounded heavenly, but I was cautious not to get my hopes too high as the last place that was deemed a "paradise" Taghazout, Morocco was a disappointment.

By the time I had reached Madras in the deep south of the country I had traveled India for almost three months. I found India the most fascinating, exhilarating and colorful place I had ever been. However, I also found India exhausting, frustrating and demanding to travel.

I needed a break from India. The idea of a "mellow paradise" appealed to me very much. I needed not just some "R&R." But a big dose of "S&L" – Sri Lanka!

From the south of India, via a three hour ferry crossing to Jaffna, in Sri Lanka's north; a seven hour train ride to Colombo, the capital (where I stayed the evening) and a two hour train ride heading south, hugging the coast as the aqua blue ocean unfolded . . . I arrived in Hikkaduwa.

On arrival, I immediately fell under the spell of its tropical seduction. The village enveloped in lush jungle vegetation with the ocean right at your feet. When I say "at your feet" this is in the literal sense.

My lodging was a small thatched hut, with one window, a floor of sand and a hammock tied between two towering palm trees. When the pounding surf was at high tide the water would surge onto the beach and come within ten feet of where I stretched and swung in my hammock.

But it was more than the sublime setting that made Hikkaduwa such a special place. It was the atmosphere, so relaxed, easy going, friendly. There were about twenty-five travelers in Hikkaduwa, several countries were represented, these being; Germany, France, Norway, Switzerland, Canada, England and even a man in his thirties from Oregon.

Without question the singular main reason why there was such good harmony and chemistry between travelers was that we all had something in common. And that was that each of us had arrived from traveling in India.

India, we all shared stories of our times traveling, from the most memorable fantastic moments, to hellish horror stories. We were all so crazy happy to be in Sri Lanka. However, we also knew that we eventually would be leaving Sri Lanka to re-enter India and this brought up colorful conversation also.

During the day packers went their own way doing their own thing. For me, my "goal" in Hikkaduawa was simple, to RELAX, RECHARGE and RENEW.

So each day my basic agenda consisted of; lie on the beach, lie on the beach and read, walk up the beach, walk down the beach, snorkel, swim in the ocean, take a nap. I achieved my goal with flying colors. I felt so at ease. My most pressing decision each day being; do I prefer fresh pineapple or coconut from the young Sri Lanka boy carrying both as he would cut it right in front of me on the beach.

Come sunset, all would gather on the beach to watch the sun dip into the Indian Ocean, as we would drink beer or pass around grass and listen to music (someone playing a guitar, or a taped cassette). The Eagles' "Hotel California" was especially popular.

Later the travelers would retire to one of the village's four small restaurants, named: Mamma's Cafe; Reef's End; Farmhouse; and Sun, Sea and Sand. Each serving up hearty, eclectic western dishes, such as: spaghetti and meatballs, grilled chicken, hamburgers, macaroni & cheese, French toast, and banana fritters.

The place had such a laid-back atmosphere, was so incredibly beautiful; it was a soothing, healing cure to the brutal rigors of travel in India. But it was also the type of place that was so seductive that you could easily wake up to discover you had been there for a month, then three months, then a year. Some did. I stayed five days.

Was this my "paradise?"

Glorious beach setting, delicious food, no stress, and even a long legged Norwegian blonde who inspired me to re-enact Burt Lancaster's lusty beach scene with Deborah Kerr in *From Here to Eternity*.

In one sense it was "paradise." But not completely.

On the sixth day I woke up and knew that I needed more . . . not more of "hedonistic" paradise, but more of "discovering" Sri Lanka. More discovering of the the people, the culture, the history. Hikkaduwa had so much going for it.

It was fun. But that pure pleasure was not enough for me. I needed more authenticity, more substance. I know many packers for whom Hikkaduwa was it! They would only stay in Hikkaduwa; they needed nothing more of Sri Lanka. But for me I found it too "internal," I needed more in finding my "paradise."

For the next three weeks I would travel freely, dividing my time between the beaches of the south coast and the verdant green mountains of the interior.

As stunning as Hikkaduwa was, the beaches further south I found even more so. The beaches wider, the vegetation heavier, these were the most spectacular beaches I have ever seen . . . and they were empty! I took my time, as I traveled the south coast's charming ocean perched villages: Koggala, Unawatura, Dickwella, and Weligama.

Sleeping on the beach at night and during the day trying to convince the local fishermen to take me out in their boats. They were friendly towards me, but they were clear that they did not want to take me out fishing. Though the fishermen sometimes allowed me to help them unload their catches of the day, when they would return in the early evening.

One of the fishermen I got to know was a young man named Supun. He was probably only in his late teens. He was tall, very dark, and attractive. His English was good and one evening he invited me to his home to meet his parents and younger sister to have dinner. The family lived in a simple thatched hut with a partial dirt floor. His father was a big man and exuberant giving me a big hug. On the floor was a blanket with an array of Sri Lankan food items.

I was instructed to sit down on the floor as they joined me. His father, who did not speak English, said something to him and Supun translated for me.

"Scott, my father wants to know if you have ever eaten Sri Lankan food before."

Although I had been in Hikkaduawa I ate only "western comfort food," so I answered, "No I have never had authentic Sri Lankan food before."

Supun, added quickly, "My father wants you to be careful, as it is very hot."

I responded back to Supun with a confident, reassuring attitude. "Tell your father not to worry. I have traveled India for three months and eaten their hot food. I love spicy."

Supun translated back to his father. And with that translation, his father, as well as his mother and younger sister started to chuckle slightly; as if they were in on a secret. They passed me a plate with a bowl-shaped pancake. This was called a "hopper," Supun informed me, and was one of the staples of Sri Lankan cooking. Inside the hopper was goat curry.

I bit into the hopper, acting "cool," in full control. I smiled at the family of four shaking my head, saying: "delicious, delicious."

About ten seconds later the BURN came. The burn was HUGE!! This made everyone laugh. The mother quickly handed me a prepared bowl of grated coconut, and instructed me to eat it to cool the burn down.

Make no mistake about it. Sri Lankan food is the hottest food I have ever eaten, and remains so today. As I traveled along the coast I tasted an array of curries bursting with heat, be it on fish, chicken or goat.

Leaving the coastline, I headed inland into the Central Highlands, an area of green lofty misty mountains, its uncommon beauty and tranquility I found especially appealing. Little villages in the Badulla District, such as: Ella, Bergala and Hapatule teetered on mountain sides.

The view provided two distinct breathtaking views; looking south the open plain ran to the coast, looking north was a sea of hills, hill after hill folding into each other. This view especially in the early morning in a surreal blue hue was magical.

The Highlands with its magnificent landscape and fresh mountain air was conducive to moving slowly. And move slowly I did. My goal was to get to Kandy, the ancient capital and largest city in the Highlands.

It was only forty miles, but I would take my time, six days, as I walked leisurely drinking in the bucolic surroundings and the genuine warm hospitality of the people. The local children with their deep rich dark skin, animated giggling smiles and gleaming white teeth would often follow as I walked, encouraging me to rest and come visit their home and parents. I would do this at times, sharing a home-cooked dinner and sleeping on their land in my sleeping bag, all which I found very rewarding.

As I walked, cars would caringly stop and inquire if I needed help or a ride.

I would smile and thank them and continue walking. However, one day leaving the town of Nuwara Eliya, Sri Lanka's highest elevated town at 5,960 feet, and known as "Little England" for its British Colonial "feel," a car stopped. I got in.

The man's name was Simon. He informed me that we were now officially on the Neuwara Eliya - Kandy Road, famous for its dramatic vistas, profusion of tea terraces and hair-pin- turns. Simon was probably about thirty, had curly dark hair, a slight beard and greenish eyes. He was open, gregarious and easy to talk to.

After about fifteen minutes he said, "I am turning in here, but you are welcome to stay with me and my family if you want."

"Thank you," I said. In the distance I could see a large impressive house setting atop the hill. The drive to the house up a private paved road was carpeted on both sides as far as I could see with bright green bushes.

"Tea?" I inquired.

"Yes, tea," he said matter-of-factly.

It was not until over two hours of being in his home, a very tasteful and affluently decorated home, that I learned that he was the supervisor of the entire tea plantation. He mentioned it almost with embarrassment. His wife, Heather, at least three inches taller, wore her auburn hair long; she was both pretty and charming.

They were both delightfully spirited, engaging and well-traveled. We enjoyed sharing comparable stories of cities in Europe, as I would sip tea and eat little tea sandwiches served by an official servant dressed all in white. It was such a pleasing environment, including my spacious room with a grand marble bath tub. Now this is sheer heaven I thought, as I soaked for over an hour; this my first tub in over a year.

That next morning I was planning to leave. Over a classic English Breakfast, Simon and Heather informed me that they were going to be gone for three days to pick up their two children in Colombo, who were staying with his parents; and that if I wanted, I could stay on the Tea

Plantation in their home. Heather, saying: "Scott, please do, it is so lovely and James, our butler, will cook and look over you."

Wow, tea plantation, my own servant to take care of me. How very special for a weary backpacker. "Thank you very much, Heather and Simon!

And so it was, for three days I had free reign to explore the tea plantation and its surroundings. I would go for long walks through the narrow pathways of the tea bushes, amazed by their manicured precision. Wherever you looked it was rolling tea fields everywhere. During my walk I would smile at the "pickers," all of them women. They would smile and nod, but not stop to talk.

In the evening I would retire to the plantation house. I was extremely well attended to by the butler James. He was a light skin Sri Lankan man about fifty with a distinguished well-schooled British accent. The dinner for each evening would be formally announced by James in the morning, following a hearty breakfast.

James always inquired if this was "satisfactory," and met with my approval.

"Mr. Scott, this evening the dinner will be roast pork tenderloin; would this be satisfactory?"

The following two dinners would include the British classics: Shepherd's Pie, and Beef Wellington. I let James know that I found the food delicious and made mention of it on my last evening with a nod of approval to British cuisine. As James cleared away the dishes, he said to me:

"Mr. Scott, don't forget the British were here from 1948-1972, and many of their dishes are still beloved."

James loved that phrase, "is it satisfactory?"

My stay so transcended "satisfactory," it was more like I was in "Hog Heaven!" I felt so "pampered", a word I can't recall uttering in the last year and a half of roughing it on the road.

Following dinner each evening, James would draw me a hot bath, and lay out a plush robe and slippers. He would suggest I retire later to the 'library.'

The library was a handsome, dark walnut-paneled room with floor to ceiling book shelves, housing leather-bound books. Especially impressive and of interest to me, was the over-sized illuminated world globe. A huge, burgundy leather wing back chair was positioned by the roaring fire, which James would dutifully tend.

I felt like I was on the set of *Masterpiece Theatre*, as James would inquire if I cared for Cognac, Port or Scotch; and pointed out the classical music record collection. I would be left alone, but about an hour into my library stay, a light knock would be heard and James would appear and ask politely:

"Mr. Scott, is all satisfactory?"

As I lounged, oh so comfortably, in the big overstuffed chair, sipping on my Graham 20 Year Old Port; as the haunting melody of the British composer Edward Elgar filled the library, I thought: travel is so amazing. Just ten days ago I was sleeping on the beach, and sharing the closeness of a simple fisherman's family. And now I am sitting in the lap of luxury.

I loved BOTH experiences! I whole-heartedly embraced both. This is a classic example of what makes travel so memorable and special to me. It is the unexpected, and the wide range of living that one experiences that is so enriching.

On my second day, walking about an adjoining tea plantation I met one of the local "cutters." The men cut the strong bushes, as the women picked. His name was Henry, about sixty, spoke some English and informed me that all the women who were pickers were Tamil, the minority who came down from southern India.

He was Tamil himself, and went on to say that the Tamil people were not treated well, and the women had an especially hard life. "If they don't get forty pounds of leaves picked each day, they don't even get paid." He took me to where the pickers and cutters live, in a long, communal concrete bungalow.

It was a very heart-warming experience to accept his invitation to attend their special celebration later in the day. This was a festive occasion, including their Hindu worship with sparklers; and even a Bollywood movie projected on a make-shift screen. After the celebration, because of the darkness, Henry and several co-workers kindly escorted me back to the property line of the plantation where I was staying.

Time had been passing so pleasantly, I could scarcely believe I had been in Sri Lanka nearly a month. And there was still more I needed to see. Because I wanted to travel longer, I had to return to Colombo to get my VISA extended. The country had an official rule: "To spend an additional month in Sri Lanka, it was required that you spend at least $3 a day." This I found difficult to do. I marveled at so much good living for so little money.

The next month I would travel across to the east coast of the country to Trincomalee, Sri Lanka's second largest city. However, my major focus was on visiting the antiquity and religious sights, which the country is famous for.

These included the ancient and sacred kingdoms of Polonnaruwa and Anuradhapura.

They both were remarkably well preserved and displayed an abundance of impressive ruins: huge bell- shaped stupas, temples; and palaces with ancient pools, and a reclining Buddha.

Anuradhapura contained "Sri Maha Bodhi," the oldest living tree in the world, Buddhists believed. A branch had been brought from the tree in India, where Buddha attained enlightenment in 245BC, and it was planted here.

I traveled north to Sigiriya. Known as "The Fortress in the Sky," and to many as the "Eighth Wonder of the World." Sigiriya is a huge block of granite set deep in the jungle, which rises abruptly (700 feet high) from the ground. Sigiriya contains one of the oldest landscape gardens in the world, and it is one of the finest examples of ancient urban planning.

However, it is the frescos that I found astonishing. The entire western face of the granite rock, which runs nearly 500 feet is covered in frescos. The frescos, estimated to be over 1,500 years old, yet were in excellent condition. The paintings are delicate, depicting beautiful, voluptuous female figures, called "Sigiri Apasara" (celestial nymphs).

Sri Lanka is 76% Buddhist. This is not as high a percentage as other south Asian countries such as Thailand, or Cambodia. However, devout Buddhists the world over consider Sri Lanka one of the foremost sacred destinations for worship. This can be especially witnessed in its pilgrimage sites of Kandy and Adams Peak.

Kandy is a charming city surrounded by dense green mountains. It is home to "Temple Of theTooth." This is where the Lord Buddha's tooth presides, as it is said was smuggled from India seven hundred years ago. My imagination was flying, what a tooth from the Buddha would look like. However, despite the colorful "pomp and circumstance," filled with energetic chanting and beating of drums, the actual tooth was never shown. Instead the tooth was inside a small case, within a large glass encasement, covered in jewels and flowers.

There was one last place I had to go. I was deliberately saving it for the end of my Sri Lanka travels: Adams Peak. Adams Peak is the highest mountain in Sri Lanka (7,359 feet), and is dramatic in its isolated setting.

It rises up alone from a jungle plain in almost a perfect cone shape. But what makes it especially important is that it is a sacred mountain, a place of heavy pilgrimage; as on top of the mountain resides Buddha's footprint. This is the belief of devout Buddhists. Tamil Hindus say it is the footprint of Shiva. And the Christian followers who make up 5% of the population, say it is the footprint of Adam.

Because Adams Peak was so important for me to see, I planned it so that I would see it at its best, during a full moon. On the night I went, arriving at the base of the mountain around ten o'clock, the night air was clear and chilly; the moon resplendent in its illumination.

It was crowded, but organized, and I with thousands of others slowly made our way up the narrow but well- defined trail. The trail contained large wide steps, and in parts the incline felt as if you were walking straight up a wall. I made good contact with those pilgrims that were positioned close to me, as we made the climb. Those coming down would sing to us, it being translated as: "We are blessed, we have seen Buddha, and you soon will be blessed."

It took me four hours to reach the top. Looking out, though dark I could make out the distinct outline of mountains. The platform at the peak was crowded with pilgrims. But it was not the overly- jammed; there was order and a controlled energy to view the "Sri Pada," the sacred footprint.

The wait was forty- five minutes, before I made my way up the broad steps which led to a walled enclosure of the footprint. The pilgrims were passionate, as they prayed and chanted and adorned it with flowers.

It was now about 2 a.m., and it was cold. However, I was not heading back down; but instead stayed on top, as the ultimate goal in worshiping is to be on top of the mountain at sunrise to see "The Shadow of the Peak." This referring to the distinctive shadow the mountain casts at sunrise on the surrounding plain.

I had struck up conversations with several Sri Lankans, all thrilled that I had found their country such a rich travel experience. From them I learned that the sunrise was expected at six o'clock.

I had four hours to wait, to sit cross-legged jammed in with other pilgrims on the cement platform of the mountain peak. As the night went on, it became colder. The wind was harsh, biting. To generate warmth we physically huddled together embracing each other. As the time passed from two hours more, to one hour left, there was demonstrative spirit among all, making the cold seem more tolerable. It was interesting that of the dozen pilgrims that were in my area: nine were Buddhist, two Hindu and one Christian. They all spoke openly and comfortably about their faith.

From the left side of the platform I heard a rising collective "ah," as over a distant mountain an orange glow could be seen. This was where the sun would rise. The pilgrims that were sitting were all now standing and focused in this direction as the sky turned pinkish with orange streaks. Everyone breathlessly waited. It seemed to take a while. Then an exploding sunrise! It was brilliant in its radiance. All around you could hear, "AH, AH," expressed by the pilgrims.

But, of course, there was more drama to come . . . within about fifteen minutes the "Shadow of the Peak" appeared. Down below off to my right, the well-defined shadow of Adams Peak, the mountain I sat atop appeared. There was a quiet reverence that enveloped everyone witnessing it...A magical moment.

It was overwhelming. And as I sat there, I reflected on the unforgettable two months I traveled Sri Lanka. I was filled with powerful heartfelt memories; and in awe of how a country the size of Sri Lanka (smaller than West Virginia) could posses such a diversity of landscapes and cultural riches. I began to slowly join the other pilgrims as I walked the path down, singing the "Blessed Song."

I indeed did feel blessed for discovering Sri Lanka . . .

My "Paradise" found.

* Note:

"Paradise," that is what Sri Lanka was like when I was there (1978).

However, then the tragic, horrific bloody Civil War. (1983 – 2009). The Tamil Tigers, a separate militant group, fought for their "independence," resulting in 70,000 deaths.

The Tsunami in 2004 on the east coast cost a loss of another 35,000 lives. It is heart-wrenching to think about the tragic cloud that had come over the country.

Let us hope now that peace will return for good to Sri Lanka, so others can continue to travel to this exquisite "Paradise."

CHAPTER 33

PALEMBANG – BUKITTINGGI AGONY EXPRESS (SUMATRA, INDONESIA)

I did not have to take it. It could have been avoided. But I just had to take it. The bus that is… the bus ride, or let me correct myself, the bus journey from Palembang to Bukittinggi on the Indonesian island of Sumatra.

This bus journey was not just another long ride on a bus in Asia. This ride was one of legend, the ride (journey) that all others were measured against. Time and time again, I would come off a grueling bus journey, blistered ass, feeling sick, cold, nauseous, but if my fellow bus traveler had experienced "The Agony Express," as it came to be known, the typical response would be: "Man, this was nothing. Just wait till you take the Palembang to Bukittinggi bus. Now, that is tough!"

It had gained mythical status among fellow backpackers. And any traveler who had been to Indonesia almost always was greeted with:

"Did you do the Palembang to Bukkitinggi bus ride?"

"How was it?"

"How long did it take?"

The bus journey which departed from Palembang, located in southern Sumatra, to Bukittinggi some 800 kilometers (600 miles) to the north on the island's west coast, was well documented to be made up of primitive rough roads, landslides, possible flooding, crazed drivers, and busses that constantly broke down.

Those that I spoke with who had experienced the journey were definitive and direct about their feelings: "brutal," "agonizing," "a nightmare," "terrifying." "Avoid it!" The record time for doing the trip was reported at forty-three hours. Although most I spoke with came in around fifty-two. And there was that guy from Scotland, though I had never met anyone who had met him. But his bus trip became one of lore, as it took him an astonishing 118 hours to do the ride.

But I did not avoid it…I mean how could I? As a traveler wanting to experience the most authentic, unusual and memorable experiences as possible, how could I let this ride, the ultimate bus journey, pass me by?

I could have easily avoided this trip, as my destination from Singapore was Lake Toba, a bucolic traveler's hangout, located off the coast of northwestern Sumatra. The logical thing to do would have been to take the short direct flight to Bukittinggi. But instead I opted to actually go out of my way, flying all the way down south to Palembang, just for the "experience" of this 600 mile "killer" bus journey.

Most would call me crazy, out of my mind, a masochist. But I can't help myself. I am in love with long Asian bus journeys! And when I say "bus," I am NOT referring to the special charter bus variety for pampered tourists, with dark tinted windows and piped in Kenny G music. I mean buses that the natives take, the local buses, which serve as a lifeline for the common folk; be it they live in the most remote mountain village in Nepal, to that hamlet resting on the burning central plain of India.

As a traveler, it is not just the destination. It is the process: the ride, the journey, those you meet, the landscape you travel, what you experience, and what you feel. And, yes, it is true that much of what you feel on a long Asian bus journey is discomfort and excruciating: be it the bone rattling roads, the sardine-crowded conditions, annoying animals, the stench, screeching music, dare devil drivers; and busses that at times become extremes of ice boxes or a sauna on wheels.

But for me, putting up with these headaches and discomforts is very much worth it. Not just because it gets you to your destination, but what you experience on the journey. On a bus journey, as almost through osmosis, an intimacy develops with the native travelers. You feel more of their culture, sharing food, drink, laughter or hardships. There is a bond that develops. And the contact is strong.

The natural beauty of the landscapes I have witnessed from my bus seat, with my face pressed against the glass, or in many instances leaning far out the glassless window, has been astonishing. For me, watching a new land unfold, as the bus rolls on, fills me completely with wonderment. There is something about how a bus hugs a curve of a mountain, or dips into a valley, that you feel the landscape more intimately. It becomes part of you.

The riveting images linger. I recall it all ... a creaky, battered bus slipping and sliding in the snow, as it grinds its way up an 18,000 foot mountain pass in northeast Nepal. And at the peak, the early morning light breaking on the valley floor, covered in glistening white crystals.

I recall... weaving in and out of the lush jungles and waterways of south India's Kerela and touching the banana leaves from the open window.

Or on the island of Luzon in the Philippines, our bus clinging to the narrowest of gravel roads, as the remarkable rice terraces fall directly below. . . Or Sri Lanka's southwest coast with its miles of uninterrupted pounding surf, the bus so close you can taste the ocean spray. All these breathlessly beautiful and at times perilous bus journeys never to be forgotten.

Arriving in Palembang, after my short flight from sterile, controlled Singapore, I discovered this city one of the filthiest, most chaotic in Asia. And I loved it! It greeted me like a smack in the face with its dirt, stench and disorder.

Although Singapore was a refreshing, change-of-pace respite I now sensed it was time to move on. I ached for the Asian freneticism and the bigger-than-life high drama in the streets. That is one of the true fascinations of travel, the various moods each locale can cast. And how each place and its people must be valued and appreciated for its own unique authenticity.

I had spent more time in Singapore than I intended. I had planned to spend just four days. However, I ended up staying eleven days. I met a delightful English girl named Emma. I met her ironically the next day following my horrific run-in with the nasty Singapore brothel. She was living in Singapore teaching French at a private school. It was the first relationship of any substance that I'd had in some time. So that was a welcomed pleasure. But even her lovely charms could not keep me in Singapore. The city was just too stifling. I yearned to get out, to hit the road again, and embrace the down and dirty delight of Asia once again.

In addition to my romantic interlude with Emma, there was something else I valued, that I left without. Despite my most valiant efforts to get the coveted "S.H.I.T." (SUSPECTED HIPPIE IN TRANSIT) stamped on my passport, I did not succeed. Even not shaving for four straight days, or crazily talking to a palm tree right in front of a police officer, I could not convince the authorities to condemn me a hapless "Hippy" and deserving of excommunication.

My departure time for the Palembang – Bukittinggi "Agony Express" was tomorrow at eleven o'clock. It was now 3 pm, my time was limited. I had to make the most of it. I needed my south Asian "fix." This meant hitting the streets, taking in the vibrancy, color and crazy madhouse atmosphere. I was like a man in the desert craving water. I was drinking in the unique, warped vitality of Palembang, which I cherished after uptight, sanitized Singapore.

To get the best panoramic perspective of the "scene," I positioned myself on this overpass with a huge KANSAS cigarettes billboard that ran through the heart of the city. From my perch, I looked down with appreciation on the manic circus and mass confusion below me.

It was an absolute nightmare of a traffic jam. But in some respects there was a surreal beauty, almost a ballet-like quality in the intricate rhythmic movement and patterns created: cars (mostly big old Sixties Chevys) inching their way against the on-going flow of bicycles, motorized scooters and rickshaws; while thin, stick-like men, crunched over, balancing enormous loads on their backs would zig-zag between the traffic; and still others would push and pull varied loads in wooden carts (a refrigerator, stove, car parts, and the most immense pig I have ever seen). This visual circus was accompanied by the cacophony of every type of discordant, blasting horn, screeching to be heard.

Now looking in the opposite direction, I could see the river, a tired, dull brownish color. Speed boats moored at its bank competed to take passengers across. To the right was an outdoor market, bustling with humanity. I could make out the open air shoe maker, a dentist and barber shop, all working their trade amid the raw garbage, piled five or six feet high. As the late afternoon light became softer, way off to the left a single mosque minaret was visible, silhouetted against the darkening sky.

The next morning I arrived an hour early for the eleven o'clock bus departure. The weather was humid, but not oppressively so. One thing I had in my favor, from a weather point of view, fortunately this was a good time of year to take the journey. It was not during the monsoon, and not during the hottest time of year. I was wearing a cool, cotton dark blue shirt and my only pair of shorts, tan and well-worn. I felt good. My weight was up to 141 pounds, still looking like a stick; but up nineteen pounds from the worst days in Burma.

Although it was early, already there were many people milling about. However, with my assigned ticket I could relax. I did not have to get anxious and do my usual jockeying for position for the preferred seat, or for any seat at all. My white paper reserved ticket had a small typed "48."

The bus, not surprisingly, was very colorful. Asian bus companies encourage and appreciate this decorative style, painted in vivid yellow, red and blue stripes, with the bold "ALS" letters on the side. Pakistani buses especially go to extremes in their décor. It is almost a rule that they have to resemble a glitzy Christmas tree on wheels. I noticed the bus was somewhat small in size. It looked odd. It appeared short, like a toy bus.

Those waiting to board seemed to be mostly Indonesian, with a small smattering of ethnic Chinese. It seemed strange that there were no young children, as if the bus, like a film, had a strong "R" rating. The youngest person I saw was a guy, perhaps seventeen, who seemed to be with his parents.

I did not see one Western face, which I actually preferred. Being a lone wolf by nature, I find I experience and feel more, and get more contact, on my own when traveling, as opposed to being with another Westerner, where you are apt to be drawn more into "things back home." Also, being on your own, others reach out more to you. They see you are alone, and it encourages better contact. Although I assure you, there are times when I do certainly relish the companionship of a fellow Western traveler. But this trip, the momentous Palembang-Bukittinggi bus journey, was not one of those times.

I was pleased and surprised when at 10:50 am. we were allowed to board. Will we actually be leaving on time? This was an unusual occurrence in south Asia bus travel. With ticket in hand I boarded. With number

"48," I knew immediately that I would be in the back. But please "No!" I hope not, but damn, my seat number "48," was not only two rows from the back, but right over the wheel. This was the worst place on the bus, the place for maximum bone-shaking misery.

Was it the luck of the draw that I got this unlucky number? Or did they save this special seat for the "gringo?"

There is an important thing to know about this bus to Bukittinggi, which made my #48 position on the bus all the more punishing. I had never experienced it before, but had heard about it from other travelers who had made this bus journey. There was much that was primitive about this bus, I knew.

But the most barbaric thing was that there are no seats, only benches with no backs. This was a sobering realization, as I quietly took my place on the bare bench. I was about to subject myself to a torturous bus journey for at least fifty hours with no back support. What made it more painful: I had been warned.

I was determined to document every detail of this bus. The infamous benches were made of wood, some painted pale blue, others a bilious green. There were seven rows of benches, fourteen rows in total, with about a two foot space for an aisle running down the middle. Each bench contained four seats, with the passenger's number printed on the bench.

Amazing! At eleven o'clock the bus turned on the engine. It lurched forward right on schedule! Outside the bus, friends and family members waved an enthusiastic send off. I leaned out the narrow window and waved as well, pretending to spot a family well-wisher. It made me feel good being caught up in the spirit of the occasion. I had a sense that to the locals, as well, this trip was regarded as a brutal ride, and the passengers needed all the love and support they could get.

On the road again! My backpack, like all the passengers' baggage, was stored on top of the bus. However, valuables as always, my passport and money, I kept tight around my waist in my money belt.

I took a quick overview of the passengers. The bus seemed full from what I could tell. One thing that I liked right away, that although the bus was full, it was not packed. So many south Asian buses are over packed to capacity: with people just crammed in; or standing and sitting in the aisle, and often with huge, cumbersome bags; and sometimes with noisy, smelly animals. This seemed more civilized. I was feeling good, almost buoyant. The paranoia had dissipated.

Yes! Bring on the Agony Express! We're certainly off to an auspicious beginning. Perhaps that forty-three hour time record will be beaten.

These positive vibes, however, were put on hold, as after traveling maybe just two minutes the bus stopped. It had blown a tire. The bus turned around and limped back to where we started. I recalled hearing stories of past backpackers who did the journey, that blowouts and breakdowns were so frequent, that it was necessary to carry a full-time mechanic, in addition to the two drivers who alternated at the wheel.

The delay lasted about an hour, as they struggled with the tire. During this time I noticed the ceiling of the bus. I was correct. The height of the bus was low; in fact very low. I could not stand straight up, as my head would hit the ceiling.

So it gave me time to introduce myself to my traveling bench companions.

To my left was a middle-aged couple, named Dong and Yi, certainly of Chinese origin. They spoke no English, but through some basic Chinese I knew, we communicated. They were living in Palembang, going to visit their daughter in Bukittinggi. On the very end of the bench sat a very old Indonesian woman. She was tiny, dressed in a colorful blue local costume that almost swallowed her up. I offered her a slice of orange. She beamed a grateful smile, showing her one tooth, and pecked at it like a bird.

Okay, tire fixed, we headed off again. This time just as we were out of Palembang, on the road for less than fifteen minutes, the bus stopped, turned around and headed back again. What was going on here? At this pace forget the speed record. It was more like the 118 hour record was in jeopardy. There was a suppressed mumbling amongst the passengers, but nothing more than that. It was as if they were well aware of the reputation of this bus trip, and were well prepared to be calm in handling any fate they were dealt. Whereas, Americans are more action-oriented, more "can do" types: What can I do to change things?

So again back where we started, the driver got off and spoke to an Indonesian couple with luggage by their side. He took their luggage, putting it on top of the bus. The couple got on the bus and sat in their place in the third row. What a system! I hope we are finally full now. If not, do we keep turning back to pick up more passengers?

For the next three or four hours the trip was quite pleasant. The road was smooth and the scenery lovely, with abundant lush green mountains.

Soon we pulled into a restaurant, supposedly to get some food, but the main reason seemed to be mechanical problems. During this time I did eat, regretfully. All the kitchen had left this late in the evening was a plate that served an orange colored hardboiled egg on rice. It was hardly edible. Unfortunately on this journey I would come face to face with the orange egg on several occasions.

I also spent the down time: sitting on the bus, exchanging words with my neighboring bench partners, the Chinese couple; and hanging outside the bus with the other passengers watching the mechanic examine the bus, as he crawled in and out beneath it. I also met two young Indonesian passengers, both guys in their early twenties, who spoke no English. They insisted on wanting to touch the blond hair on my arms. I let them to satisfy their curiosity. But when they gestured to see my chest hair under my shirt, I let them know that the show was over.

So now it was about eleven o'clock. According to my Sumatra map, we had traveled just one inch (80kms), yet we left almost twelve hours ago! Studying the map closer, our destination looked to be a full twelve inches, a foot away (700 kms). Ugh!

As soon as we regrouped, getting back into the bus, and started off, the orange egg resting uneasily in my stomach, we immediately turned off the paved road to a dirt surface. Instantly you could feel the ttthhhhdddd, as if a basketball were being dribbled inches off the ground. It was here that the real NIGHTMARE and AGONY of this ride truly began.

This ttthhhhdddd went on mercilessly for over an hour. I hoped that it would end soon. But no, instead of letting up, you could feel the pavement change to an even rougher more primitive surface. And the road went from bad to worse. You could feel the bus slow down and lurch deep into what must have been a massive gopher hole, and another, and another. BAM! The bus hit what must have been a loose rock, and sent me airborne, crashing my head on the metal ceiling.

It was dark and you could not see the road, only feel the lurching and shaking. You just had to hope that it would end eventually. But it did not end. It was unrelenting in its brutality. It remained this way for the next thirty-eight intolerable hours. I have traveled on many rough roads, this was nothing new. But what made this ride so exceptional, so punishing, deserving of being condemned as "The Agony Express," was the distance and duration of this unforgiving road.

For thirty-eight hours the bus rattled, rocked, rolled and jarred on. What made these bumps excruciatingly bad was because of the low height of the ceiling of the bus. I had to continually brace myself from my head hitting the ceiling. This was especially difficult at night, when I became exhausted, and it became increasingly hard to keep my arm up continually to protect me. When it fell down, needing to relax, WHAM! it would send me flying, my head whacking off the ceiling. Being tall made the challenge greater. Despite my best efforts to brace for the impact, I probably hit the ceiling with my head 15-20 times.

And it was not just my head which took a beating, but it was my back. I had sharp, shooting, unbearable pain from not having any back support. It was just a barren, wood bench. For relief I would alternate from bending over, to sitting up straight to every position in between.

Sleep was impossible. My eyes burned. And my stomach churned; the orange eggs were making me nauseous. Several times I would be forced to lean out the window to vomit. This was difficult in itself, as the constant bus jarring caused me to mostly vomit on myself.

I was not alone in my puking and misery. Many times the passengers were hurled from their seats. The bus stopped three times to administer aid to those that were cut and bruised from the impact of hitting the bus walls or floor. During this nightmare on wheels, the bus stopped, mercifully, four times for mechanical problems, and two other times to change blown-out tires.

There was absolutely no interaction between passengers during these thirty-eight hours on the bus. People just concentrated on survival, on bracing themselves against the violent jarring, on just focusing to get through it. However, each time now that we disembarked, there seemed to be a caring coming together, as if fellow survivors of something monstrous, we were all enduring together.

I especially would seek out some of the older people, who looked especially worked over, and offered them some fruit and water and much needed encouraging words. I quickly learned the words in their language for "bad" and "shit."

After being on the bus for a good length of time, I made an interesting observation. The two drivers had two distinct styles of driving. Granted, with these impossible road conditions, there was no driver that could give you a smooth ride. But one of the drivers was much more cautious and caring and seemed more concerned than the other.

The driver who seemed to have more compassion for his passengers and was more professional was tall, muscular and probably in his mid-thirties. He had a very nice, easy way about him. He spoke no English, but I understood that his name was Ismaya.

The other driver looked older and was small and frail. He wore a constant, disgruntled look, and smoked continually. He seemed fiendishly empowered by putting all our lives at risk. I called him "Little Napoleon."

When he made a scheduled stop at the town of Solok, several passengers got off, and there was now room to spread out. I had an entire bench to myself. Lying down, trying to sleep, it felt good to stretch out. I was holding my arms around the bench ready for the bumps, but they did not come. I began to think that the worst was over. It had been a nightmare in every sense, even more terrible than I imagined. But I was feeling, as I looked at my map, that we were now "home free."

It felt good to play back some grim facts in my mind, the "survival statistics" of the trip, as if it were the stats of a football game replay:

* 48 hours of travel over impossible terrain
* 5 tire blow-outs
* 4 stops for mechanical problems
* 7 "questionable" restaurant stops

* 5 orange eggs eaten and regretted
* 4 times vomited
* Stops for toilet break: not enough! (1 time peed in pants)
* 15-20 times estimated hitting head on ceiling

As the pavement improved, so did the landscape. And so did my spirits. We began to climb higher and weave around the bends in the mountains. The verdant tropical scenery was thrilling to see as I relaxed and took it in. Checking my map, we were only fifty kilometers from Bukittinggi.

I was feeling good now. The worst was over. Soon, probably in another couple of hours, we would arrive at our destination. I checked my watch. It was now ten o'clock. The journey was going on two full days. Right now was the 47th hour since leaving.

With the paved road this brought forth a sense of joy and happiness on the bus. One of the passengers brought out a guitar and started singing, and we all joined in. An older woman, whom I had not noticed before, stood up clapping and danced a lively jig.

My two new-found Indonesian friends were passing around their home brewed "Brem" an Indonesian rice wine as well. Yes, the worst seemed behind us, and all of us were in high spirits, creating a party atmosphere.

Sipping on the overly sour "Brem" which I normally find disgusting, but at that moment I was feeling wonderful and it tasted just fine! Though I was in a celebratory mood, I still was sober and sane enough to notice that our driver, "little Napoleon," was driving at a reckless speed. But what especially concerned me was he would pass the slower vehicles on mountain curves. These were blind curves, with no knowledge of what was coming. This frightened me, and after seeing what I was sure was going to be a head-on crash, I could take it no more. I went up to him and said, "What are you doing? Are you crazy?"

The driver had not heeded my warning. So I alerted Ismaya, holding out my hand and twirling my finger by my head to say, "This driver is crazy. Help me." He understood and I am sure was in agreement, as he went to talk to him immediately. But this only spurred "Napolean" on, and he defiantly drove even faster.

Minutes later, with a car in front of us, he started to pass it on a totally blind curve. At the same time another car came straight at us. Our lunatic driver swerved to avoid it. But he went too far, and teetered for a moment on the edge of the road, before rolling over, flipping twice hurling down the hill.

The experience was certainly unnerving, but it was weird, it seemed as if it were in slow motion. I was conscious of the bus flipping over once, and again, but during the rollovers, I just felt it is going to be okay. And I was okay, except for some bleeding under my eye. But there were others on the bus badly shaken up, bleeding and in need of assistance.

Crisis, it seems, brings its victims together. Soon I was consoling, comforting and helping those that were strangers before. I immediately checked on my "bench buddies," the Chinese couple, and helped them carefully and cautiously climb out of the window on its side, and guide them to a safe place.

I turned my attention to those most urgently in need, the old and infirm. Clearing the bus was a first priority. Both its unstable condition and the threat of fire were prime concerns.

Being one of the few young and healthy passengers aboard the bus, I was glad to join others strong and energetic; in carrying or assisting them out of the bus to safe seating on the grassy hillside, making them as comfortable as possible.

We gave them water. And cleansed and bandaged their wounds, with the limited first aid supplies Ismaya provided. But important medicine, too, was lots of positive reassurance that help was on the way; and a replacement modern city bus was scheduled to arrive soon.

It was three hours before the replacement bus arrived. Plenty of time to think. During this time, after making sure all my fellow passengers were well cared for, I felt like being alone and walked up a little rise that looked out over the valley. It was a pretty setting, so calming, yet down below was our wrecked, overturned bus. I felt very fortunate. The "Agony Express" could have had a deadly ending.

It seemed miraculous, that despite a lot of minor injuries, no one on the bus suffered serious bodily harm.

These people were amazing. This bus trip was tough alright. But so were its passengers. After the traumatic bus accident rolling over the cliff, everyone shaken up and bleeding, there was some quiet sobbing, but no screaming, wailing or hysteria or rage (or threats to call their lawyers).

These people were not strangers to suffering. They knew discomfort and disappointment on a daily basis. They were an undemanding people with low expectations and high tolerance for frustration. As a result, they were gutsy, adaptable, and exhibited a quiet acceptance of their unfortunate fate.

I had chosen this fate. I chose to take the Palembaug-Bukittinggi bus. I could have avoided it. Everyone had warned me: "Avoid it!" Veteran travel adventurers cautioned me. I took their words to perhaps be hyperbole or bravado: "brutal, grueling, agonizing, terrifying, a nightmare." They were wrong: it was worse.

So in retrospect, I asked myself: "Would I take the "Agony Express" bus trip again?" Would I subject myself to this senseless, life-threatening torture? Short answer: Yes.

Agreed, there would be no prestigious medal awaiting me. No Silver Star For Valor awarded me. But there would be deep satisfactions impossible to explain or describe to the sane and rational.

*   It was a consummate travel adventure challenge.
*   My coping and survival skills had been tested and found worthy.
*   We sense and savor life most in "contrasts."

Like beating one's head against a concrete wall, it felt so good when the bus stopped: safe, secure, free.

And so damn exhilarating to be ALIVE!

But would I take the trip a second time?

Short answer: No. That would be crazy!

When the replacement bus finally came, it was a modern city bus, as promised, with real padded seats with backs, windows with glass, a high ceiling and everything. We all slowly hobbled aboard, piling in a few at a time.

Thankfully, Ismaya, and not "Little Napoleon," was behind the wheel at the controls. I gave him a big, appreciative pat on the back. When the purr of the motor started, a ROAR went up from the long-suffering bus passengers.

As I sat comfortably right up front, the bus smoothly cruised the remaining two hours on a well-paved road, around the alluring landscape of northwest Sumatra. At 3:12 p.m., after fifty-two hours, the bus pulled into Bukittinggi.

INDIA: "THE AGONY AND THE ECSTACY"

Chapter 34

INDIA WEAVES ITS SPELL

Y ou can't travel India and emerge unchanged. India weaves its spell.
Mark Twain called it: "bewitching, bewildering, enchanting."
Understatement! There are no words to adequately describe it:
its multi-faceted, richly textured diversity, its tradition, color, staggering
beauty, and its spirited people.

Revered writers like Rudyard Kipling have tried and failed. India must
be experienced. Imperial England called it: "The Jewel In the Crown."

I call it: "The most extraordinary destination on my world journey."

There are many Indias . . .

The India... of elegance and grandeur. It dazzles: marble palaces
of Maharajahs, castles of kings and royalty, temples, fortresses, and formal gardens and fountains. Extremely impressive is its magnificent wide
ranging architecture: exotic and one of a kind, such as the Konark Sun
Temple, the bewitching ruins of Hampi, the erotic carvings of the temples
of Khajuraho, and of course the Taj Mahal.

The India... of crazy, colorful carnival street life. Its pageantry, parades,
processions and ceremonies with fireworks, brilliantly costumed people,
and extravagantly decorated elephants in full regalia.

The India ... of its sprawling crowded cities of Calcutta, Bombay,
Delhi and Madras, with their explosion of sounds and images. A booming
confusing cacophony of noises and colors bombard the senses. Radiant
orange, hot pink and purple saris dot the ceaseless sea of moving humanity. Jostling for position, they compete with livestock for space and garbage scraps. Pigs squeal. Chickens cluck. "Holy" cows wander aimlessly.
Rickshaws rumble. Barterers taunt and mutilated beggars plead.

Strident sounds of raucous laughter, boisterous shouting, and human
wailing fill the air. And the stark silhouettes of the silent, "unseen" Muslim
women, draped in layers of black cloth, vanish into the night.

Sensual delights delight: the Indian sitar; music and dance; and zesty aromatic foods. Smells delight and disgust: spicy, steaming Indian curries and fragrant incense intermingle with the stench of excrement and rancid garbage.

On the other extreme is India's spectacular array of diverse landscapes; from the pristine towering mountains of the Himalayas, and the idyllic beaches of Goa, to the sweeping dune deserts of Rajasthan, and the lush coastal waterways of Kerala.

And the other India . . . a place of sharp and cruel contrasts. The fortunate privileged and educated live well. The others, the masses, exist in grinding poverty. I had an opportunity to observe both worlds. Divided: so close but chasms apart.

The India . . . of many sources of outrageous fascination, from the annual Pushkar Camel Fair to Varanasi, the eternal city, on the banks of the sacred Ganges.

At sunrise the throngs gather on the ghats (stairs) to partake of its holy water.

It is here they choose to come to die, achieving instant nirvana, freeing the soul from the normal cycle of birth and rebirth.

And finally India is its people . . . Hindus, Muslims, Sikhs, Janists, Buddhists, Christians, form an intricate mosaic of religions and races. A country with twenty-one major languages, and one hundred and ninety ethnic minority groups. As a country they have made great achievements and progress, overcoming insurmountable obstacles.

As individuals, they are a remarkable people with an uncommon exuberance for life and an indomitable spirit, regardless of the harsh realities of their existence, their karma.

India is the land of Gandhi, Mother Teresa, Nehru, and the Indian poet Tagore, who wrote: "YOU ARE INVITED TO THE FESTIVAL OF LIFE."

India is the "Festival of Life!"

Chapter 35

THE HINDU PILGRIMAGE: ON BEING DEIFIED

Backpacking around the world, you never knew what to expect on any given day. But you could always expect something amazing in India, embracing "the sublime to the ridiculous." So extraordinary; I had to create a new word to describe them: "amazingness."

But on this day with the searing early morning sun of Southern India pounding down, I felt sluggish; as I ambled along the potholed road, which led to the dreaded Kattayam bus station. I knew bus stations always meant two things. Neither was good: endless waiting for late busses; and oppressive, curious crowds. What I didn't know . . . this was to be one of the most "AMAZINGNESS" days of my life.

As I approached the station, I braced myself for the unwanted attention I knew would greet me from the persistent locals. "Hello, you speak English?"

"Where you go my friend?" I heard, as two young boys, one on each side, tugged on my sleeve, showing me postcards.

A short armless man, holding his tin begging cup in his toothless mouth, danced before me. The disfigured beggar made odd disturbing noises and kept bouncing in front of me like a pesky mosquito that I could not escape. I would move faster and there he was. I would turn right suddenly, and there he was, jumping up and down like a human pogo stick, as he gnawed on his cup. But luckily there was a distraction, when two striking Nordic beauties with backpacks caught his attention. He was no longer interested in me, and off he went.

Instead of heading over to the busy ticket counter, I made my way to a distant, isolated corner and sat on the dirt floor resting against my backpack.

I felt at peace tucked away in my corner. I relished its quiet open space in the midst of Indian bus station chaos.

This spot on the floor felt nice, alone, unnoticed. But I wondered how many seconds it would take before I was discovered. Before a young man would sit next to me and ask with all sincerity if I was on "a government mission," or someone proudly tell me at great length about his "uncle Navin in California," and if I knew him; or some giggling school girls would request I "sing an American pop song."

The Indians, they would drive me crazy with their overblown attention to a foreign traveler. However, to travel India, to survive India as a traveler, you had to deal with this. Fortunately I was able to, as I kept repeating to myself the mantra: "They mean no harm; they mean well; they are just curious."

I found that the Indians especially enjoyed staring at you in gathered groups, most sitting on their heels. During long train delays, which there were many, these groups could grow to near one hundred people.

Some travelers I knew could not handle this, and would grow agitated. I have seen travelers angrily shout, curse, and even spit at the over-attentive Indians. Ignorant, arrogant behavior like this is not acceptable. It is rude and unkind. And it doesn't work. It only increases their interest and intensity level.

My style in dealing with Indians like this was to be easy, let it be, and just "go with the flow." Sure there were times I was not in the mood to talk too much, but I would always do my best to be civil. Other times I would make the most of the situation and not only communicate with the people, but make an effort to put on a show and entertain them. This entertainment was not juggling or a card trick, or tap dancing (although I thought of it), but what I called "Show and Tell."

The S&T, as I liked to call it consisted of two parts. Part one was postcards from my travels. This consisted of either showing only the best of the best postcards, a selection of ten, to the full collection of thirty. The collection that made the TOP 10 included: Paris with the sun setting on the Seine; the Alhambra in Granada; a bull fight in Seville; the Parthenon in Athens; Michelangelo's Pieta; India's Taj Mahal (this always brought out spontaneous yelps of patriotic pride); Fjords of Norway, the canals of Venice; the Matterhorn in Switzerland; and the Mona Lisa.

Please know that when I presented each postcard I did not just show it, and flip casually to the next card. Oh, no, I would take my time discussing each card with grand animation, as if I were a school teacher in the midst of a group of wide- eyed first graders.

"Oh, yes", I would say, "take a look how the sun plays off the river. And there that is the Cathedral of Norte Dame, so beautiful. Can you see why they call Paris the 'City of Love'?"

After a dramatic pause and direct eye contact. "Do you see it? Can you say 'Paris the City of Love'?" Amazingly, they would nod and repeat: "Paris the City of Love."

If the postcard display was the warm up or Act One of the S&T, the Final Act was "Photos from Home," and this especially stirred the emotions. "Photos from Home" was a collection of five to seven choice photos. Whereas the travel postcards garnered a curiosity of a far off exotic place, the "Photos from Home" captured the heart and created greater intimacy, as each person I addressed could relate to family.

There would be a special order to the photos from home, as I would show them, starting with general pictures of our house; one of the lake setting where our house was located; a picture of me on the baseball team; and one of the campus of my university.

But the two favorites that always generated the greatest glee, no matter what country I was in, was of course a picture of my mother and girlfriend. I must admit I egged on their reaction by being somewhat theatrical in displaying the picture. For instance, when I showed the picture of my mother, I would utter "mama", with great sensitivity and pretend to shed a tear and wipe it away as I said this.

And on the word "mama" everyone would seem to edge closer to me; or if in the back would move up, craning their necks to see the "mama." I would let loose with another impassioned "mama" and there would be some laughter; especially from the older people with a nodding of their head, as if to say "we understand."

I could guarantee that the photo of "mama" and how it was tenderly presented, and the sincere longing I had for my own parents brought me in amazing contact with mothers and fathers from all over the world. Often after presenting the "mama" photo, older people would approach me, and if they could not speak English, which was usually the case, they would pull on my sleeve and make a gesture of eating or sleeping (with both hands pressed together to the head) and I would be taken to their home. The world is big, with many languages, but the muttering of "mama" is universal, deeply felt and understood.

But the photo that was saved for last was that of the "girlfriend." The photo I presented was a close-up of me and my college girlfriend, looking our best to go to the Homecoming dance. Linda, tall and blonde, had an appealing all-American perky cheerleader look, which played especially well in far-off countries.

Whereas the photo of mama brought on a respected response, the "girlfriend" brought on absolute bedlam. Everyone wanted to get as close as possible to see the girlfriend. And when I showed the photo, hamming it up, I would put my right hand over my heart, pat it a couple of times and shake my head, as if being slightly forlorn. It is interesting when the photo of mama when passed around it was handled with reverence, but the photo of Linda, the girlfriend, was almost fought over. Because of the enthusiasm to view the photo of Linda, it was often torn and required repeated tapings to keep it in tact.

Today marked my fourth month in India. I found myself in a reflective, almost dreamy state thinking of the over 120 days spent in this country. I pulled my longi up to study my legs. My legs, never muscular, but before well developed, now took on the look of sticks. I could now sadly form a circle with my hands that would go around the thickest part of my thigh. Yes, India had indeed taken a toll on my body.

But despite, the hardships of the travel, the heat, the teaming crowds, the constant gawking of others, the filth, the living in rat infested rooms, the bouts with dysentery I had a deep love of this country. Actually, it was a love-hate relationship. But more love. No country had displayed such color, diversity, and life in the streets, and such an array of "amazingness." By that, I meant it seemed each day would provide something that just amazed me, and make me shake my head in wonderment. Yes, I was a long way away from home and Hickory Island.

Suddenly my reflective ways were jarred by the screeching of voices and banging of a snare drum. A line of about sixty Indian men, all dressed in white longi and painted with orange streaks across the forehead, paraded through the station. They were yelling something, which sounded like; "Ayappan, Ayyappan."

I pulled myself up from the corner to examine the commotion closer. It was probably a festival, a celebration of some sort. And it is this type of "happening" that is one of the major reasons why I find India so stimulating. It seemed a day did not pass that there was not some God or Goddess to celebrate, as only the Indians can celebrate with such noisy spectacle and color.

And what an incredible selection of Gods and Goddesses they had to celebrate. The three major Gods in Hinduism are: Brahma, the "creator" of the Universe;" Shiva, "the destroyer"; and Vishnu, "the preserver." And beyond the big three, how many Gods are there in India? I have asked this question of many Indians and the figure ranges from 1,000 to a staggering 100,000 deities.

More and more Indians continued to flow into the station. All dressed the same, and chanting over and over "Ayyappan, Ayyappan." Some carried a large picture of a deity. The picture appeared to be of a young man sitting in a lotus position, covered with beads and holding a bow and arrow with a rainbow over his head. The station now was swarming with worshipers, the atmosphere heightened in its excitement. There was something about the procession that seemed more than just a passing "festival du jour," as each of the Indians seemed to carry extra belongings, as if they were going on a trip or perhaps a pilgrimage.

I was persistent, but still could not get an answer as to what was going on. Then a bus arrived. The Indians, who had been somewhat contained in one area now scattered running to the bus. In classic Indian transport fashion, they attacked it.

I did not even bother to inquire where it was headed. Who cared about the specific destination? To me it was obvious that the "destination" led to a place obviously with heightened spiritual significance that aroused fervor and passion. So off I dashed to the bus, throwing myself in with the wave of humanity, as I twisted, dipped and wiggled my skinny frame pressing through the small door opening.

I felt relieved that I got on the bus, as those that did not jostled angrily below. I could see the ticket collector forcing his way through the bodies on the bus. Soon he was in front of me and snarled, "Ticket, ticket."

"I have no ticket", I said searching for some rupees in my neck wallet, which was held by a string underneath my shirt. "How much?" as I presented him a wrinkled ten rupee note.

"No, ticket, OUT," he ordered.

"How much?" I asked again.

"No you OUT!" He grabbed my arm and started to pull me. He was determined to get me off the bus despite the money I offered.

Some man behind me, I could not tell who it was as it was so crowded I could not turn around, seemed to be shouting at the ticket collector. I could not understand what they were saying. It looked fairly heated as the ticket collector waved his arms about angrily and continued to bark. Glaring at me with a very pissed-off expression, he snapped the ten rupee note out of my hand, and surprisingly gave me two rupees back. Muttered something and pushed deeper in the bus to collect tickets.

I caught the eye of the man who assisted me, and said in English "thank you," followed by a "namaste." Because of the number of people I could scarcely see him, but he looked to be young, in his mid-twenties and had a neatly shaved beard.

Now, on the bus, pressed in, ticket in hand, the bus began to roll. What experience would this lead to? What was I going to witness? Being a veteran of many Indian jam- packed busses and trains, I could handle the press of bodies okay. However, because of the large exposed boil on my foot, which I acquired from unwisely swimming in the Ganges in Varanasi with an open cut, I had to be careful not to put much weight on it; or get stepped on by an over -zealous pilgrim. My flimsy footwear, consisting only of a cheap pair of rubber Indian sandals gave me no protection.

The bus ride was not long, about an hour. When it arrived the station was flooded with pilgrims, super congested. I had lost sight of the man who had helped me on the bus. Finally after about ten minutes of just standing in one spot and scanning the station, I saw him about thirty yards away.

He was surrounded by three older men engaged in an animated conversation. When these men left, I slowly approached him and said: "Thank you for helping me on the bus. I appreciated that."

He smiled and said: "Oh, no problem, those conductors can be difficult at times." He went on to ask: "What is your name? Where are you from?"

"My name is Scott Stone. I am from the United States." As I reached to shake his hand, he said: "I am Dakshi."

Looking at him now close up I felt certain he was in his twenties. With his neatly trimmed beard he looked rather bookish. His face seemed sensitive, and open. He had a gracious way about him. Even when he asked where I was from, one sensed he was genuinely interested.

"Dakshi, can you tell me what is going on here? Is this a pilgrimage of some kind?"

He became quite demonstrative, as he answered: "Yes, this is a pilgrimage for Swami Ayyappan. You are very fortunate to be able to take part in the pilgrimage, if you can."

Feeling good that I had someone that I could talk to who could explain what was happening, I pressed on with questions. "Is this the beginning of the pilgrimage here? How do I take part in it?"

"Scott, it makes me happy that you have expressed interest in Ayyappan and the pilgrimage." I brought out an apple and cut it in half and shared it with him. He gestured to a cement slab where we could sit. He began to share with me the details of Ayyappan and the Hindu pilgrimage.

"This pilgrimage, the Celebration for Lord Ayyappan, is one of the most famous pilgrimages in all of India. This is my seventh pilgrimage to Ayyappan, and every year it has brought me more inner beauty and harmony." His face became calm as he spoke. But at the same time it glowed with a special radiance. He explained that there would be probably thirty lacks, this being three million Indians taking part in the pilgrimage. And on January 14th the pilgrims would gather at a temple called Sabarimala, where between 6:00-6:30 p.m. a magical light called the Jyothi would appear in the sky.

He continued explaining that after January 14th, the date that the pilgrimage reaches its climax, the next sixty days following there are many restrictions: No sex or physical contact with women; eat only fruit and vegetables; bathe twice a day; no shaving of facial hair; must sleep on a hard surface with no pillow.

As I looked around, I noticed there only seemed to be men, and asked if women were allowed on the pilgrimage.

"Only women that are not fertile, or girls before age twelve, and those over fifty are allowed," Dakshi responded.

The bus arrived in Erumeli after a short ride of about thirty minutes. The atmosphere was electric. There were thousands of pilgrims converging. Music blared. Loud speakers with urgent announcements crackled. Many of the Indians were dancing, prancing, jumping and shaking wildly. They were dressed only in their longis, with no shirt, and with an inflated balloon wrapped around their head. The balloon was about an inch in diameter. It stuck straight out in front, resembling the shape of an erect penis. It was a comical, clown-like, extremely colorful sight and carnival atmosphere.

Following Dakshi, and his companions, whom I had not met yet, we turned the corner of the bus station. And there, as far as I could see, masses of pilgrims were gathered. Many were stretched out, resting, some praying, some setting up tents, and rolling out sleeping bags for the night. The surreal sight took my breath away.

What incredible adventure was about to unfold I asked myself. I was in their hands, and we walked carefully between the hordes of pilgrims that had laid claim for their spot to rest. It was so crowded that we had to step over people who sat or slept on straw mats; often going right over their bodies and plates of food. Despite the close quarters and everyone jostling about, there was an understanding and ease about the cramped conditions.

After about half an hour of weaving our way amongst the masses, we found a small space between a tent and a couple of blankets.

As we all sat down; Dakshi officially introduced me to his friends. One named Romakrishna, about thirty, was short but had a strong -looking body. His skin color was very dark. He seemed on the quiet side, but spoke excellent English.

Next to him was a somewhat older man, perhaps mid-forties with slightly graying hair. His name was Musthoul. He was warm and friendly, as he welcomed me with a broad smile and hearty handshake.

He added with a laugh, "sorry, my English is not good." Dakshi proudly added: "Musthoul has been on the pilgrimage twenty-one times."

Musthoul seeming to appreciate the kind comment; looked at me with folded hands and said: "Scott, pleased you are here."

Dakshi turned and gestured towards another man about ten feet away, and said with a reverence, "Scott, this is our Chief."

"Chief?" I asked, genuinely confused.

"I think in America you might know the word as 'guru' better," Dakshi added.

The chief's age was hard to tell. His face was weathered but not old. Dressed in orange, his dark hair was piled high on his head, with a tiny gold spear going through it. But mostly it was his translucent green eyes that created a mesmerizing aura about him. When you imagine what a guru should look like, he was right out of Hollywood central casting.

I was not sure how I should address him. I thought of dropping to the ground to touch his feet, as I have seen Indians do in the presence of a holy man. But instead I opted to fold my hands together, and in the most pious way, offered him my most sincere "namaste."

The Chief looked at me directly with those otherworldly penetrating green eyes. But he said nothing. His face showed no emotion. He turned his head and gazed out into space.

Peeking out from behind the Chief, was a young Indian girl about ten years old. Her name was Pandit. Her shyness broke into giggles as I introduced myself.

The Chief continued to look off in the distance as if in very deep thought. I wondered what he thought of me. Did I make a major faux pas by not touching his feet? If he doesn't like me, will this be bad karma for me?

My self-preoccupation was interrupted as Romakrishna asked, "So are you going to join us on the walk?"

I looked at Dakshi who nodded and said, "I hope you do. We plan to sleep here tonight and leave early tomorrow morning."

Musthoul said something in Hindi to Dakshi and Ramakrishna. They talked and laughed a little between themselves. Dakshi looked at me and said, "I want to make sure you are aware that the pilgrimage will be a walk of fifty-two miles through the jungle and mountains. It is not an easy walk, and takes good strength. We will do this in four days." At the same time Musthoul was gesturing with his right hand the motion of climbing up and down, as in the mountains.

There was quiet. I looked out across the pilgrims to the high sloping green hills. I had no hiking boots. It would have to be done in my rubber sandals. It would be difficult. The three of them were looking at me. The little girl, Pandit, was smiling. And the chief had his back to me, as if lost in more deep thought.

I felt excited about the idea of taking part in the walk. But with the weak state I was in and having just the flip flops to walk in, and my nasty boil, I questioned my physical ability to do it. I was not sure.

Dakshi looked at me and said, "Scott, because we are doing the same walk that Ayyappan did, you have to do the walk as he did; and that is you have to walk with no shoes."

What, no shoes? My initial thought was they might be testing me, playing some type of joke on me, humiliating me: you know, hey it's his first pilgrimage; let's tease him a little and see how he responds.

"Barefoot, really?" I questioned.

Dakshi looked at me seriously and nodded "Yes" with finality.

My mood had changed from questioning if I would do it; to I don't want to take part. I am sure they could read my doubting expression and the three of them moved closer to me. They each looked at my extremely skinny feet, their eyes focusing on the one with the disgusting boil. The three began speaking in Hindi again, and I could sense they were reconsidering my difficult situation, and feeling sorry for me.

The Chief then broke away from his far-off gazing fixation and came forward. He moved close to me, probably only four inches from my face and fixed his stare in my eyes for what seemed an uncomfortably long time. He slowly moved down on his knees and examined my feet, with special attention on my boil. He had his face so close to the boil, that I could feel his breath. He stayed down there for a good minute, looking at it from various close angles. He moved his hands over my feet, first slowly, then quickly, back and forth, as if he were putting a magic hocus-pocus on them. I was starting to feel uneasy. Finally, he rose up and faced me. He solemnly stared at me; once again with no expression and softly touched the top of my head twice. The Chief nodded to the others.

What was going on here?

Musthoul, who claimed he spoke just a little English, expressed himself well as he said: "The Chief says he knows the journey will be difficult, but you have a special blessing from him. He wants you to know that Lord Ayyappan will be looking over you to guide you, and to make the walk safe and your journey possible."

I was feeling the pressure. Here the Chief does his "thing" and blesses my foot, guaranteeing the fifty-two mile walk with no shoes will be smooth sailing.

All eyes were expectantly on me. I looked at Dakshi. His face was relaxed with a soft smile. Musthoul and Romakrishna were nodding their heads about in that classic confusing Indian fashion, where you can't tell if they are nodding for yes or no. Cute little Pandit had a huge grin on her face. The Chief had now returned to his distant gazing.

I took a quick glimpse at the surroundings, a sudden feeling of invincibility poured through me, I yelled with arms raised, "Hell with my foot, I'm ready to walk!"

Now all arms were raised cheering for me. The guru looked up at me with a slight nod.

Dakshi was clapping his hands and said in a joyous tone, "Let's go dance now!"

I was not sure what he meant by dancing, but I eagerly followed along and was told that we all must strip down to our underwear.

We walked into the village. The narrow main street was jammed with pilgrims, most looking similar to us only in briefs. At a store front, we jostled with other pilgrims in buying colored chalk, some branches of leaves, a balloon, (the funny shaped one that I saw before) and some vegetables.

Musthoul showed me how to apply the colored chalk, spreading it all over the body freely, the colors being red, blue and yellow. There was no set pattern just be as colorful as possible. It was fun joking with Pandit, as we applied the chalk on each other. I put on my penis- shaped balloon around my head. All of them laughed. I felt that I must have looked very silly.

Those branches that we acquired, what do you think we did with them? Campfire? Heck no, we stuck the branches in our underwear, as instructed. Ramakrishna explained to me that some of the branches were to be held and waved about as I danced. And the vegetables we purchased were put in a small bag they provided, and attached to a long pole that the pilgrims carried.

Moustal came up to me, and taking a strand of beads off his neck, he placed them around me. "Scott, these are the beads that are to be blessed for Ayyappan. You should wear them during the pilgrimage."

I thanked Moustal and touching them closely, brown in color, I noticed that Dakshi and Romakrishna wore them as well.

The dance we were going to take part in symbolically dramatized the story of God Ayyappan. When he was in the woods hunting and he could not find any food, he ran into a Muslim God, who helped him, and they became close friends. And because of that meeting, as I was informed before, to this day the Temple of Sabarimala is the only temple attended by both Hindus and Muslims. The dance was to represent his hunting in nature.

I noticed that many of the pilgrims carried knives and spears made of wood and danced in an extremely frenetic way, jumping up and down, and shaking their bodies to the nonstop pulsating beat of the drummer. I could make out this loud chanting as the dancing continued. It was hard to tell what it was, but sounded like "Swami inot go" "Swami inot go" "Swami inot go." This phrase was repeated over and over accompanying the dancers.

As we were swept up into the jostling dancers, we as well began to shake and dance about. The intensity of the music felt natural to join the wild scene of the dancing line. As we danced on, with non-stop music and chanting we approached a temple with gaudy flashing lights.

On top of the temple there was a statue of Ayyappan sitting on a tiger with an umbrella over his head. We entered the temple dancing about with the other pilgrims, carefully dancing backwards, as we exited.

The dancing around the temple had become even more crazed than before. Some pilgrims were becoming out of control, with spastic movements, as they squirmed and waved their branches about. I noticed one young pilgrim laying flat on the bank of the river. His eyes were rolling about and his mouth frothing almost as if he had been on a drug overdose.

We crossed a small wooden bridge jammed with the colorful dancing Indians. Below hundreds of Indians swarmed about bathing in the muddy river waters.

We soon approached a larger temple. We continued to dance around and then circled back still dancing, and all the time chanting:

"Swami inot go."

"swami inot go."

Now back in front of the temple we joined the screeching, hysterical masses of pilgrims, as we took our penis-shaped balloons and broke them with our hands.

Then grabbing our branches, we took off the leaves and threw just the branches on top of the temple. It was an outrageously colorful and festive "happening."

The entire top of the temple was covered in green branches and balloons which we also tossed up as well. The ground was covered thick with the leaves from the branches; where hundreds of pilgrims stretched out face down in front of the temple, praying with loud moaning.

In the crush of pilgrims I lost sight of my comrades for a few minutes. During this time several pilgrims would approach me,

"What are you doing here?

Where are you from?"

I heard, "Scott," and saw Dakshi waist deep in the water waving to me to join him.

"You must be clean, wash away the bad for Ayyappan," he said, as he dunked his entire body underwater.

The little river was crammed with hordes of pilgrims. It looked dangerously polluted, and if I had come directly here from the States, there would have been no way I would have gone in that water.

But this was India and I was well aware of the sacred significance of water to Indians. Having bathed in many Indian rivers, including the holiest of holy the Ganges, in the holiest city of all Varanasi, which contained carcasses of both floating people and dead cows; this in comparison was like jumping into a sanitized swimming pool of purified sparkling water.

Totally into the spirit of the moment, I freely submerged myself four times. With folded hands I prayed going back to the temple; then turned and faced the late afternoon sun. Closing my eyes, the sun, now felt warming, not hot. And the "sounds" of the pilgrims were enthralling.

Dakshi and I joined Ramkrishna and Musthoul on the banks. Dakshi said, "We go back to our campsite now." We headed across the wooden bridge and through the village with the masses of pilgrims.

The atmosphere was quieter now. The respite from the ferocity of the few hours felt good. This provided me with an opportunity to ask Dakshi a question which was on my mind.

It concerned the Chief.

"The Chief seems like an amazingly deep profound man." I said.

With that Dakshi stopped walking, leaned in closer to me and said, "To us he is the closest to talking to God."

I mulled this over for a few seconds, looking around, before I responded, with the most sincere tone I could muster asked,

"Is there a reason why he seems so quiet? I have never heard him say anything. Nothing at all."

Dakshi made an odd face then responded, "It is because the Chief has taken a vow of silence not to speak."

"Not at all?" I inquired.

"Nothing, he has not said a word for over four months," Dakshi replied.

I shook my head in confused amazement.

He added gravely: "They say his first word spoken, if he is angry with you, has the power to kill you."

I could just envision the Chief unleashing his first lethal "word" on me: "Ugly American!"

I am sure I looked freaked out from hearing about the power of the first word because Dakshi added, and I am glad that he did as it made me feel more comfortable:

"Believe me, the Chief thinks good of you, and is moved by your involvement with Ayyappan."

We started to walk, the Chief was still on my mind.

I stopped and asked Dakshi another question:

"If the Chief can't speak to you, how do you receive this wisdom from him?"

Dakshi shook his head and looked disappointed by my question.

"That is regretfully the typical western response," he said. "You must understand that words are not important. They are not needed in his presence. You sense his knowledge. You feel his wisdom. You grow from this."

We headed back in silence.

The sky was getting softer in muted colors of pink and purples. As we walked to our campsite, you could see the little campfires starting. I was starved and delighted to see two men busily cooking. They were older and also much heavier, with a comfortable, generous layer of fat running above their longi. They also looked just like each other.

"Scott, this is Navin and Domshel. They are twins and very well known as the best cooks in the valley."

They both smiled broadly; Navin gestured with a theatrical patting of his stomach that it was time for dinner. And their reputation certainly proved correct, as they served up a very tasty rice and vegetable dish with a delicious pepper sauce, eaten on the ubiquitous large banana leaf, which is so common in southern India cuisine.

Our entire crew was now enjoying the dinner serving, even the Chief whom I had not seen all day had accepted the food, and responded with a nod. We sat in a small circle, the Indians so at ease sitting cross- legged.

Pandit giggled in my attempts to sit in the lotus position. As I stretched one leg on top of the other, and it feeling absolutely uncomfortable, I admitted my lack of flexibility. I made fun of myself, falling over in a backward somersault, delighting the young girl.

I noticed two pilgrims, both young possibly only in their late teens and very dark, achingly thin, standing hesitantly over to the side watching Navin stir the cooking pot.

Musthoul whispered to me, "Very poor. Ayyappan always say must help others." He gestured that they sit down, where Navin served up two heaping hot plates to the pilgrims, who gobbled down the food.

Following dinner I spent some time sitting on my sleeping bag writing in my journal by candlelight, when Dakshi came over and offered me a cup of tea.

He sat on my sleeping bag close to me.

"Did you enjoy today?" he asked.

"Enjoying is not the right word. It was a day like none I have ever experienced."

Looking serious, he asked, "Do you feel Ayyappan?"

To be honest, I didn't really know what I was to feel, and how to answer this. But I replied: "His spirit seems all around us," which was certainly true.

He caringly patted my shoulder and got up to leave, "I am very glad you are here. And believe me Ayyappan is very happy with your presence also."

It was 10p.m. and wherever you looked you could see the little fires burning and hear the chants of "Ayyappan."

Lying on my sleeping bag I just gazed up at the sky. It was packed with more stars than I had ever seen. I let my mind wander over the past day and all the impressions that I witnessed. Today was indeed a day filled with big time "amazingness." I felt blessed I was here.

The dawn broke. The sky a streaky orange was visible through the mist. Off to my left I could see a long line of pilgrims stretching for at least a half mile, moving in a slow close forward motion, as if they were tied by one string.

The pilgrims were beginning their solemn, sacred walk. As the line snaked its way ever onward, the pilgrims almost all dressed in white longi, all barefoot, marched with the same prayerful posture of the hands on the head, supporting the "gift" for Lord Ayyappan.

There was an undeniable beauty to the scene. And now it was our turn to join the line. To begin the fifty-two mile walk for Lord Ayyappan.

I looked down on my foot, it looked worse; the boil seemed even bigger and more inflamed. But at this moment, I determined that Ayyappan would give me the strength needed to complete the pilgrimage.

Off came the flip flops and we began our walk.

For the first thirty minutes on a surface that was fairly soft and level my feet held up okay.

We soon began to climb steeply; the narrow rocky path filled with pilgrims each walking carefully over the loose rock surface. It became painful, but I pressed on, I could do this.

But about an hour into the walk, I slipped badly and my bad foot gashed open with a deep cut. All my friends stopped and called for one of the many Marshals along the way for assistance. I was told by the marshal that my cut would need ten stitches and I should stay off the foot for a few days.

It was a unanimous decision that my foot was in too serious a condition to continue the entire walk. I was devastated.

Dakshi, came forward comforting me and said, "Scott, there is a shorter six mile walk to the temple that you can do."

A happy amazement surged over me.

He went on to say: "on the fourth day of our trek we will pass through a nearby location called the Information Center that you can get to by bus. We can all meet there and walk together. You can get four days of rest. It will be January 13th, say at 3p.m."

They all seemed to agree that the shorter route probably was best. I hugged each of them, and let them know how much I was looking forward to our reunion in four days, and wished them safety in their walk.

It was then that the Chief came forward. I was nervous from yesterday's conversation that he might let loose with a lethal word.

I tensed up as he walked toward me. But instead his face looked sympathetic and comforting in some way. He handed me a small orange, about the size of a golf ball. He put it in my palm and closed my hand around it.

I, with folded hands, bowed to him.

Dakshi said, "This is very meaningful what the Chief has done. This is the sacred fruit. Always keep this and the feeling of Ayappan will always be with you."

Without my friends, for the next three days staying in this congested base camp was a test in too much Indian "attention." I would miss my new found friends. Their kindness and teachings about the Ayyappan pilgrimage gave me much greater insight. Their being with me also served as a protective buffer from the compulsively curious Indians.

From my long stay in India I was accustomed to the excessive attention from the India people. But here at the pilgrimage, this "attention" had reached a new level of intensity.

It was unnerving. On my first morning I woke up in my sleeping bag to find six Indians looking straight down at me. They were leaning over me, focusing in as if I were a breakfast buffet being examined.

When I raised myself up I could see that behind these six was a crowd that looked four or five deep. They were all jammed together, probably fifty people, all pressing in to get a close look.

But their kindness was immediately demonstrated. Without asking, two youngsters ran to get me Indian chai (tea). Soon a man arrived with some idly and dahl, and another placed flowers at the foot of my sleeping bag.

Wherever I went the Indians wanted to talk to me. They were curious and amazed as to what I was doing at the pilgrimage. I was peppered with questions:

"What are you doing here?"

"What are your thoughts of Ayyappan?"

But their interest was more than just passing chit-chat, as most wanted me to spend time with them, to feed me and comfort me. I would find my arms being pulled and going from one straw mat to another for yet another dosa or biryani. They would not take "no" for an answer.

It was as if being in my presence was some kind of special karma. My presence seemed to bring out impassioned feelings in some of the pilgrims. A couple of times fights would actually break out deciding with whom I would eat.

So much hospitality and well-meaning, but it became extremely tiring. As word spread about a young American on the pilgrimage, the attention level to me became more oppressive.

As my celebrity status increased, I became overwhelmed from all this focus. In desperation I would limp away to the forest in the dawn, and hide. It was not to contemplate the ways of the world, or to further my closeness to Ayyappan, but simply to be alone.

With this overwhelming pattern of life, I was thrilled when the final fourth day came. My foot was better. I took a short bus ride around noon to the Information Center to meet my friends; and to begin the final six mile walk to the Temple of Sabarimala.

Arriving at the Information Center around 2:45p.m., there were hundreds of pilgrims milling about the wooden structure. I pressed into the crowd trying to locate Dakshi, but did not see him. I did not panic as certainly on finishing their long walk, it was understandable if they were late. I sat under a shady tree as a slew of curious Indians gazed on.

It seemed every fifteen seconds the loud speaker would crackle calling out the names of those trying to be located. I felt certain they would show up eventually and my name would be called.

At 4p.m., I heard the announcement loud and clear: "Mr. Scott Stone, Dakshi is seeking you. Please come to the Information Center."

There they were, five of them. Four of them waving and running up to me. The guru stood below nodding his head. We hugged and laughed. They all inquired about my foot and were happy to learn it was better. I felt as if they were my family at that moment.

We stayed the night at the camp near the Information Center.

The next morning, I felt great anticipation as I prepared myself for the day ahead. I stood in line for over an hour to use the water pump to wash. My body and hair were caked with thick dirt. I was washing for my own cleanliness, but as well for Lord Ayyappan and my arrival at the holy temple.

This is the day . . . the climax of the pilgrimage.

I wanted to show my reverence as best as I could.

By nine o'clock following the usual breakfast of rice and dahl, we prepared to leave.

There were some things to do for preparation. Musthoul brought out some red ointment. I was instructed to put it on my arms and forehead in broad, thick strokes. Romakrishna was cracking open a coconut, and the Chief was pouring ghee into it. The Chief looked at me. He did not speak, but motioned and gave me half a coconut.

He poured the substance into mine. I was not sure what this was for; or how to react to the Chief, with whom I still felt awkward. Dakshi came to my rescue and instructed me that I was to carry this. He cautioned me to be careful not to spill it, as I was to take it to the temple and give it to the Hindu priest to pour over the deity.

Backpack on, and carrying my half-filled coconut in one hand and the full coconut in the other, we were off.

I walked beside Dakshi, with Romakrishna closely behind.

My feet, surprisingly, held up well. The path was up and down; however, not too rocky or steep. It was quite the balancing act, concentrating on my delicate feet, while carrying the coconut filled with the liquid ghee from spilling, as it was extremely crowded. I stayed on the side of the path as much as possible for a softer surface and to prevent my bandaged foot from being stepped on by the other pilgrims. Perhaps the Chief's vision was right, Ayyappan would look over me and take care of my feet.

This smooth orderly procession changed about four hours into the walk. The line began to climb a steep hill; there was more commotion, more pushing up front and uncontrolled noise. The wailing for "Ayyappan" had increased. The closer we got to the top of this hill, the greater the energy and noise was:

"Ayyappan!"

"Ayyappan!"

At the top of the hill, Dakshi stopped me and pointed down below in the valley where I could clearly see the golden phallic tower rising up, and the impassioned throngs of Indians snaking their way toward it.

"It is the Temple of Sabarmila."

Soon the line began to lose its form, as some sprinted ahead trying to cut in front of others. Those in front objected noisily. Shouting and pushing began to break out. The marshals arrived with their sticks and began to swing at those seeming to cause the problem.

For the remaining part of the walk, now downhill as we headed straight toward the temple, this unruly activity became the norm. Despite the marshals with their barking orders and batons, it did nothing to quell the high tempered excitement of the crowd.

Approaching the temple, powerful emotions erupted.

With each step closer to Sabarmila, the passions of the pilgrims became stronger. After five days of wilderness walking; after the ceaseless chanting through the night; there at last down below was the climax of the pilgrimage.

I, as well, was swept up in this energy and felt the spirit of Ayyappan.

We were probably now just one mile away from the temple. In "normal" conditions walking down would have taken perhaps twenty minutes. But from here it was slow going. The walk now turned into a grinding, halting, pushing affair.

It was now about two o'clock, the sun was beating down. It was hot. India HOT! It was easily over 110 degrees. My foot with the boil was ripped open again. It hurt, but I thought of Ayyappan and the throbbing seemed to subside some.

My coconut filled with ghee was beginning to spill, as I would be jostled about in the crowd. I did all I could to protect the ghee carrying it close to my body; and even wrapping it up with a t-shirt to cover the top.

There appeared to be some problems down below near the base of the temple. Dakshi explained that there were reported to be serious "manifestations" (a favorite Indian word for "trouble"). Some kind of fighting had broken out between a few pilgrims and marshals. He told me that this sort of behavior seemed to happen every year on the final descent to the temple.

Because of these problems and all the commotion, the jammed line took a couple of hours to cover this short distance. As we slowly inched forward toward the temple, the pushing and shoving increased. When finally reaching level ground within the shadow of the temple, the crowd became even more frantic and raucous in its desire to get to the sacred steps of the temple.

Those behind pushed full force, determined to break through. The masses of human flesh pressing, squeezing; I felt I was in a human vise. I heard myself yelling: "stop, stop!" My cool western sensibility played in my head. I could not understand why people had to be so crazed and agitated. I mean, we will all get there, right? Yes, you will make it to the temple. But the closer I got to the temple, the madness intensified.

And then it happened. As if a dam had broken and the flood gates opened, the crushing pushing had now taken on another level. Frenzied, the pilgrims were fighting and clawing, as if caught in a fire and had to escape. Down I went a human stampede.

I was being run over, stepped on, kicked. I tried to get up, but only to be knocked down again by this avalanche of violence. The full coconut still stayed with me as I held it tightly to my chest. But the half coconut with the ghee was gone from my other hand.

I had no idea where it was. I tried my best to crawl to the side, out of the frenzied line and stampeding of bodies. When I finally did, I felt exhausted but more than this I felt distraught. Where was my half coconut with the ghee, my gift for Ayyappan? I had come all this way, and now I could not find it. And my friends, where were they? During the onslaught, the stampede, I had lost them.

Out of nowhere I felt a hand on my shoulder. It was forceful.

Looking back, it was the hand of a marshal. He was an imposing figure.

Not tall, but strapping, muscular. His legs bulged beneath his khaki uniformed shorts. His face was distinguished with a black classic handle bar moustache against his olive complexion, and with dark green piercing eyes.

He extended his hand and pulled me up. Incredulously he had a half coconut in his hand.

"Is that mine?" I gasped. I don't think he knew for sure, but nodded that it was. The ghee was, of course, no longer in it. He gestured and in broken English he said "Ghee at temple." I was not sure what that meant, but he said: "take arm" and whipped out his baton and barked authoritatively something in Tamil or Hindi. And with that, there appeared to be a small opening in the mass of bodies.

He took hold of my arm and powerfully pulled me through, right to the base of the temple and its sacred steps. I felt I was with Moses parting the sea. He smiled at me and said: "Go up." His look, his actions, I had the feeling I had been rescued by my own personal Bollywood Hero.

In the midst of this impassioned chaos, I stole a moment despite the over-zealous pilgrims pushing behind me, to pause to take it all in. For maybe ten seconds, that's all. But to me it was important to drink in the experience. In front of me were the renowned seventeen steps that I had heard so much about. The steps were massive. Each step at least two feet high and about ten feet across. The steps were covered in smashed coconuts. The chanting was ferocious in its fervor.

"Swammy Ayyappan"

"Swammy Ayyappan"

The pilgrims called out, as they smashed their coconut.

I held my coconut, and like the three million other pilgrims on the journey, I smashed it with gusto; yelling out the Lord Ayyappan's name.

My smashing was on the first step, as this was my first visit to the temple. Up the steps I went. Most of the Indians seemed to run up the steps. I attempted to take my time in absorbing the experience of each step, and thinking of the millions and millions over the years that had come before.

That thought was short-lived, as the pilgrims surged forward, and the crush became frightening. I assumed that perhaps once at the base of the temple things might have mellowed out, and the tone become more reverent. No way! That was not the case. If anything, on making it up the steps and finally seeing the deity, their outward actions dangerously intensified.

The deity was a small black stone image of Ayyappan, about eighteen inches high. It was on display in front of a Hindu Brahmin priest, who poured the ghee over it. He had a protective barrier around him to keep the pilgrims from getting too close. But CLOSE is where the pilgrims yearned to be, and they did all they could to get as close as possible. They would twist and turn and shove and crawl; then ceremoniously present the priests their sacred coconuts with ghee, and watch worshipfully as ghee was poured on Ayyappan.

I did not push. I did not shove. I stayed cautiously away. The crush of the people was too serious. I refused to subject myself to it. I just stood off to the side observing. I must have looked strange and out of place: this tall, skinny white guy, holding my half coconut without ghee. I felt empty, deflated. I felt incomplete not having the ghee.

Had this just been an endurance test in futility, to come all this way and not complete the ritual? And where in this bloody mob were my good friends Dakshi and Romakrishna?

It was then an old Brahmin priest, with the classic string across his bare chest, fought his way through the hysterical crowd and approached me. He was white haired, his body withered with age. But he was animated and energetic.

"Where is your ghee?" he questioned. I started to explain, but he interrupted me: "No worries hold on to my waist and duck a little." And this wild old Brahmin was like a torpedo, as he bulldozed forward.

"Out of way, out of way" he ordered. It was more than just his forceful physical pushing. There seemed to be some built-in respect and recognition of him. When he spoke the pilgrims seemed to listen and clear a path for us.

Within two minutes of this waist holding and ducking, he had positioned me right at the railing with the sacred deity Ayyappan no more than six feet away. It was almost anti-climatic when he requested: "Ghee, give our friend some ghee." (said with all the casualness of just, "Pour the guy a beer.")

One of the Hindu priests, inside the fenced area, took my empty half coconut, filled it with ghee, and gave it to me. My new-found Brahmin friend instructed me: "Now give him back your coconut."

I handed the half coconut back to the priest. He passed it on to another priest, who in turn took it, muttered something and poured it over the Ayyappan statue, which was covered with flowers and surrounded with fruit.

I bowed to Ayyappan with great respect, though hurried, as I worried for my own safety to escape.

I have never known the desperation of self-preservation. Like an animal I began to claw my way out; whatever it took to get out of this human death trap. Pushing, fighting, crawling, until I broke free to the less congested other side of the temple. Gasping for breath, I pulled myself together and exited the steps.

Just as I tried to catch my breath, yearning to be alone, a Brahmin priest approached and stopped me. He was an old man, probably in his seventies, slight, balding and walked with a limp, supported by a cane.

His first words were spoken with a perfect Oxford-educated English accent: "You are Mr. Scott, from the states. Is this correct? My name is Mr. Samuels."

Taken by surprise, I nodded, and he went on, "May I say that all the pilgrims and I are most impressed that you travel so far away for the pilgrimage of Ayyappan. Has the pilgrimage been good for you?"

I responded "yes," feeing curious how he knew my name.

He persisted, "Mr. Scott, I have a favor to ask of you. I want you to address the pilgrims. They are very moved by your presence being here, and I request you speak about your thoughts on the pilgrimage."

Before I could even respond to his question, he commanded: "Now please, follow me." It did not matter what I had answered to his question, he was determined to have me speak. Following behind, I noticed he hobbled. Somewhat bent over, and with his balding head and cane, and spectacles, reminded me of the great Gandhi. I fell under his persuasive spell.

Why not? I challenged myself. Why not speak? Despite being exhausted, this once in-a lifetime "happening," so colorful, impassioned and culturally enriching; and filled with such kind people must be acknowledged.

I was proud, when I heard myself stating: "Yes, I would be pleased to speak and honored."

We walked slowly, inching our way through the crush of people. He looked back to check on me from time to time, calling to me, whenever we got separated. After navigating through a thicket of small trees, we came upon a clearing.

And there on the hillsides, as far as the eye could see, in front of me were thousands, no, hundreds of thousands of Indians gathered. They seemed to be focused on a stage in the distance.

As we got closer to the stage I could see some exotic dance group performing on it. We walked behind the stage and made our way up the side stairs, and were now waiting in the wings behind the curtain.

He looked at me and said, "After these dancers, we go on stage."

The performers soon finished and exited the stage to polite applause. We then walked out.

My Gandhi-like friend went first. I noticed there was not much response. However, when I came out, following a few steps behind him, the place went nuts! It was as if every pilgrim in the crowd, if not having seen me, was familiar with "that guy from America here to praise Ayyappan."

The masses all seemed to rise at once welcoming me with wild, spirited cheering and clapping.

Mr. Samuels, taking the microphone, said a few words first in Tamil, then Hindi. I did not understand the exact translation, but did hear: "Mr. Scott from America." There was a roar of approval that swept through the crowd.

Turning to me, he spoke in English to the crowd:

"I am pleased to be standing here with Mr. Scott Stone, who traveled all the long distance from the United States to take part in our pilgrimage. This is Mr. Scott's first trip to India. And his first pilgrimage. I have a question for all the audience: IN THE NAME OF AYYAPPAN, SHOULD WE WELCOME HIM?"

His question generated a deafening response of thunderous applause, shouting and cheering. Mr. Samuels had to wait until the noise quieted down. And again he spoke. This time he directed a question to me:

"So, Mr. Scott, I have a question for you. Can you express to these pilgrims, your feelings about Ayyappan, and the pilgrimage you have taken part in?"

This time, however, his question was met with mass silence, with the eager, curious pilgrims in rapt anticipation of my response.

How do you handle the SILENCE of millions?

I paused. I froze. Never had I seen so many people in one place. It seemed to go on forever. I could not tell where it ended. And all waiting silently to cling to my every word. (My college course, Public Speaking 101 had not prepared me for this). I was tongue-tied. The pressure. The stress. The human body can play cruel tricks in crisis situations. I was sweating profusely. WAS I HAVING AN ANXIETY ATTACK?

Finally, I stammered out a weak, inaudible "Namaste," almost timid in its delivery. And as if Ayyappan was sitting on my shoulder like a movie director, I heard a whispering in my ear: "Take two." Once more with feeling. More spirit. Show your passion! Was it Ayyappan? And suddenly I heard my voice booming out over the loud speaker to the crowded hillsides.

"N-A-M-A-S-T-E!" clear, strong and inspired.

With my hands firmly together, I gave a reverential bow of my head to the pilgrims and bellowed a bold, impassioned:

"AYYAPPAN! AYYAPPAN!"

"DO YOU FEEL HIS SPIRIT?"

"DO YOU FEEL HIS SPIRIT?" I repeated even louder.

The crowd was ecstatic, chanting back "AYYAPPAN, AYYAPPAN".

Now I no longer felt exhausted but alive, energized, empowered.

I waited for the crowd to quiet down before speaking further. It took a good couple of minutes for this quiet to come. This quiet when it came was powerful. I could sense the pilgrims' sincere interest and heightened anticipation of what the young American would say.

I paused. My dear friends were very much on my mind. Even now at this crucial moment I was still concerned about Dakshi, Romakrishna, Musthoul, little Pandit and the Chief. They were so vital to me in making the pilgrimage possible, and making it so meaningful, so joyful. Were they out there somewhere?

I then delivered my thoughts . . . "This pilgrimage has been a deeply moving, spiritual experience for me. My sincere thanks and gratitude for the kindness I have felt from everyone, and the privilege of being part of it. Most powerful is your unwavering love and belief in Ayyappan, the son of Shiva and Vishnu."

There was a roar from the crowd; those that were seated came to their feet. Mr. Samuels came to the microphone to translate. But none seemed needed. They understood. Once again waiting for the noise to subside, I continued:

"This pilgrimage with over three million strong is so remarkable and inspirational, because both Hindus and Muslims come together peacefully, as brothers, in their shared devotion and tribute to Ayyappan and his great goodness."

I had just finished my concluding remarks, and the masses of pilgrims were on their feet chanting: "Ayyappan", when a thread-like man, very dark suddenly climbed on the stage and came toward me. He had a wild, disturbed look. It made me anxious.

But he stopped a few feet in front of me, and placed his hands together, lowered himself to the ground and touched my feet. He began to mutter a mantra, over and over again, which I could not comprehend. His actions certainly were not harmful. Six or seven others, following him, were making their way up to the stage, crying out fanatically: "Ayyappan! Ayyappan!" Two of them went for my feet, touching and bowing their heads; while the others circled about me, tugging at my shirt and pants. They kept grabbing at my clothes, pulling the material. I was confused a little and thought about getting my ass off the stage.

But I grasped at what they were doing. They were pinning rupee notes on my clothing. When I knew this was the purpose, I stood still and let them continue, although I had no idea why they were doing it. I thought Mr. Samuels would intervene, but he did not.

I looked at him pleadingly and asked: "What's going on?"

He replied simply: "It is good, peaceful. It is their way of saying they love you. Let it be. Let it be."

Over a half hour of "letting it be" passed, as pilgrim after pilgrim approached me. Some going directly for my feet with their hands; others put garlands of flowers around me, and many continuing with the pinning of money.

I could not estimate how many pilgrims stormed the stage. Perhaps two hundred, this continued with no let up.

And the chants continued even louder: "AYYAPPAN!" as they gazed at me, covered like a money tree.

Mr. Samuels finally walked over to me and putting a caring arm around my shoulder, said he must speak to me about a matter of "much importance."

He confided in hushed tones: "Many of the pilgrims feel that you could be a reincarnation of the God Vishnu."

I looked at him confused and alarmed. "VISHNU?" I stammered. "VISHNU?"

He nodded and said something about Vishnu's 11th reincarnation had been questioned; and that I could be this form.

He gave me his best interpretation of "reincarnation:" Hinduism believes that the human spirit returns to earth in different form again and again, he explained.

Yes, I knew this! That is why I was so agitated. When he said that many felt I could be the reincarnation of Vishnu, I was shocked, shaken. It freaked me out.

I told Mr. Samuels, I in no way wished to appear insensitive to Hindu beliefs, but it had disturbed me what he had told me. It is one thing to read about Hinduism in a <u>Comparative Religions</u> college text book. It's quite another thing to be living it.

With apprehension, I felt the energy of the crowd intensifying, as more and more spastic pilgrims piled onto the stage to honor me. Their tactics were frenzied with extreme jumping and leaping about. The bizarre behavior escalated with high-pitch screaming; and so many grasping hands reaching out to touch me. This mob hysteria, reinforced by the alarming Vishnu reincarnation statement was deeply troubling. A red flag of dangerous complications, I could not control. I must escape this stage. I must make a gracious exit NOW!

And so, ceremoniously, with my hands folded high over my head, I shouted a final "AYYAPPAN! AYYAPPAN! NAMASTE!" with flourish; and exited the stage hurriedly, pushing through a jungle of groping, worshipful hands. Mr. Samuels called out to me. But I was compelled to keep going. I waved again, ceremoniously but pressed on. A quick escape was not easy. Perhaps not possible.

No matter how fast I walked, I was pursued by a relentless surge of fanatical pilgrims, each wanting to make contact and be in my presence. Wherever I walked, the pilgrims followed. I felt suffocated, overwhelmed. Here I am surrounded by the masses, but I feel alone. So alone. I have lost my kind pilgrim friends. I prayed pleadingly and playfully, in desperation: "Where are they, Lord Ayyappan? Can you help me? Can you give me a sign?"

Just as I felt I had reached my breaking point . . . miraculously, out of nowhere there was precious Pandit. Was I hallucinating? Call it what you will: coincidence, luck, or divine intervention. I choose to call it incredulous, amazing.

And just perhaps . . . Ayyappan is looking over me.

Pandit wore that brilliant endless grin, but turned and ran away.

"Pandit, Pandit," I called.

"Come back!" Where was she going? She was a fleeting symbol of sanity, reality. Where was she?

But soon she came skipping back toward me, holding the hand of Dakshi. What a relief to see him and filled with the warm feelings of joy to be together again in this vast sea of strangers.

Predictably, here came the Chief several paces behind, ever silent, ever searching, ever gazing into the great beyond. But unpredictably, when he saw me, it was shocking and surprising, he acknowledged my existence with an energetic "thumbs up!"

I returned his "thumbs up!" and an ear-to-ear grin. How satisfying.

I would have liked to embrace him too, but could not risk his wrath (the lethal word), so restrained myself and gave my usual respectful "namaste."

It was so comforting to find my family of friends again. I felt peaceful in their presence. It was as if they were a safe, secure fortress, protecting me from the masses of over-zealous pilgrims, whose interest in me now escalated to scary, God-like proportions.

"We saw you on stage," Pandit chirped cheerily.

"Yes," added Dakshi, we were touched by your words. The pilgrims could feel your love for Ayyappan." He was beaming with a touch of paternal pride, as if I were his son or disciple.

It was now almost five-thirty. Dakshi telling me we had to move fast to find a good position to view the Jyothi, the mystical star which would be appearing soon. As we walked Dakshi's face looked serious as he said, "Scott, it is important I explain more to you about the Jyothi. I know I have spoken about it, but I want you to know as much as possible. Between 6:00- 6:30 tonight, on this day, January 14th, and only in this place, Sabarimala, does the Jyothi appear."

He continued: "The Jyothi is a mystery, which no one can explain. There is no scientific, rational explanation. But to those here, both the Hindu and Muslim, believe it is the sign of God Ayyappan giving all his blessing."

We positioned ourselves on a slight rise and looked out toward three distinct sloping hills. "It should show up probably over there." Dakshi, pointed to the perfectly shaped "U" curved hill furthest to the right. There was a sea of pilgrims as far as you could see, all focused on the distant sloping hills.

It was now 6 p.m. There was a stirring in the crowd in anticipation of the sacred star. Soon chanting had begun, joined by pounding of drums, first slow, then rapid. As the time moved closer to the Jyothi appearing, the ceremonial pounding of the drums exploded into an even louder, faster, more frenzied beat.

Suddenly I heard screams. A scream like never heard before. More hysterical screams, some people near-by started to point.

Had the Jyothi been seen? I tugged on Dakshi's shirt and shouted to him, to make sure he heard me over the noise: "Where is it? I don't see it!"

Dakshi looked confused as well. "No not seen yet" he said, not looking at me, but focused only on the sky and hills. Had we missed it?

I got on my toes, straining, looking everywhere. Dakshi yelled, pointing: "Scott over there!"

And there hovering in the middle of the valley of the second hill was a light. The light looked like a star. It was dim, and could be clearly seen. It seemed to move slowly and flicker in its brightness. This went on for about thirty seconds before fading out. I looked at Dakshi and belted out a wondrous "WOW!" And gave him a huge hug. I felt such powerful emotion. I had witnessed the mystical Jyothi!

Should I start looking for my "good fortune and divine blessings?" I knew historically, there had been controversy about the sacred light's validity. But never disputed by devotees. Tonight I was a devotee, clinging to the magic, and awaiting my "divine blessings."

I had experienced quite enough miracles and madness for one day, so I thought tonight I would instantly crash, when I finally hit my sleeping bag.

I desperately needed sleep. Tomorrow I would be leaving. Had I ever been so exhausted? So exhilarated?

But sleep would not come . . . Too much stimuli, the circuits were overloaded. The Pilgrimage had been such a compressed time of sensory stimulation: the immense crowds; the other-worldly sights; the excessive attention focused on me; that I scarcely had time to reflect, or to think my own thoughts of what I had witnessed.

As I looked up at the riot of stars in the vast open night sky above me, I questioned if I were still on the same planet, part of the same universe. Is that the same crescent moon? What about Times Square? Where is Disneyland? Has anyone in Yankee Stadium cheered for Lord Ayyappan lately? Is this what my parents meant by "broadening my horizons?"

The Hindu Pilgrimage had been totally surreal. It had been referred to as one of India's largest pilgrimages. And I was the only non-Indian among millions. I had not only survived it, but had been deified. And had addressed the throngs. Moreover, I had escaped Vishnu's reincarnation. And Hallelujah! Even the infected boil on my big toe was healing.

As the promise of a new dawn was breaking . . . the impassioned pilgrims now in silence, still sleeping, the little fires still burning on the hillsides; my last conscious thought was how inspirational and transformative it all had been, in ways unable for me to adequately express. Except to say: Just another day of "AMAZINGNESS" in India.

As for being "deified," . . . what a profound relief to be free, to just be me. To pick up my pack and open that world map to see what else was out there . As my eyes finally closed in sleep, I'm sure I had a blissful smile on my face.

On the Hindu Pilgrimage

HOMEWARD BOUND

Chapter 36

HOMEWARD BOUND

My global odyssey had come to an end. I had circled the globe: from New York to my next and last destination Los Angeles, then back to my Midwest home and Hickory Island.

As I settled comfortably in my seat for the flight home, I thought: "This is bliss." I was glad no one was sitting beside me. I didn't want to talk. I just wanted to be suspended in time and space to be alone with my overpowering thoughts. Time to reflect . . .

It was deeply satisfying now during this long flight to have uninterrupted time to re-live my world journey. I also welcomed the opportunity to finally finish my Journal.

So, "NO!" I did not wish to talk. I did not wish to sleep. I was too excited about my homecoming. And I did not want to read. I could not concentrate.

Although I was eager to finish the book I had from my last book swap. This book was Henry David Thoreau's *Walden*. I had read it in college. It was assigned reading. But now it had renewed meaning for me. I had underscored a passage from Chapter 2 that powerfully resonated now, and had copied it in my Journal:

> "I know of no more encouraging fact than the unquestionable ability of man to elevate his life by a conscious endeavor. It is something to be able to paint a particular picture, or to carve a statue, and to make a few objects beautiful; but <u>it is far more glorious</u> to carve and paint the very atmosphere and medium through which we look . . . <u>To affect the quality of the day, that is the highest of arts.</u>"

The profound words of Thoreau, that followed, spoke to me, eloquently expressing the purpose of my world journey:

"I wished to live deliberately... and see if I could not learn what life had to teach, and not, when I came to die, discover that I had not lived ... I wanted to live deep and suck out all the marrow of life."

"TO LIVE DEEP AND SUCK OUT ALL THE MARROW OF LIFE," I repeated to myself. Yes, that had been the purpose of my world journey.

But right now I decided my purpose was to finish my Journal, I promised myself. That is what I insisted on doing during this long last leg of my journey, while I had free time to do so. I felt an urgency to complete it now, before the rest of the world came rushing in.

Here were my treasured Journals close beside me now, in their protective covering. Always my constant companions. I had safeguarded them during the whole trip backpacking around –the-world. To protect them, I always slept with them at the bottom of my sleeping bag, when I felt vulnerable in a strange, questionable dangerous area.

I had documented it all in my Journals. But I wanted to SEE it all too. I wanted to play it all back again in my head; like a cinematic movie reel to keep the images imprinted on my brain, my gut, my soul ALIVE forever!

As I adjusted my seat back, and closed my eyes, I could visualize it all now . . . I had left just a kid out of college with my life savings ($914). Nearly two and a half years later, I was returning a RICH MAN with a WEALTH OF LIVING. And $11 in my pocket.

The visual reel was revolving rapidly in my mind with vivid images of "the wealth of riches" I had experienced:

Being enthralled with the awe-inspiring natural landscapes of the world. I could see it and sense it . . . the fjords of Norway, the Himalayas of Nepal, the jungles of Indonesia flashed before me.

And the magnificent man-made wonders of the world. I had fantastic footage churning in my head of the Alhambra, the Taj Mahal; the twin Buddhas of Bamiyan.

The wealth of experiences from living in a cave in Morocco, to romance and rapture in the Hindu Kush; to being deified on a Hindu Pilgrimage (of three million Indians) in India.

Being inspired by the world's people! Their vibrancy, diversity and kindness; and witnessing the goodness and greatness of which mankind is capable.

Now in mid-flight I had been remembering not only the good times with the world's people and their unforgettable hospitality, food and fellowship. But I was compelled to remember as well the difficult times.

These tough times cause one to reflect that travel, like life, contains both the good and the bad, the highs and the lows. It goes with the territory, accentuating the best of times, while coping with the hard times: being hungry, being cold, lonely or lost, or gravely ill. Sometimes scared shitless. And constantly being tested.

But mostly being abundantly enriched, awaking each new dawn to the surprise pleasures and challenges to greet you each day. And it was the "unknown," which I found so enticing and seductive. Not knowing what is around the bend, to me was a thrill in itself. Be it a colorful festival in a tiny village you stumble upon; or a hitched ride taking you home to good food, talk and laughter; or a spectacular vista that greets you over the next hill; or perhaps a spontaneous meeting that results in romance. Ah! Travel . . . the "unknown" is enthralling.

It was deeply satisfying now during the flight, to have uninterrupted time to re-live this remarkable, spinning reel of images. And to know they were all documented in my Journals, where important details could never be forgotten.

And never to be forgotten . . . images that I couldn't get out of my mind or heart, and kept returning, were those of my home and family. I could hear my mother's laughter . . . I could see my little sister's red hair in the sunlight; so pretty and sweet, I had renamed her "Rose." I could see my fun, sports-loving brother, my favorite pass receiver, as he ran into a tree. But caught the pass. And I could feel Big Dad's crunching bear hug around me now . . . I could hear myself laughing out loud in anticipation. I was HOMEWARD BOUND!

Recapturing these powerful, deeply meaningful memories of my world journey had been totally absorbing; it made the flight go much faster. But there was still time for a brief summing up for my Journal.

I had done the math:

With little money and lots of grit (and grace), I had amazingly financed this priceless global odyssey myself. On less than $2 a day!

I grabbed my beat-up, beloved Journal and flipped the worn, weathered pages to my last entry:

"The global scope and vision of this journey transcends travel. I am a world traveler, but I am a 'life' traveler as well. Mine is a journey exploring the world; but a 'growth' journey exploring self as well.

Travel serves as the powerful vehicle that propels the pistons of this PASSION-FOR-LIFE journey to a higher, larger place. And the world journey serves as a metaphor for the greatest journey of all . . . LIFE."

With a triumphant grin on my face, and my eyes tearing, I fumbled to find my pen, and scrawled in giant BOLD CAPS, my final entry:

"WHAT A WORLD!"
"WHAT A LIFE!"

The End. The Beginning . . . FOREVER INSATIABLE!

UPDATE: Current Travel Photo (Yunnan Province, Southwest China)
AND THE JOURNEY CONTINUES . . . THE BEAT GOES ON . . .
Since my global odyssey, I have continued to travel during my professional
life . . . I still travel as I did: with backpack; at an unhurried pace; off the
beaten path; seeking close contact.

My upcoming travel to the Balkans (Albania, Macedonia, Bulgaria)
will be country number seventy-eight. Time to hit the trail, fellow travel
adventurers. You will have some wild and wonderful tales of your own to
tell. I encourage you to contact me to share your journeys: wscottstone@
aol.com.

ABOUT THE AUTHOR

SCOTT STONE is a long-time resident and champion of New York City, when not traveling. He resides there with his wife Zehua, who shares his enthusiasm for travel. Since college graduation (Michigan State University 1976), Stone has held executive positions in both magazine publishing and the cruise industry. A "man for all seasons," he has varied interests from opera, jazz and art, to sports and cuisine. His greatest passion continues to be travel, especially to remote destinations that are culturally rich with indigenous minority groups and dramatic landscapes.

Made in the USA
Middletown, DE
02 February 2015